T0277680

New Orleans

The neighborhoods of New Orleans have given rise to an
extraordinary outpouring of important writing. Over the last
century and a half or so, these stories and songs have given
the city its singular place in the human imagination. This
book leads the reader along five thoroughfares that define
these different parts of town – Royal, St. Claude, Esplanade,
Basin, and St. Charles – to explore how the writers who have
lived around them have responded in closely related ways
to the environments they share. On the outskirts of New
Orleans today, where the book ends, the city's precarious
relation to its watery surroundings and the vexed legacies of
race loom especially large. But the city's literature shows us
that these themes have been near to hand for New Orleans
writers for several generations, whether reflected through
questions of masquerade, dreams of escape, the innocence of
children, or the power of money or of violence or of memory.

T. R. Johnson has taught at universities in Louisville
and Boston and is now a Professor of English and Weiss
Presidential Fellow at Tulane University. He has written
books on Lacanian psychoanalysis, the teaching of writing,
and prose style, and is the editor of *New Orleans: A Literary
History*. Since the late 1990s, he has lived in the 9th Ward
of New Orleans near the Mississippi River and hosted a
contemporary jazz radio program.

Imagining Cities

Editor
Chris Morash, Trinity College Dublin

Imagining Cities is a series of books by leading literary scholars, each of which explores the ways in which writers have created cities of words that overlay the stones and pavements of the places where they lived and worked. Each book in the series is dedicated to an individual city – whether it be New York, London or Dublin – in which the words of its writers have shaped the experience of urban life.

Books in the series

New Orleans
A Writer's City

T. R. Johnson

CAMBRIDGE
UNIVERSITY PRESS

University Printing House, Cambridge CB2 8BS, United Kingdom

One Liberty Plaza, 20th Floor, New York, NY 10006, USA

477 Williamstown Road, Port Melbourne, VIC 3207, Australia

314–321, 3rd Floor, Plot 3, Splendor Forum, Jasola District Centre,
New Delhi – 110025, India

103 Penang Road, #05–06/07, Visioncrest Commercial, Singapore 238467

Cambridge University Press is part of the University of Cambridge.

It furthers the University's mission by disseminating knowledge in the
pursuit of education, learning, and research at the highest international
levels of excellence.

www.cambridge.org
Information on this title: www.cambridge.org/9781316512067
DOI: 10.1017/9781009057493

© T. R. Johnson 2023

First published 2023

Printed in the United Kingdom by TJ Books Limited, Padstow Cornwall

A catalogue record for this publication is available from the British Library.

ISBN 978-1-316-51206-7 Hardback

For my brothers,
Clark and Ben

Contents

A Writer's City
Series Foreword

New Orleans

The *Writer's City* series of books grew out my own experience of the city that I know best – Dublin. Like New Orleans, Dublin is a place where the city's true self is not immediately apparent in its pavements or buildings. My own sense of Dublin, from the moment I first arrived here in the mid 1980s, was that it was not so much a city of great buildings, as a city of words, both written and spoken. So, when my editor at Cambridge University Press suggested that the next book in the series might be on New Orleans, from the start it seemed intuitively right; for, when I think of New Orleans, what first comes to mind is not monumental architecture, but words – in this case, not only written and spoken, but also sung.

New Orleans is a city whose place on the imaginary map of America – indeed, of the world – always seems somehow out of proportion to more empirical measures of significance. I am continually surprised by the fact that that New Orleans is actually relatively small, as cities go. The total population is just under 400,000, less than, say, Mesa, Arizona, or Aurora, Colorado, and outside the top fifty largest cities in the US. At the same time – and there is no real way of measuring this – I expect that if you asked anyone, anywhere, to name half a dozen well-known American cities, New Orleans would feature. And if you limited your pool of respondents to people who love books (never mind those who love music), New Orleans would probably be among the first two or three American cities inscribed on that map of the imagination.

There are a number of reasons for this, not all of which involve music. For many decades now, New Orleans has not only been producing great writers, it has been attracting them. From Kate Chopin to Tennessee Williams to Eric Nguyen, New Orleans has been a city in which writers have felt at home, where they can write, and, for many, where they can confront things that matter. T. R. Johnson begins his literary map in *New Orleans: A Writer's City* with John Howard Griffin arriving in the city to begin the odyssey that would become *Black Like Me*; he ends it with the poetry of Karisma Price, whose work is deeply marked by the experience of having had her family home destroyed by Hurricane Katrina in 2005. When we experience New Orleans through its literature, we see that it is big enough to contain two of the biggest questions facing societies everywhere: racial discrimination, and the effects of climate change. At the same time, that experience is on a human scale that saves us from abstraction. Here, we feel, some of our greatest challenges can be encountered in a neighbourhood that is uncannily familiar. And that must be part of what makes a great city of literature.

Chris Morash
Dublin, 2022

Chronology

1815   General Jackson wins War of 1812, after pardoning Lafitte in exchange for his help

1817   City Council officially permits dancing in Congo Square, but restricts it to that space

1821   John James Audubon moves to New Orleans, soon begins to publish *The Birds of America*

1828   Abraham Lincoln's first flatboat journey to the city, the second three years later

1830   Population 43,085. Free people of color: 11,562; enslaved: 14,476; white: 20,047

1834   The LaLaurie family on Royal exposed for torturing and mutilating those they enslaved

1836   La Société d'Économie et d'Assistance Mutuelle founded, scores of similar groups follow

1837   Bras Coupé captured and hanged

1841   St. Augustine Catholic Church opens

1842   Sisters of Holy Family, first religious order for women of color, founded

1843   *L'Album Littéraire*, a literary journal created by Afro-Creoles

1845   *Les Cenelles*, nation's first poetry anthology by people of African descent

1846   *La Patria*, a Spanish language newspaper, begins publishing in New Orleans

1848   Walt Whitman visits New Orleans

1849   Pontalba Apartments completed

1853   Solomon Northup's *Twelve Years a Slave*; Yellow Fever kills nearly 8,000 people in the city

1860   Population 170,024. Free people of color: 10,939; enslaved: 14,484; white: 144,601

1861   General Beauregard of nearby St. Bernard Parish fires on Fort Sumter, ignites Civil War

1862   *L'Union*, nation's first Black newspaper, launches shortly after Union captures city

1863   Emancipation Proclamation

1866   White supremacists massacre Afro-Creole activists

1869   Straight University and New Orleans University, both for Black students, founded

1870	Kate Chopin arrives in city, stays nearly a decade
1872	Louisiana elects Pinckney Pinchback as governor, first Black governor in all of US
1871	Lafcadio Hearn arrives in city, stays nearly a decade
1874	Several thousand former Confederate soldiers try to overthrow state government, fail
1879	George Washington Cable's *Old Creole Days*
1880	George Washington Cable's *The Grandissimes*
1881	Marie Laveau dies
1890	Population nearly 250,000, one-fourth African American; three-fourths white
1892	Corbett v Sullivan at the Olympic Club begins modern era of boxing
1895	Dockworkers riot, white union-members massacre African-American non-union laborers
1896	*Plessy v Ferguson* ruling launches Jim Crow era of "separate but equal"
1897	Storyville opens
1899	Kate Chopin's *The Awakening*; also Alice Dunbar-Nelson's *The Goodness of St. Rocque*
1900	White riots in response to Robert Charles's shooting of police
1901	Louis Armstrong born
1907	Buddy Bolden incarcerated for remaining twenty-four years of his life
1911	*El Mercurio*, a Spanish-language magazine, is born, links city to Latin literary world till 1927
1915	Major hurricane causes widespread damage
1917	Storyville closes
1921	*The Double Dealer* magazine begins, lasts five years
1922	Louis Armstrong leaves for Chicago; Mother Catherine Seals opens her temple
1924	William Faulkner arrives in city, lives at what is now 624 Pirate's Alley for about sixteen months
1925	Louis Armstrong records with the Hot Five, yielding first Jazz masterpiece of recorded era

1926   William Faulkner's *Sherwood Anderson and Other Famous Creoles*

1936   William Faulkner's *Absalom, Absalom!*

1937   Charles B. Rousseve's *The Negro in Louisiana: Aspects of His History and His Literature*

1939   Katherine Anne Porter's *Pale Horse, Pale Rider*; Dew Drop Inn opens at 2836 LaSalle

1944   D-Day Invasion made possible by the Higgins Boat

1947   Tennessee Williams's *A Streetcar Named Desire*; Robert Penn Warren's *All the King's Men*

1948   Truman Capote's *Other Voices, Other Rooms*

1949   Fats Domino's "The Fat Man." William Burroughs arrested, flees the city for Mexico

1950   Population 570,445, about one-third Black, two-thirds white

1951   Lillian Hellman's *The Autumn Garden*

1952   Louis Armstrong's *Satchmo: My Life in New Orleans*

1953   Professor Longhair records "Tipitina"

1954   *Brown v Board of Education* ruling seeks to end Jim Crow era of "separate but equal"

1955   Robert Penn Warren's *Band of Angels*; Little Richard records "Tutti Frutti"

1956   Nelson Algren's *A Walk on the Wild Side*

1958   Tennessee Williams's *Suddenly Last Summer*

1959   John Howard Griffin takes on Black disguise; "Battle of New Orleans" becomes hit song

1960   Ruby Bridges desegregates Frantz Elementary; Lillian Hellman's *Toys in the Attic*

1961   Walker Percy's *The Moviegoer*; Shirley Ann Grau's *House on Coliseum Street*; first issue of *The Outsider*; Ernie K-Doe's "Mother in Law"

1962   Irma Thomas's "It's Raining"

1963   Kennedy assassinated; John Rechy's *City of Night*; Irma Thomas's "Ruler of My Heart"

1964   The Free Southern Theater moves to New Orleans; Dixie Cups' "Chapel of Love"

1965   Hurricane Betsy; Bob Dylan's "Mr. Tambourine Man," composed after carnival visit

1966 Construction on Claiborne overpass begun; Aaron Neville's "Tell It Like It Is"

1967 Robert Stone's *A Hall of Mirrors*

1968 Marcus B. Christian's "I Am New Orleans" in *Times-Picayune*. Dr. John's *Gris-Gris*; Tom Dent and Kalamu Ya Salaam publish first issue of *Nkombo*

1969 Hurricane Camille

1970 Black Panthers' showdown with New Orleans Police in Desire Housing Project

1972 Ishmael Reed's *Mumbo Jumbo*; Mahalia Jackson dies

1973 Sniper Mark Essex avenges killings of Black students at Southern University by killing nine

1974 Final issue of *Nkombo*

1975 Nine slayings of those slated to testify before Congressional probe into JFK killing

1976 Anne Rice's *Interview with the Vampire*; Michael Ondaatje's *Coming through Slaughter*

1977 The Dirty Dozen Brass Band forms, a new era of brass music follows

1978 City elects first Black mayor, Ernest "Dutch" Morial

1979 Wynton Marsalis, age 17, leaves New Orleans for New York, where he has lived ever since

1980 Population 557,482 and now a Black majority city: 55 percent Black, 42 percent white, 2 percent other

1981 John Kennedy Toole's *A Confederacy of Dunces* wins Pulitzer. Ellen Ghilchrest's *In the Land of Dreamy Dreams* wins National Book Award

1983 James Booker dies

1984 Tom Robbins's *Jitterbug Perfume*

1986 Jim Jarmusch's *Down by Law*

1988 Harry Crews's *The Knockout Artist*

1989 Everette Maddox dies

1990 Anne Rice's *The Witching Hour*; Paula Fox's *The God of Nightmares*

1992 MC T Tucker and DJ Irv release first Bounce single, "Where Dey At?"

1994 Erna Brodber's *Louisiana*

1997 Brenda Marie Osbey's *All Saints*; Tom Dent's *Southern Journey*

1998 Johnny Adams dies

2000 Population 484,674. African Americans a two-thirds majority

2002 Natasha Trethewey's *Bellocq's Ophelia*. Dean Paschal's *By the Light of the Jukebox*

2003 Valerie Martin's *Property*; Peter Cooley's *A Place Made of Starlight*

2005 Hurricane Katrina

2008 Tom Piazza's *City of Refuge*; Lil Wayne's *Tha Carter III* outsells entire genre of Jazz

2009 Dan Baum's *Nine Lives*; Peter Cooley's *Divine Margins*

2010 David Simon's *Tremé* begins to air on HBO

2011 Brad Richard's *Motion Studies*

2012 Frank Ocean's *Channel Orange*; Brad Richard's *Butcher's Sugar*

2013 Big Freedia's reality TV show premiers

2015 James B. Borders's *Marking Time, Making Place*; Rickey Laurentiis's *Boy with Thorn*; Tom Piazza's *A Free State*

2017 Margaret Wilkerson Sexton's *A Kind of Freedom*; Ladee Hubbard's *The Talented Ribkins*. Confederate monuments removed

2018 Peter Cooley's *World without Finishing*. Zachary Lazar's *Vengeance*

2019 Sara Broom's *The Yellow House*; Albert Woodfox's *Solitary*; Maurice Ruffin's *We Cast a Shadow*; Bryan Wagner's *The Life and Legend of Bras Coupé*

2020 Covid-19 pandemic shuts down indoor music, dining, and wider tourist industry

2021 Ladee Hubbard's *The Rib King*; Maurice Ruffin's *For Those Who Don't Say They Love You*; Eric Nguyen's *Things We Lost to the Water*

2023 Karisma Price's *I'm Always So Serious*

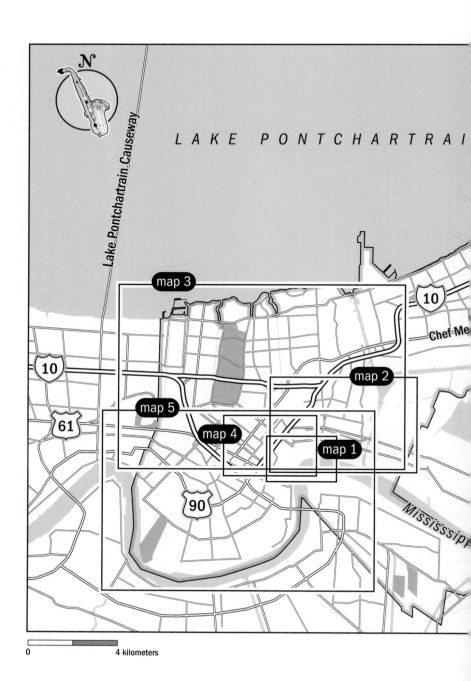

LAKE PONTCHARTRAI

Lake Pontchartrain Causeway

map 3

map 2

10

Chef-Me

10

map 5

61

map 4

map 1

90

Mississsipp

0   4 kilometers

Bayou
Sauvage
National
Wildlife

LAKE BORGNE

LOUISIANA

Mississippi R.

area of detail

Introduction

New Orleans is among the most storied cities in the world.

I first began to think of it this way in the late 1990s, when I was lucky enough to land a job in the city. As soon as I shared the news with friends and family that I would be moving to New Orleans, I made my way to a bookstore near my apartment and began to browse the travel section for something that could orient me to the world that, a few months later, I would enter. I found a guidebook that looked thick with curiosities and stood in the bookstore for an hour, thumbing back and forth in it. I then took it home and sprawled on the couch with it till well past midnight. The next morning, I picked it up again. In the weeks that followed, I began to fall in love with New Orleans through reading about it. And, ever since, my experience of the place has been intertwined with the literature and lore that has sprung up in it and about it – and that have given the city its singular place in the human imagination.

After I moved to New Orleans, I put the tourist guidebook away and began reading everything I could find that was connected to my new home. I went through novels, collections of poetry, plays, books about its music, its history, its architecture, and started watching movies about the place, all the while digging into the musical nightlife and cuisine as much as money, time, and energy would allow. I had been living this way in the city for about a half-dozen years when Hurricane Katrina struck. In the aftermath, as the eyes of the world were fixed on this place, I began teaching a course on the literature of New Orleans and thinking about it with a new kind of urgency.

After about a decade of teaching that course, an opportunity arose to start writing about the city myself: Cambridge University Press told me they were interested in publishing a comprehensive history of the city's literature, and asked me if I'd like to solicit new essays on the subject, contribute my own work, and serve as editor of the volume. I did. When that book was published in 2019, Cambridge asked me to do a second one – this one.

This time, rather than a polyphony of scholarly voices on various turning points in the history of the world's understanding of the city, as I assembled in that first book, this new project, I decided, would proceed solely in my own voice, emphasize the most recent generations of writers, and do so in a way that would appeal to non-academic audiences. Rather than restrict the book to works that are *about* New Orleans, this new one would also discuss all of the most influential writing to come *from* New Orleans. An apparently impossible task, but my life in New Orleans had taught me that simply because something is impossible is no good reason not to go ahead and give it a whirl.

And so, in the summer of 2020, hunkering down for what we were just beginning to grasp was the long, long grind of the pandemic, I committed myself to writing a book that would map, through story and song, the vast record of human experience inscribed in New Orleans. A book that would give people who have known the city their whole lives an array of new angles for wondering about it, and give newcomers a foothold in beginning to fathom the place where they find themselves. I would, in short, gather a lot of stories about the most important stories and storytellers of New Orleans, whatever their genre and mode.

To create the thickest possible context for reading one's way through the city, the chapters would combine swatches of cultural, geographical, and historical information with literary gossip and original lines of interpretation about certain works, certain connections between works, and even broad traditions of writing around the city. Part of what this would entail is more discussion of music than one might expect to find in a book about writers. But music suffuses the air that writers in New Orleans breathe, shaping their language and thought in ways that are often explicit, and framing the meaning of New Orleans for people around the world. What's more, many New Orleans musicians have written memoirs that provide keen insight into the city; other musicians – vocalists, lyricists – work so closely with language that they too belong in a book about writers. Thus, memoirists, songwriters, and singers would be in the mix, from Louis Armstrong and Fats

Domino to Lil Wayne, Big Freedia, and Frank Ocean, to name only a few, along with thoughts about the built environment, from architectural treasures to drainage canals, along with dozens upon dozens of novelists, poets, playwrights, and journalists, all of this marshalled together to locate today's New Orleans as a living flashpoint in the global collective.

But where to begin?

I chose to organize the book through five streets, each of which serves as a primary corridor through a different part of town. In each chapter, I work my way up and down one of those streets, thinking about the generations of writers whose lives were shaped by them.

Directions? No one in New Orleans explains where things are by using the terms north, south, east, and west. Instead, they'll say "uptown," meaning upriver, or "downtown," meaning downriver. The opposite axis is defined by the lake, at the northernmost end of the city, and, at the opposite end, the river. Nonetheless, some street names do use north–south, which can be a bit tricky around this sharp bend in the river, because S. Claiborne, for example, is upriver from N. Carolton, implying that the river flows South to North. It doesn't. This book will mix the two ways of locating places to keep both insiders and newcomers on their toes.

I've devoted Chapter 1 to Royal Street, as it runs from Canal Street downriver to Esplanade Avenue through the French Quarter – the first and most iconic thoroughfare of the city's literary history. Through it, we can trace the most relevant work of a range of writers who have moved along it, from Walt Whitman to Charles Bukowski, Dorothy Dix to Katherine Anne Porter, Truman Capote to Dalt Wonk, among a score or more. And we can explore, through these tight clusters of addresses, the preoccupations that their New Orleans writings share.

From there, I've proceeded farther downriver in Chapter 2 to consider what has been in some ways the opposite of that glamorous stretch of Royal Street – the long stretch of working-class blocks centered around St. Claude Avenue. Beginning in the Lower 9th Ward, on the downriver side of the Industrial Canal, I've worked my way back up St. Claude to consider the Desire neighborhood, then farther up to St. Roch, finally crossing to the other side of St. Claude to consider the neighborhood on the banks of the Mississippi River that in the 1940s came to be called the Bywater. As in the last chapter, I've taken up a wide range of writers, from Zora Neale Hurston, Kalamu Ya Salaam, Cheekie Nero, and Alice Dunbar-Nelson to John Steinbeck, John Waters, Nelson Algren, and Valerie Martin, to name a few, and the ways their interests intersect.

Next, in Chapter 3, I've moved farther back upriver to consider the street that constitutes the lower border of the Quarter, Esplanade

Avenue. The oldest passageway in the city, it moves out from the Quarter under some 3 miles of continuous live-oak canopy to Bayou St. John. I've wandered back and forth on Esplanade in the third chapter by way of thinking about the major writing and the various cultural circumstances of the adjoining neighborhoods of the Marigny, the 7th Ward, and along Bayou St. John as it reaches all the way into Mid-City. Again, a range of figures and the themes they share will focus this chapter, among them Solomon Northup and Kate Chopin, Tom Piazza and Mona Lisa Saloy, and many others, including several memoirs by historic songwriters.

In the fourth chapter, I've focused a short distance farther upriver to take up the Basin Street corridor, first by discussing the directly adjacent Congo Square, then the Storyville District through which Basin runs, and finally, as Basin bends to the north away from the river to become Orleans Avenue, the major literature of Tremé. This is the part of the city – the 6th Ward – where, some three hundred years ago, African-American music first began, and, a century ago, where Jazz itself was born, processes still rippling, through the memory practices of this neighborhood's vibrant street culture and in the major literary achievements of Albert Woodfox, Brenda Marie Osbey, Tom Dent, Michael Ondaatje, and Natasha Trethewey, among several others.

In Chapter 5, I've gone uptown via St. Charles Avenue, the well-known thoroughfare at the center of this part of the city, crossing toward the river to consider first the literature of the Garden District and the Irish Channel, then, at the uppermost reaches of St. Charles and along its other side, the University District, turning finally back downriver to consider the major writing of the neighborhood that stands across St. Charles from the Garden District, which is Central City. A wide range of extraordinary figures have shaped the meaning of uptown New Orleans, from Anne Rice to Little Richard, Sister Helen Prejean to Everette Maddox, to name, again, only a small sample.

Finally, the last chapter of the book will be called "Outskirts." Rather than focus on a particular street and the neighborhoods that adjoin it, this chapter will explore a sense of placelessness, or, more precisely, the struggle against loss in the often marshy surroundings beyond the old city. These are the suburbs that look much like all other suburbs in the US and that, during the cataclysmic hurricane and floods of 2005, bore the brunt of the hardship, grief, and displacement. Moving back and forth between the areas known as Gentilly, New Orleans East, and across the river to the West Bank, which did not flood during Katrina, I've considered the way the major writers connected to these areas are consumed with a combination of looming threats: the forces of gentrification that have pushed Black people out of the city's traditional centers of Black culture to these flood-prone, modern suburbs; the nearby swamps as places where it's so easy to get lost that they come to serve as metaphors for an undifferentiated, monster-ridden abyss of placelessness; and finally, as the coastline erodes and seawaters grow warmer and more volatile, the certainty of yet more cataclysmic storms. From William Burroughs to Beyoncé, Karisma Price to Walker Percy, Maurice Ruffin to Skye Jackson, these are a few of the very different figures discussed in this final chapter.

To arrange this survey of New Orleans writers through these major streets makes a certain kind of sense. Streets are themselves passages, freighted over time with conflicting meaning that one must learn to navigate, negotiate, and, in the broadest sense, to read. Quintessentially public spaces, streets are monuments that, on the other hand, have immediate, daily, practical use. They divide one neighborhood from another but also connect them, as much bridge as border, and their identity remains always fluid, a function of the people, moment to moment, who happen to be hanging out or racing along. And, like monuments, streets are repositories of political memory. They merge history and geography, time and space, crystallizing thereby an array of competing meanings. Thus, the legendary mystique of these New Orleans streets, their peculiar hauntedness and allure.

This book seeks to deliver a vision of New Orleans, through its writers,well beyond the familiar romance popularized in the decades after the Civil War, when writing by George Washington Cable, Mollie Moore Davis, Lafcadio Hearn, and Grace King helped drive the first stirrings of the local tourist industry and codify the city's symbolic role in the national mythology of the US. That vision – recycled again around World War II by Herbert Asbury, Frances Parkinson Keyes, Lyle Saxon, and Robert Tallant – has come to seem, as Thomas Adams rightly notes, narrow and shopworn as we make our way into the twenty-first century, guided as we are in new ways by questions of racial justice and the precarity of the city's relation to its watery surroundings. Hence, this new, more expansive, and fine-grained reading of the city also invites writers of today to follow the lead of writers of color like Sarah Broom, Eric Nguyen, Margaret Wilkerson Sexton, and

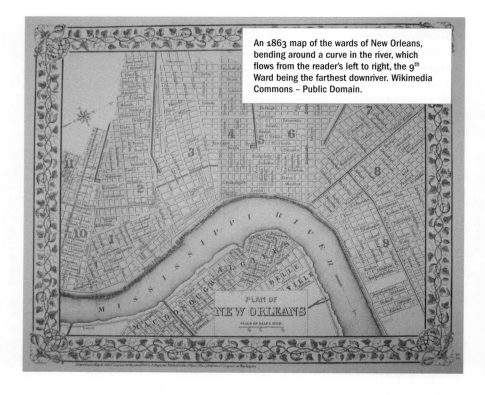

An 1863 map of the wards of New Orleans, bending around a curve in the river, which flows from the reader's left to right, the 9th Ward being the farthest downriver. Wikimedia Commons – Public Domain.

Maurice Ruffin in telling new kinds of stories about dimensions of New Orleans that have only begun to be voiced for literary audiences on a national scale.

As Lafcadio Hearn noted of New Orleans in the 1870s, "Every race the world boasts is here, and a good many races that are nowhere else." Across these races in this paradoxical capital of the old frontier, the distribution of resources and responsibilities has been not simply uneven but rather as pitched and tilted and jaggedly angled as the French Quarter skyline. Such power dynamics explain why a central motif in much of the literature of New Orleans is trauma and the struggle to recover from trauma by telling one's story. In addition to slavery, the key context for this theme is water – the swamp, the river, and the ocean – sponsoring as they have successions of outlaws, epidemics, floods, hurricanes, and high-risk dreams of escape.

Given the ways the politics of race and the pervasive presence of water have combined to make of New Orleans a volatile, ever-changing, ever-improvised entity, an additional word about the book's arrangement. Dr. John has observed that in New Orleans, "You can't separate nothing from nothing ... everything mingles each into the other ... until nothing is purely itself but becomes part of one fonky gumbo";[1] and Rebecca Solnit and Rebecca Snedeker note, in particular, that, between land and water in New Orleans, there are a "thousand degrees of marshy, muddy in-between,"[2] a metaphor, in turn, for the impossibility, as Richard Campanella notes, of drawing, in this place, any sort of hard line.[3] How then to separate a part of town into a distinct literary legacy and nexus of meaning?

By following a poetic logic, as inclusively as possible, and with as much sensitivity to nuance, conflict, and exception as one can, remaining always provisional, even fatalistic about the prospect of satisfying everyone: this has been the organizing principle of this book.

The challenge of mapping the literature of New Orleans arises still more pointedly when one starts asking to which neighborhood one should assign a given writer: Kate Chopin, for example, lived in the uptown, "American" sector, but her most important book is set in the downtown, Creole world; so, in which chapter does Chopin's novel belong? Similarly, Tennessee Williams felt that the French Quarter was the place in the world where he felt most at home, but *A Streetcar Named Desire* takes place a few blocks below the Quarter in a rather different area, and his *Suddenly Last Summer* is probably the most evocative work ever written about the Garden District. So, where to put Williams?

For practical purposes, I've decided on a simple answer. Although I'll note, in passing, the part of town where a particular writer has lived in the chapter devoted to that part of town, the bulk of the book will be devoted to discussing particular works in terms of the neighborhoods where those works are set. Thus, *Streetcar* will be discussed in the chapter on St. Claude Avenue, for example, and *Suddenly Last Summer* in the chapter on St. Charles. And because Armstrong's memoir, though anchored around Basin Street, reaches a climactic moment at the outermost end of the ridge upon which Esplanade Avenue sits, it will be discussed at the very end of the chapter on Esplanade. When a writer's settings are not local, as in the case of Tom Piazza, his work will be discussed simply in terms of the part of town where that work gets done – in his case, not far from Bayou St. John and hence in the chapter on Esplanade Avenue, even though where he writes is a fair hike from Esplanade.

This, then, is the book's ultimate goal: to delineate the primary, historic threads that run through the literature of various neighborhoods of New Orleans and the way these threads reach into the present; to showcase, in turn, the literary scene as it flourishes today; and finally to open this global gateway anew for future writers and readers who will continue to redefine the place. After all, given the scale and the speed of the changes that this city has always undergone and will continue to undergo, one cannot, to adapt an old chestnut, step into the same New Orleans twice.

Except of course through books, which give us a relatively fixed point against which to witness change. As the world becomes more urbanized and globalized, and coastal communities in particular begin to brace for increasingly frequent and large-scale cataclysms, we need precisely these fine-grained visions of how cosmopolitan, multicultural communities like New Orleans have managed to hang on and hang together as long as they have.

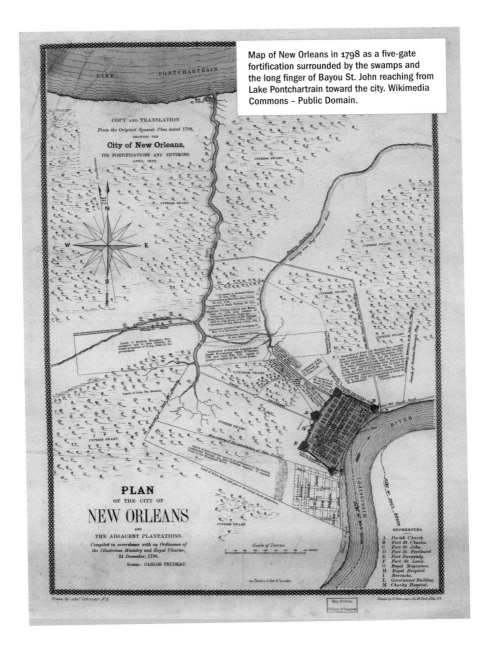

Map of New Orleans in 1798 as a five-gate fortification surrounded by the swamps and the long finger of Bayou St. John reaching from Lake Pontchartrain toward the city. Wikimedia Commons – Public Domain.

1. Hotel Monteleone – 214 Royal
2. Monkey Wrench Corner – Royal at Canal
3. Offices of The Double Dealer – 204 Baronne
4. George Cable's fictional home for Madame Delphine – 253 Royal
5. Adrien Rouquette's boyhood home – 413 Royal
6. Lee Harvey Oswald's home as a teen – 126 Exchange Place
7. Office of La Tribune – 216 Exchange Place
8. Paul Morphy's home 417 Royal
9. Mollie Moore Davis's home – 505 Royal
10. John James Audubon's home – 505 Dauphine
11. The Arts and Crafts Club – 520 Royal
12. Adelina Patti's home – 631 Royal
13. John and Gypsy Lou Webb's home – 648 Royal

14. Truman Capote's apartment – 711 Royal
15. St. Louis Exchange Hotel – 621 St. Louis.
16. William Faulkner's apartment – 624 Pirate's Alley
17. Upper and Lower Pontalba – 500 St. Peter/500 S
18. Alice Heine's girlhood home – 910 Royal
19. Home for Lestat in Rice's The Vampire Chronicles
20. Madame LaLaurie's mansion – 1140 Royal
21. Tennessee William's home – 1014 Dumaine
22. Home for Rheinhardt and Geraldine in Stone's Ha
    Mirrors – 920 St. Philip St.
23. Norma Wallace's brothel – 1026 Conti St.

Map of the Royal Street corridor: between Canal and Esp

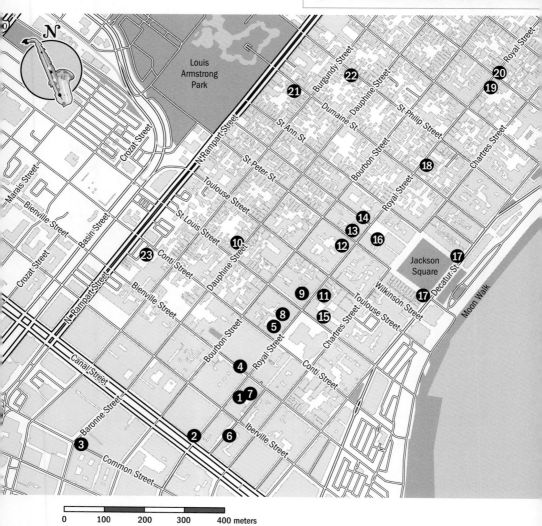

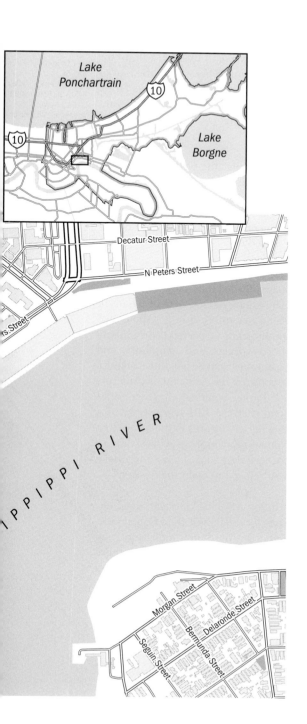

Royal Street – A Masked Ball
Between Canal and Esplanade

1

A white man left Dallas the day after Halloween, in 1959, on a flight for New Orleans. Landing just after sunset, he made his way to the foot of Royal Street in the French Quarter to check into the glamorous Hotel Monteleone. He hadn't yet figured out how, a few days later, he might check himself out as an African American. That could present difficulties, even dangers.

He made an appointment with a dermatologist the next morning and told the doctor he wanted to darken his skin as much as he could. He got a prescription normally used to treat vitiligo, a disease that leads to the loss of skin pigmentation, and was told to sit under an ultra-violet lamp. It worked. Within a few days, he could pass for Black. And thus began his experiment.

His name was John Howard Griffin. He kept a journal of the daily experiences his false identity as a Black man afforded him. He spent most of his time in the French Quarter, shining shoes, but returned each night to a boardinghouse on Dryades Street a few miles upriver. About two weeks into his project, he noted one morning a particularly gloomy mood among his African-American co-workers and neighbors, and when he asked about it, they showed him newspaper headlines about a Mississippi jury's refusal to indict anyone for the lynching, six months earlier, of a young man named Mack Parker some seventy-five miles north of New Orleans. Griffin learned that the FBI had presented a large dossier of evidence that identified the key figures in the group that dragged Parker from his jail cell late on a Friday night and drove him to a lonely bridge over the Pearl River, where they took his life and tossed his body over the rail. But the jury had refused to open the dossier.[1]

Griffin decided to travel the region in his African-American disguise. On a Greyhound bus, he passed through Slidell, and then Poplarville, where Mack Parker had been abducted by the lynch mob, and then onto Hattiesburg, where the sham trial had just ended; from there he hitchhiked to Mobile and then passed through some tiny swamp hamlets in Alabama, circled back to New Orleans, and then set out again to experience Biloxi, Mobile, Montgomery, Tuskeegee, and finally Atlanta. After some three weeks away from New Orleans, he returned to the city to masquerade one last week there; he then flew home in mid December, roughly six weeks after his experiment began, and allowed his complexion to fade back into the whiteness he had always known.

A few months later, he was famous.

He was interviewed for TV talk shows, most notably by Mike Wallace, and hanged in effigy in front of the courthouse of the little township in suburban Dallas where he lived with his family. Soon thereafter, he fled to the safety of Mexico, so he could turn the diary he kept during those six weeks into a book he would call *Black Like Me*. The book has now sold more than 10 million copies, been translated into fourteen languages, and turned into a movie. More than a half-century after its initial publication, *Black Like Me* is still a standard presence in high-school and college courses.

Today, some readers might dismiss what Griffin did as an outlandish stunt with troubling echoes of blackface minstrelsy; others might complain that it foreshadows the strange shenanigans of Rachel Dolezal, a woman of European ancestry who prefers to present herself as Black, her "true self," and expects the world around her to play along. But Griffin's intent differs from these, for nowhere does he suggest a trace of caricature, as in minstrelsy; nor, as in Dolezal's case, does he suppose that his manufactured identity is in any sense authentic. Griffin, in fact, acknowledges the limitations of what he did in the first lines of the book's preface: "[T]his is a white man's experience as a Negro in the South, not the Negro's." What Griffin renders is a relatively fleeting and wholly optional visit to the bottom end of the white supremacist system, one that he probably could have ended the instant the risk of running afoul of that system ran too high. Nonetheless, a few years after the book made him famous, he did pay a price: travelling through Mississippi, he stopped to repair a flat tire and was recognized; a mob quickly assembled and tore into him; five months would pass before he recovered from his injuries.

Griffin's life before this experiment and sudden leap to fame had hardly been uneventful. Some twenty years earlier, as a 19-year-old medical student in Nazi-occupied France, he helped deliver Jewish children from Austria to safety in England. Betrayed by an informer, his name appeared on a Gestapo death list, and, after a narrow escape, he ended up serving with the Army Air Corp in the Pacific. Wounded in an enemy air raid, he woke up blind – and didn't regain his eyesight until ten years later.[2]

These experiences, particularly in Europe, might explain why he chose to drift the way he did down Royal Street and around the surrounding region in the late 1950s, as those who suffer acute trauma are often inclined to re-create, at least in loose outline, the basic dynamics of their traumatic memories in hopes of taking control over them and quelling the terror they carry. To travel the backroads just north of New Orleans, as a Black man, in the aftermath of the lynching of Mack Parker – this was probably as close as he could come, in 1959, to the experience of being chased by the Gestapo.

And perhaps he chose to begin his journey near the foot of Royal Street, at the Hotel Monteleone, because he knew that to walk down Royal toward Esplanade, where the French Quarter ends a dozen or so blocks later, was to walk, in a sense, into the American literary imagination itself. For, particularly in Griffin's time, there was no street in the US that could rival Royal for the depth and density of its literary significance. The sheer volume of books produced on and around these blocks or that take their settings among them, the range of the drama and lore that has unfolded along Royal Street has made this thoroughfare a kind of muse to American writers, each successive generation, from the mid nineteenth century till near the end of the twentieth, inspiring the next to take their turn there. This self-perpetuating dynamic reached extraordinary peaks in the twentieth century, particularly in the 1920s, the 40s, the 60s, and the 80s, a cyclical flowering the first iteration of which can be found in the Afro-Creole poetry of the 1840s and 60s, as well as in some of the most famous fiction of that century.

All of the writing that has sprung up on, around, or about Royal Street hinges on the way that stretch of blocks – its rows of stately townhouses with their iron-lace galleries, flickering gas lanterns, and private courtyards of contained jungle – seems to inspire those moving up and down it to undergo the most profound changes, either adopting double identities or experimenting with that theme, as Griffin did, finding thereby considerable fame and even, for some, roles in far-reaching social, aesthetic, and political revolutions. In short, on Royal Street, writers have learned to experiment with new identities and to witness, through these masks, the hemispheric riptide of history.

A fine example is Walt Whitman: a little over a hundred years before Griffin began walking down Royal in his disguise, Whitman too jostled his way along these same blocks, encountering in the course of his work for a local newspaper a range of social types that outpaced anything he'd ever seen in his life, electrifying him. Immediately afterward, there began to appear in his notebooks the sort of language that would become, less than a decade later, *Leaves of Grass* – surely the most innovative and influential body of poetry ever produced in the US, a vision of urban democracy and cultural diversity as America's mystic salvation.[3] Whitman's experience, in particular, of the markets where the enslaved were auctioned off moved him: he cut an advertisement for an auction out of a newspaper – or tore it off a wall – and kept it next to the desk where he did his writing for the rest of his life. It was a "warning," he said, and also an emblem of all that his writing must always push against.[4]

As much as New Orleans emboldened Walt Whitman, Griffin went a step farther, for rather than merely bonding in imagination with the sufferings of African Americans, he took on for six weeks the identity of a Black man. When he first saw himself in a mirror in his Black disguise, he writes, "The transformation was total and shocking ... . my [first] inclination was to fight against it," for his new identity, though only temporary, registered as a threat to his survival.[5] A sign of this sense of abject powerlessness appeared a few days later when, exhausted after a long afternoon of walking in the French Quarter, he decided to rest for a moment on a bench in Jackson Square. No sooner had he sat down, he writes, than he saw "a middle-aged white man across the park slowly fold the newspaper he was reading, get to his feet and amble toward me ... . With perfect courtesy, he said to me, 'You better find yourself some place else to rest.'"[6] Griffin took the remark as a friendly warning, as intended to prevent him from far worse trouble. Later, he found out that he was not violating a law by sitting there – that the man was simply ordering Griffin out of his presence, as if it spoiled the view, and Griffin, psychologically defeated by the racist logic of the moment, did exactly as he was told, without hesitation, something he otherwise would never have done.

The contrast to Whitman couldn't be more complete than when Griffin adds that he seemed to spend most of his time and energy in search of things that, before he became Black, he could take for granted, such as a place he was allowed to eat or rest, a toilet he could use.[7] Whitman, of course, voiced a free and total access to every dimension of existence as his American birthright, such that simply pressing his way through a crowd created a kind of euphoria that bordered on the erotic.

An additional and even more pointed contrast to Griffin's experience appears in the life of essayist and editor Anatole Broyard, who was born of Black parents in the same year as Griffin (1920) in a part of

New Orleans then not widely known beyond the city (Tremé); Broyard was able to pass as white and lied his whole life about having grown up in the French Quarter. As a critic for *The New York Times*, he eventually became one of the central literary gatekeepers of his generation. Broyard named his daughter – who would write *One Drop: My Father's Hidden Life* (2008) – exactly what one would expect, given the feelings Griffin ascribes to the opposite transformation. He named her Bliss.

The Two Faces of Royal Street

Despite the grief, terror, and sense of self-disconnection that Griffin equated with his experiment in double identity, he experienced the setting for the immediate launch of his adventure – Royal Street – with "intense excitement … entranced." In the opening paragraphs of *Black Like Me*, right after he checks his bags at the Monteleone and begins his walk down Royal, he writes, "Strange experience. When I was blind, I came here and learned cane-walking in the French Quarter. Now, the most intense excitement filled me as I saw the places I visited while blind. I walked miles." Griffin continues, thrilled to discover with his eyes a world he "once knew only by smell and sound." He adds, "Every view was magical, whether it was a deserted lamplit corner … or the neon hubbub of Royal Street."[8] Perhaps what excited Griffin was the way the neighborhood had itself long presented to the world a similar kind of double identity. On one hand, that dozen-block stretch of Royal is a primary corridor of a neighborhood that stands as an international symbol of drunken debauchery, and yet the same area is also known for a cultural legacy of the highest seriousness. Griffin likely would have known the former reputation as codified in Herbert Asbury's *The French Quarter*, a colorful retelling in the mid 1930s of much of the lore about this Babylon at the end of the Mississippi River. The book offers a scandalous parade of backwoods ruffians and pirates, decadent, aristocratic duelists, voodoo queens, high-stakes riverboat gamblers, and varieties of conspirators and mercenaries with their eyes on Latin America, crystallizing thereby a popular mid twentieth-century understanding of the city as a white adventurer's paradise.

The other side of the New Orleans story might well have been known to Griffin too through *New Orleans: City Guide 1938*, a product of the Works Progress Administration's Federal Writers Program – a program that, as Lawrence Powell notes, generated roughly 400 such volumes. Published just two years after Asbury's book, the *City Guide* was reissued in 1952 and 1983, and has been called "the masterpiece of the whole [guide] series."[9] The project was directed by Lyle Saxon, and, rather than simply spinning thrilling tales in the manner of Asbury, he records actual addresses and the histories associated with them in a sober setting forth of the cultural treasure he knew New Orleans to be.

The French Quarter today is a theme park, as Ned Sublette quipped, the theme being alcoholism. New Orleans has more bars per capita than any other major American city – double the per capita number of Denver, Boston, Portland, Phoenix, and even Las Vegas, and five times the figure of other large cities.[10] Those first blocks of Royal are, historically, ground-zero for this phenomenon: in 1868, nearly half of the city's 468 saloons were located within a half-mile of the corner of Royal and Canal.[11] As Saxon explains, this spot was known as Monkey Wrench Corner by seamen all over the world, adding that every major port has a similar intersection. Even today, maps refer to that corner where Royal meets Canal by that name – "monkey wrench," according to the *Urban Dictionary*, being a verb with several different meanings linked only by their graphic sexual nature. Incidentally, Monkey Wrench Corner is the setting for an early short story by Tennessee Williams called "The Yellow Bird," where the main character, Alma, does sex work and eventually dies, her death however followed by a vision of her favorite lover bringing her a vast treasure from the sea which she then bequeaths to the Home of the Reckless Spenders.[12] (Williams later developed this story into the play *Summer and Smoke* in 1948 and then revised it to become *The Eccentricities of a Nightingale* in 1964.)

As celebrated New Orleans geographer Richard Campanella explains, port cities inevitably take on a certain reputation owing to the significant presence of male transients. In 1831, there were 55,000 permanent residents in New Orleans, but another 25,000–50,000 "strangers" were usually in town each winter.[13] Port cities, with so many men coming and going, are historically more tolerant of brothels, gambling halls, and taverns. And, as Campanella adds, given the Latin-Catholic, as opposed to the far more judgemental Anglo-Protestant, tradition, New Orleans soon took on the same devil-may-care ethos as Rio De Janeiro, Vera Cruz, San Juan, and Havana. All of these hubs of the Creole Atlantic celebrate some form of carnival and court tourists by gloating over their roguish reputations.[14] The pattern has only been amplified in the years between Hurricane Katrina and the dawn of the Covid-19 pandemic, when a city of well under a half million people hosted roughly 18 million visitors every year, most of whom likely arrived intent on having a few drinks. In this context, the lore about the old apothecary at 437 Royal is no surprise: a man named Peychaud brought with him from Saint-Domingue (now Haiti) a secret recipe for compounding cognac and bitters, which he served from his drugstore in an egg-shaped cup, known in French as a *coquetier*. This word was mispronounced by American visitors so regularly that it became known as the "cocktail," which, in the ensuing generations, became a central term in the culture of alcohol across the US and beyond.

Royal Street's doubleness was probably on Steve O'Keefe's mind when he remarked that New Orleans is the place where America's greatest writers have gone to drink, for in addition to the boozier tradition, there is another face, one of highest seriousness. In fact, the *City Guide 1938* lists more than thirty-five addresses on those twelve blocks of Royal of historic importance to architecture, politics, and the arts, especially literature. Consider, for example, 631 Royal: known as Patti's Court, it was the home for several months from late 1860 to the spring of 1861 of the opera star, Adelina Patti. (Opera, incidentally, was thriving in New Orleans in the 1790s, some thirty years before a company was founded in New York City.) In the autumn of 1860, one of the principal women in the opera company fell ill and another broke her leg. Adelina Patti, an essentially unknown 17-year-old at the time, was asked to perform both roles. Though the New Orleans audience was notorious for its exacting standards, Patti brought the house down, her triumph absolute, her planned departure delayed by several months as her fans seemed unwilling to allow her to leave the city. She finally sailed to London, where her success marked the official European debut of one of the greatest musical careers of that century. Some twenty years after this historic New Orleans debut, Verdi wrote that he believed her to be the very greatest singer who ever lived.[15]

Turning back up Royal to walk toward Canal, one would pass on the next block, at 505 Royal, the home of Mollie Moore Davis, who grew up in rural Texas but married the editor of *The New Orleans Picayune* and hosted for nearly thirty years a lively literary salon visited by most of the key writers in the city of the late nineteenth century. She had a national reputation for her two short-story collections and five novels, as well as plays, poems, and travel essays. She also published three largely fictionalized memoirs, most notably *Jaconetta: Her Loves* (1901), that concealed the reality of her itinerant, hard-scrabble Texas girlhood under the fabrication of an upbringing on a wealthy plantation.[16] Moving farther up the next block, one passes at 417 Royal the home

An early twentieth-century postcard depicting the Old French Opera House, built at the corner of Bourbon and Toulouse in 1859. It burned down in 1919. Wikimedia Commons – Public Domain.

FRENCH OPERA HOUSE BY NIGHT, NEW ORLEANS, LA.

of Paul Morphy, who in the late 1850s established a reputation as a master of chess: at age 5, he was known to be the greatest player in the city; at age 12, he defeated visiting Hungarian chess master Johann Lowenthal in a match of three games; at 21, he travelled to London and Paris, where he defeated most of the greatest chess masters of that era in Europe, usually winning easily. Hailed as the game's world champion, he returned to the family home on Royal Street in New Orleans the following year, and retired from the game altogether.

Across the street, at 413 Royal, is where the poet Adrien Rouquette spent his childhood. After his father's suicide, the family moved a few miles north to Bayou St. John, where Roquette began to interact daily with the Choctaw before heading off to school in France. In 1841, just short of his thirtieth birthday, he published *Les savanes, poésies américaines* in both Paris and New Orleans, celebrating the natural environment where he used to play with the Choctaw in and around what is now City Park and its surroundings. He returned home the next year, enrolled in a seminary, and was ordained as a Catholic priest three years later, publishing a few years after his ordination a second volume of verse, this one in English, called *Wild Flowers: Sacred Poetry*. He spent most of the rest of his life on the far side of Lake Pontchartrain, near Bayou Lacomb, where he preached to the Choctaw and wrote.

Royal Street's dozen blocks between Canal and Esplanade are dense with famous addresses, where early governors, senators, generals, and architects lived, all of them adding to the glamorous high-stakes sizzle of the street's reputation as the city boomed through the nineteenth century. A sign of Royal Street's social reach: Alice Heine grew up at 910 Royal Street,[17] and, at age 18, she married Armand Chapelle, the seventh Duc de Richelieu in Paris; when she was widowed seven years later, she began to host what would become a celebrated literary salon that would be frequented by Marcel Proust, for whom she became the model upon which he based the character Princesse de Luxembourg in *Remembrance of Things Past*. After ten years, she married Prince Albert and became thereby the Princess of Monaco; she then turned Monte Carlo into a glamorous cultural destination and took the opera singer-composer Isidore de Lara as a lover.

But perhaps the most extraordinary of all the neighborhood's former denizens is John James Audubon. His life constellates the essential forces that created the French Quarter. Born on a plantation in Saint-Domingue about five years before the revolution began that would rename the place Haiti, his father a French Naval officer, his mother a chambermaid, he had several mixed-race half-siblings; at age 6, he was taken to France to be educated, but by his late teens he was living in Louisville and then other towns along the Ohio River. He spent most of the 1820s and 30s in New Orleans, where, just a few blocks off Royal, first at 706 Barracks and then at 505 Dauphine, he worked on his magnum opus, *Birds of America*, which made him a central figure in the arts and sciences of that century.

These then are the two faces of Royal, one being the raffish assemblage of saloons and gambling dens spiraling out from Monkey Wrench Corner, and the other a corridor of high culture icons, local and global. These two faces of Royal, so central to William Faulkner's sense of the city as "foreign and paradoxical,"[18] are written into the built environment of these blocks, perhaps most vividly in that first detail that Griffin noted as he walked down Royal, the iron lace of the balconies.

Iron Lace

First, some background: a sign of its long-standing legacy of elitism, Royal Street has the special distinction of being the first street in the Quarter to be paved,[19] an event of 1822 that coincided with the centennial of the French colonial administrators' laying out of the original grid of the city's streets. Historically at a slight remove from the noisy bustle of the riverfront and also from the mosquito-ridden and flood-prone blocks a short walk toward the opposite end of the old city, Royal attracted from the start the wealthiest homeowners, people who had the means to signal their status with the most ostentatious architecture. Other parts of the Quarter feature smaller cottages and even some shotgun houses; storefronts too proliferate along the riverfront and again toward the rear of the neighborhood. But Royal – and its parallel neighbor Chartres – strike a contrasting, ostentatious pose.

Most of this architecture along Royal can be called Creole. It may have come from Normandy, perhaps by way of French Canadian settlements, but its most obvious sources are in the West Indies, where African motifs merge with those of Europe, and include the kind of hut associated with the indigenous Arawak tribes of South America and the Caribbean.[20] The style's signature features of steep roofs and piers were deemed the best solution to heavy rainfall and minor, episodic flooding, and the balconies answered the need for breezy shade against blazing sunshine.[21] The same forces explain why that 1722 plan for the city's streets refers to blocks as *îles* or islands, for heavy rain and poor drainage frequently turned the streets into canals, and, why, in turn, as sidewalks took shape on the edges of these sometime waterways, they were called – as they still are – banquettes.[22]

The central blocks of the Quarter, anchored around Royal, contrast with the blocks of cottages and storefronts that dominate the periphery in featuring the largest concentration of grand, multistory townhouses. These urban mansions, as Malcolm Heard notes in his classic architectural study, *French Quarter Manual*, often feature arched carriageways and cavernous stairwells up which the steps swirl in sweeping spirals of impossible grace. The densest cluster of these townhouses is on Royal Street between Conti and Dumaine: of the nearly one hundred extant structures in the French Quarter that predate the year that Royal was paved (1822), roughly half of them are on this six-block stretch of Royal. These creations are still here today because they were built soon after the big fires of 1788 and 1794, when strict safety codes were set forth, and, being in the heart of the Quarter, they are far from the demolition-happy developers who find their easiest prey on the peripheries.[23]

The first detail of Royal Street that Griffin notes in *Black Like Me* and that has become iconic to the French Quarter as a whole is the dazzling ironwork of the balconies. Known locally as iron-lace galleries, the largest concentration of them is on those blocks of Royal between Conti and Governor Nichols. They were probably on William Faulkner's mind when he referred to New Orleans in *Absalom, Absalom!* as "that city … at once feminine and steel hard."²⁴ As Malcolm Heard portrays these iron-lace galleries, "Their room-like volumes, outlined with dense cast-iron vines, heavy with sculpted flowers and fruits … [enact] a new vertical layer of filigree and air." They are "elevated, stacked, spacious outdoor cages – [that extend] over the sidewalks to the very curb of the streets."²⁵ These iron-lace galleries, Heard adds, are at once outdoor sitting rooms, deeply shaded and well above the clangor and stench of the street, but also viewing platforms for the parades and other dramatic pageantry that roll along below. Moreover, they are stages of their own in their delicate balance of public and private. On rainy evenings when the combination of moonlight and gas lanterns makes them glisten, they come to seem, as many have noted, like masks or veils woven of jewels.

The vogue for iron-lace galleries began in the 1850s, when the Baroness Pontalba put up the residential buildings that flank Jackson Square and that bear her name.²⁶ Born Micaela Almonaster in 1795 in the final years of Spanish colonial rule, her wealthy, elderly father, who resurrected St. Louis Cathedral from a charred ruin the year before she was born, died when she was 3 years old; a dozen years later an arranged marriage took her to France, whereupon her increasingly deranged father-in-law began a decades-long campaign to commandeer more and more of her wealth. Eventually, in a fit of rage, he shot her four times in the chest at point blank range with a pair of duelling pistols, destroying one of her hands and one of her lungs, injuries that confined her to a long recovery. (When it became apparent that she would survive, her father-in-law shot himself and died.) Thenceforth, she began to devote her money to building, starting first with the famous Pontalba Hotel in Paris (now the US Embassy), and then returning to New Orleans to focus her architectural passion and genius on the old Place D'Armes, creating in its place the plaza known as Jackson Square, and renovating St. Louis Cathedral, the Cabildo, and Presbyter. She then constructed the twin residential structures that face each other across Jackson Square, the Upper and Lower Pontalba, which came to figure prominently in the neighborhood's literary legacy. She was constantly involved in the design and execution of this project, scrambling, for example, to the top of the scaffolding – with her father-in-law's bullets still in her chest – to see to the proper fitting of the roof.

As Christina Vella observes, in her account of this extraordinary life, she also designed the "AP" insignia for the iron lace, signaling the fusion of the Almonaster and Pontalba family lines that nearly killed

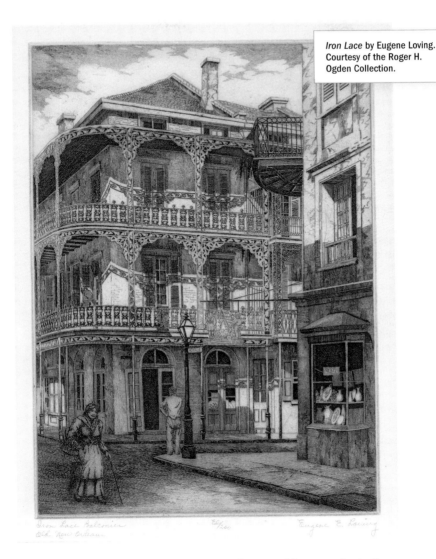

Iron Lace by Eugene Loving. Courtesy of the Roger H. Ogden Collection.

her. She located the insignia in a way that provides, paradoxically, a bold focal point for the iron lace that, as Vella notes, vanishes as soon as one stops thinking of it and thereby sustains the flowing expanse. The iron lace throughout the neighborhood can be read as an endlessly unscrolling song of praise to Baroness Pontalba for having freed herself from the horrors of her family life in France to create in Jackson Square an iconic elegance.

The iron lace has another meaning as well, for the roots of this mid nineteenth-century vogue are in Africa, as discussed in the classic *Negro Ironworkers of Louisiana, 1719–1900* by the poet, historian, folklorist, and educator Marcus B. Christian. Iron-working was well-established among the Mandingo, Jaloffs, and Foulahs, as well as groups in what later became Upper Guinea in the Sahara, and all the way to the south in Congo and Angola. So prized was this skill that it carried spiritual connotations and placed African iron-masters in a priest-like caste.[27] This esteem carried into colonial Louisiana, where the enslaved black-smiths sometimes fetched prices nearly as high as the most expensive of the enslaved, the "fancy gals."[28]

Folktales about blacksmiths have circulated for centuries in Africa. An example, collected in Heli Chatelain's *Folktales of Angola*, was said to have been quite old already when Portuguese colonizers first recorded it in the 1500s. This is the story called "The Blacksmith and the Blackbirds," wherein a blacksmith makes some hoes for some black-birds, but because he can't tell the birds apart, he doesn't know which of them should pay him for his work. He appeals to a dove to judge the case, who then begins to coo; forever after, according to the tale, this process of judging on behalf of a blacksmith is what it means when doves coo. Perhaps a trace of the ancient story surfaces in the famous metal-clinking melody, "When Doves Cry," by Prince, all four of whose grandparents were born and raised in Louisiana.[29]

Iron lace points to another fund of stories that weave their way onto Royal Street from the opposite direction. The iron worked by enslaved blacksmiths came to New Orleans from the area around Pittsburgh, brought down the Ohio and Mississippi Rivers by rough and rowdy riff-raff known as Kaintucks.[30] These people have such a rich presence in folklore and were such able purveyors of folklore themselves that they can properly take credit for the first English-language literature associated with New Orleans. Most of them could barely read or write at all, so the fund of stories that orbit around and animate these figures constitutes an oral tradition that was nonetheless memorialized in the 1850s with Baroness Pontalba's creation of Jackson Square in homage to their archetype, Andrew Jackson.

These figures who constitute the other face of the African-derived iron lace came from the forests west of the Appalachian Mountains in Ohio, Indiana, and Illinois, with Kentucky being the central territory, but plenty too coming from as far south as Tennessee, as Andrew Jackson did. They were understood to be brawlers and drunks, crude and lawless – but also unsurpassed as marksmen, and masters of the art of the practical joke. One contemporary report suggests that a signature characteristic of the type was their obscene language: "the delight they appeared to take in cursing and blaspheming were only equaled by the profligate novelty of the execrations with which their most indifferent observations was interlarded and which exceeded everything that I could have possibly imagined."[31]

After the US took possession of New Orleans in 1803, they poured into the city in large numbers. In 1807, more than 120 flatboats docked there, usually with a five-man crew – at a time when the population of the city was barely 10,000.[32] In fact, in the decade before the Louisiana Purchase, it was the pressure they put on the Spanish administrators of New Orleans to do business with them that largely paved the way for the Purchase.

Pirates Around 1810, as the population boomed with Kaintucks and those fleeing what was becoming Haiti, the pirates reached their peak. Across the river, in the swamps south of Algiers, they developed their base in an area that came to be called the Barataria, alluding to a prank in *Don Quixote* and evoking the Spanish word for "cheap" – implying in this case untaxed, smuggled, or stolen goods. Jean Lafitte ruled this shadow kingdom, with as many as several thousand employees and thirty vessels, making easy prey of the cargo vessels in the Gulf and helping the Americans win the War of 1812.

Flatboat folklore begins with the heroic Mike Fink, born in 1770 in Pennsylvania and most associated with that part of the Ohio River between Cincinnati and Louisville. As early as 1820, stories about Fink began to find their way into print in the form of a play, a novel, and a newspaper serial.[33] Soon, the figure of Fink gave rise to spin-offs up and down the riverine frontier all the way to New Orleans. Twenty-five years after Fink died, one of the most popular writers of the era, Emerson Bennett, would publish the novel, *Mike Fink: Legend of the Ohio*; blackface minstrel singers like Dan Emmet and E. P. Christy, among countless others, would be performing "The Boatman's Dance," and local-color painters like George Caleb Bingham were also taking up the subject of the Kaintuck flatboatmen and inspiring scores of imitators.[34] By the middle of the nineteenth century, newspapers were tapping into and perpetuating this folklore to the degree that the Kaintucks came to be known as hybrid incarnations of a mythical power and menace – they were called "alligator horses."[35]

Although they would eventually begin to deliver the ore that would become the dazzling iron lace of Royal Street, Fink and his brethren were initially kept out of New Orleans, according to the legends Asbury collects in *The French Quarter*, by a formidable south Louisiana folk hero known as Annie Christmas, a woman who stood 6 feet 8 inches, weighed 250 pounds, and "cherished a carefully trimmed moustache." A fearless fighter, she is said to have "whipped every bully on the river and warned Mike Fink that if he ever came down into her territory on the lower Mississippi, she would send him home lashed to the bottom of a keelboat."[36] Sometimes she dressed as a man and worked as a stevedore, other times she shaved off the moustache and converted her flatboat into a brothel that became the subject of tall tales. She is reputed to have towed a keelboat single-handedly upriver, against the current, from New Orleans to Natchez, moving "at a dead run so the boat skimmed over the surface of the water like a swallow." On festive occasions, she wore a necklace with one bead added each time she gnawed off someone's nose or ear, and two for every eye she gouged out. When she died, the legend claims, the necklace was over 30 feet long. Asbury notes that an alternative version of the story explicitly casts Annie as Black and the mother of twelve Black sons, each of them 7 feet tall and all of whom she birthed at once.[37]

This whole body of fantastic tales about Annie Christmas and the "alligator horses," according to Michael Allen, grew out of the increasingly complex stresses of daily life for white people in the Jacksonian era, as industrialization spurred the fantasy of a simpler time, one that was relatively raw, unfettered, and fun, at the center of which young men reveled in clever pranks, heroic brawls, and drunken antics, eternally adrift on rivers that flowed toward New Orleans. These figures became working-class folk heroes by the middle of the nineteenth century, says Allen, even becoming, as seen in the writing of John Henton Carter, the antebellum prototype for the late nineteenth-century idea of the cowboy.[38]

This folklore, with its easy-going ethos and anecdotal structure, constitutes a defining influence on Mark Twain, for it was at the center of the popular culture of his youth. *Adventures of Huckleberry Finn*, in particular, is unimaginable without it. Such an impact did flatboat folklore make on Twain, so much had he fallen in love with the culture of the river that, by his early 20s, he began making regular trips to and from New Orleans as an apprentice to the steamboat pilots. At 24 he earned his pilot's license, which in turn earned him enough money that he could hang around the casinos and saloons of Royal Street as a dandy. After he underwent the humiliation of crashing a steamship into the levee at New Orleans,[39] he published his first piece in a newspaper, a parody of a pretentious elder colleague named Sellers that appeared in *The True Delta* in New Orleans. Sellers had been publishing his reports about river conditions under the name "Mark Twain" (the term is what the leadsman shouts to signal there is enough depth – 12 feet – for the steamship to pass) in *The New Orleans Picayune*, but after the young pilot skewered him, he stopped writing altogether, and the younger man adopted his pen name.[40]

Popular interest in the folklore of the flatboatmen surged again in the twentieth century during the Civil Rights Era. In 1951, Julian Rayford wrote the most thoroughly researched novel on the subject, *Child of the Snapping Turtle – Mike Fink*, and Walt Disney released a movie in 1956 called *Davy Crockett and the River Pirates*. In 1959, the same year John Howard Griffin began to walk the streets of the French Quarter disguised as an African American, a song written by a high-school history teacher in Arkansas to help his students remember their lessons rocketed up the pop charts to become, according to *Billboard*, the top song of that year. The teacher wrote the song under a quintessential flatboatman pseudonym, Jimmy Driftwood; the tune is based on a traditional melody for fiddle called "The 8th of January," which is the date that the War of 1812 ended in favor of the Americans. The song, of course, is "The Battle of New Orleans." It begins:

> *In 1814 I took a little trip*
> *Along with Colonel Jackson down the mighty Mississip*
> *We took a little bacon and we took a little beans*
> *And we caught the bloody British in the town of New Orleans*

The lyric then continues …

> *We fired our cannon til the barrel melted down*
> *So we grabbed an alligator and we fought another round*
> *We filled his head with cannonballs 'n' powdered his behind*
> *And when we touched the powder off, the gator lost his mind*

The song is delivered from the perspective of the archetypal squirrel-gun-brandishing Kaintuck, executed in the classic Johnny Horton version with the pugnacious nasal twang of someone accustomed to warming himself with whiskey to sleep outdoors. More than sixty years after its release, it is often played as a fight-song at North American sporting events, serving as the unofficial anthem of the National Hockey League's Calgary Flames.

The resurgence of popular enthusiasm for this particular body of folklore during the Civil Rights Era is likely a half-conscious invoking of the most important flatboatman of them all, Abraham Lincoln. Lincoln's experience of rafting down the Ohio and Mississippi to New Orleans as a young Kaintuck in the spring of 1828 and again in the spring of 1831 was entirely typical of the tens of thousands of young men from the same background who made the same trip in the early decades of the nineteenth century, except that his two river journeys to New Orleans shaped his moral and intellectual life ever after with profoundest implications for the long arc of US history. Nearly every book ever written about Lincoln, whether for children or scholars, mentions his trips down the river to New Orleans as crucial to the formation of his character.[41]

While in the Quarter, Lincoln surely would have witnessed the auctioning of the enslaved at Hewlett's Exchange or the St. Louis Exchange Hotel, and, as Campanella writes, "Innumerable histories and biographies have deduced one core narrative from Lincoln's flatboat journeys," which is that slave trading "on a large scale and in all its brutal vulgarity" in New Orleans helped him to see the institution's essential evil and "planted in him the seeds of opposition that would eventually lead to its destruction."[42] In support of this widespread understanding, Campanella points to a passage in a letter that Lincoln wrote to the Vice President of the Confederacy, Alexander Hamilton Stephens: "When I was a boy, I went to New Orleans on a flatboat and there I saw slavery and slave-markets as I have never seen them in Kentucky … I hoped and prayed [thereafter for] its extinction in the United States."[43]

Lincoln was an avid consumer of newspapers, and the blocks around Royal were the home of several, including those that published in French and Spanish. During his second visit in the spring of 1831, a particular story loomed large in the papers, and may also have shaped his impression of slavery: two boys of African descent were sold in New Orleans to a local man, but soon escaped; one was recaptured a few days later, but stabbed the man who held him eleven times and was sentenced to death; the other was recaptured too but managed to be in the crowd to witness the hanging of the first; at the very moment that first boy was hanged, the second fell to the ground in the middle of the crowd in paroxysms of horror and died. The boys' rage for freedom and the depth of their bond perhaps signaled to Lincoln, who may well have been in the crowd that day too, their humanity, and in turn, the absurd evil of the institution into which they were born and through which their short lives ended.

Another story may have influenced him too. This one took place three years later at 1140 Royal Street: when a fire broke out at the grand mansion there, the neighborhood learned that the lady of the house, Madame Delphine LaLaurie, had been slipping away during her balls to torture, even mutilate, in the attic those she enslaved. Evidence emerged that a good many of them had died at the hands of their torturer, and a number had committed suicide. News quickly spread up the Mississippi to the Ohio River, where it reached a teenaged Mary Todd in Lexington, Kentucky, who, for days, "could talk of nothing else." Eight years later, when she married Lincoln, she surely brought it up, for the story had inspired her to help her beloved "Mamie" in guiding runaways along the Underground Railroad to freedom farther north.[44] This gruesome tale has been a mainstay of tour guides for decades. The most exhaustive, archival study of the event can be found in *Mad Madame LaLaurie* by Victoria Love and Lorelei Shannon, who suggest that LaLaurie may have taken the blame in place of the real perpetrator, her husband.

Some of the auctions of the enslaved that Lincoln visited, just as Walt Whitman would in 1848, were likely on or very near Royal Street. This type of enterprise is described in the memoirs of several of the enslaved who survived them. William Wells Brown, whose *Clotel* (1853) is the first novel written by an African American, was trafficked through New Orleans at age 16, and later wrote about it, as did Jeremiah Henson, who is believed to have inspired the title character of Harriet Beecher Stowe's *Uncle Tom's Cabin* (1852); Henry Bibb too wrote in his memoir of being sold through the markets in New Orleans. He later managed to found the first Black newspaper in Canada – *The Voice of the Fugitive* – and thereby achieved enough fame to be found by three of his brothers, who, separately, had also escaped to Canada.

In addition to these historic books, another legacy of the slave markets bears emphasis, for, not having been recorded in any form, it is too often forgotten. People trafficked through New Orleans, according to contemporary witnesses, were nearly always singing.[45] Between 1790 and 1860, about a million people of African descent were moved from the eastern seaboard to the old southwest, and, for the vast majority of them, this meant passage through the markets in New Orleans, a forced migration that, in turn, forced those undergoing it to improvise a sense of selfhood and a sense of community on the road, as they were ripped away from all that they had ever known.[46] Hence, the songs. More specifically, to be "sold down the river" – a phrase that even today signifies the worst sort of betrayal – was, for those experiencing it, a passage through the most profound form of alienation, their own bodies reduced to a certain monetary equivalence. Owned by someone other than one's self, the enslaved arrived at that most bitter of discoveries, the supreme alienation: that my body is not *mine*. In this context, the function of those pervasive songs may have been to reconstitute, tentatively, on the fly, and even if only partly, a sense of one's own being, a self among others who were sharing the same wrenching dislocation and who were seeking, in song, enough sense of community to shore themselves up against this supreme alienation.

These songs would have been heard by Whitman in 1848 and by Lincoln in 1828 and 1831. Thus, these songs, emanating from the pens that adjoined the auction spaces and landing in those particular pairs of ears, would play a role in changing respectively the course of the nation's poetry and the moral and political structure of the US as a whole.

One of the best-known hubs for trafficking the enslaved, inside the St. Louis Exchange Hotel, at Royal and St. Ann Streets, was described a half-century after Emancipation, in ruins, by English novelist and Nobel Laureate, John Galsworthy in *The Inn of Tranquility* under the title "That Old Time Place." Galsworthy's gothic study conjures a haunted setting, with water dripping down the crumbling, mossy walls of its grand ballroom and auction spaces. For Galsworthy, the ruined building, with its vast rotunda, inhabited mostly by bats, served as a double-sided metaphor for the entirety of the American South, a place defined by the careless pleasures of the rich and the crushing agonies of the enslaved.[47] Between these two, however, the first properly literary writing of the French Quarter was born.

A Creole Literature
The horrific subjugation on display at these auctions bore directly upon the realm of writing, crystallizing in 1830, just between the two visits of Lincoln's youth, when a state statute imposed a sentence of death or hard labor for life on any who "shall write, print, publish, or distribute anything having a tendency to promote discontent among the free colored population of the state or insubordination among the slaves therein."[48] So supercharged thus was the act of writing about race in 1830 that, perhaps inevitably, the most important writing associated

with the city in the middle decades of the nineteenth century engaged this territory head-on and probably explains why, even a half-century after Emancipation, one of the premier physical sites of the trade would seem, to Galsworthy, so overwhelmingly haunted.

What undergirded this draconian statute was white New Orleanians' fear that the great uprising of the enslaved in Saint-Domingue, which roared through the 1790s and birthed the independent nation of Haiti – the largest slave uprising in the history of the world, and the only one that ever fully succeeded – could quite readily happen in Louisiana. The reason this fear was especially acute in New Orleans: the population of the city had doubled in 1809 as refugees from Saint-Domingue settled in the French Quarter and brought with them fresh memories of what they had fled. Moreover, in introducing so many more free people of color, this massive influx complicated the binary of European- versus African-descended peoples that defined the rest of the American South. The newly arrived Haitian-French elites gravitated toward Royal Street, seeking to recreate in New Orleans as much of the decadent splendors of their former lives as they could, while the enslaved whom they brought along were carrying the same revolutionary fire that had upended the social order in Saint-Domingue and turned their masters into refugees.[49]

But most important were the free people of color, who constituted a complex bridge between the two, fairly unique in the US, and thus a focal point through which all three categories of refugee could forge a degree of group consciousness to resist assimilation in New Orleans to the increasingly dominant cultural patterns of the US. These new arrivals, collectively, had a defining impact on all aspects of life in New Orleans in the early decades of the nineteenth century, altering its economy, its politics, its ideas about race and religion, and its languages, changes that were soon visible in the explosive growth of cultural institutions around theater, opera, music, dance, education, journalism, architecture, and agriculture, as well as the practices of cuisine and carnival. In short, New Orleans, in the decades that preceded the Civil War, deviated to a significant degree from the racial logic of the inland South, a deviation led by certain refugees of the Haitian Revolution, at least some of whom went so far as to publish poetry about their own potential to serve as the vanguard of a post-racial society.

Although a Francophone literature had already begun to flourish in Canada and in Haiti, the literary scene that developed in New Orleans in the 1830s soon caught up. The first major wave of these writers was led by Louis Victor Séjour, Michel Séligny, Camille Thierry, and Armand Lanusse, each of whom published in *L'Album Littéraire*, a journal founded by Lanusse with Joanni Questy in 1843 that didn't survive for long.[50] Its tone on the topic of social injustice was often fiery, particularly when it took up issues of race, whether implicitly, as in an anonymous essay that called for the universal education of children in New Orleans, or explicitly, as in a short story by Lanusse in which a young woman of color commits suicide when her white lover abandons her.[51] Two years later, Lanusse published an anthology of poetry called *Les Cenelles*, which many consider the first collection of African-American poetry, wherein, as Clint Bruce notes, the acerbic tone of the earlier journal yielded instead to melancholy over the way free people of color were increasingly marginalized in the steadily Americanizing city.[52] In these poems, the free people of color seek to ally themselves with the French rather than Blacks, only taking up the issue of race in the context of encouraging young women of color to remain chaste and to avoid sexual alliances with white men, for such arrangements – known as *plaçage* – were highly unreliable pathways to wealth.[53] But poems decrying *plaçage* would likely have come to seem quaint less than twenty years later, as the Civil War erupted and newspapers based just a block from Royal Street began to publish radical political verse by Afro-Creole poets.

When the Civil War first began, the leaders of the population of free-people-of-color initially offered to serve the Confederacy as a separate unit, but were largely snubbed, as Confederate officials refused them essential equipment for militia service and never called them to the front. In fact, even before the city fell to Union hands, the Confederate leadership in the city had disbanded the unit as the state legislature voted to conscript only white men. This unit – which would come to be known as the Native Guard – then reversed course and pledged their 3,000 men to the Union cause. Less than six months after Union troops took over the city in late April of 1862, the Native Guard announced that it was fully mustered and ready for war against the Confederacy, making this announcement on the same day that *L'Union* first appeared, a newspaper based near Royal Street at the corner of St. Ann and Chartres.

In this newspaper, Afro-Creole poets, who heretofore would not have identified themselves with the enslaved but rather had themselves, in many cases, owned slaves, began to ally themselves with the newly freed Black people who were migrating into New Orleans in larger and larger numbers, doubling that demographic in the city during the 1860s.[54] This conscious decision – enacted in the poems that appeared in *L'Union* during this massive influx of Black freedmen – to cast their lot with the formerly enslaved as the best guarantee of their own freedoms followed a complicated, divisive process that was never entirely resolved. It invoked the ancestral roots that many of the poets shared in Haiti, as well as the revolutionary rhetorics of the Paris of 1789 and 1848.[55] This newspaper, which insisted that the American Civil War was part of a broader trans-Atlantic and Caribbean struggle against human bondage, another phase in the process that began with the Haitian Revolution, was sent to members of congress, and the editors themselves eventually travelled to Washington, DC, to meet with President Lincoln to appeal for the rights of free people of color to vote.[56]

A few months after the visit to Lincoln, one of the editors' lives was threatened, and *L'Union* closed. But two days later, another paper, *La Tribune*, began to publish, continuing the mission of *L'Union* with yet greater ambition. The first Black daily newspaper in the US, its editor, Jean Charles Houzeau, sought to make it the voice of the nation's 5 million dark-skinned men and located it, symbolically, at 218 Exchange Alley, a half-block off Royal in the French Quarter, within sight of the infamous auction block at the St. Louis Exchange Hotel.[57]

Houzeau wrote a memoir called *My Passage at the New Orleans Tribune: A Memoir of the Civil War Era.* Though born of white parents in Belgium, Houzeau allowed New Orleans to interpret his dark complexion as a sign of his African ancestry. Near the end of this memoir, he writes of taking on a Black identity, saying that, to whites, "I was dead, more than dead even, vilified in the eyes of my race." He then continues, "By supposing me black, they minimized the moral courage that I demonstrated in attacking an entire society ... [while my supposed Blackness] helped to increase the confidence that the colored race had in me."[58]

The poetry that appeared in *L'Union* and *La Tribune* has recently been republished in a bilingual edition by Clint Bruce under the title *Afro-Creole Poetry in French from Louisiana's Radical Civil-War Era Newspapers.* Bruce separates the volume's nearly eighty poems into five categories – but only two of the categories, the realm of ideas and of the heart, are not explicitly political. For example, when Black troops in the Native Guard performed heroically against Confederate forces in the Battle of Port Hudson a hundred miles upriver from New Orleans, their Captain André Caillou among the slain, the poet Émile Honoré published in *L'Union* a poem that includes these lines:

> *What's this? You weep for the brave captain*
> *Whose worth will astonish Port Hudson!*
> *But when he fell on that naked plain,*
> *He laid to rest a vile suspicion.*
> *Let us take heart, we men of his race;*
> *Before God alone did he deign to bow.*
>
> *Yes, there, amidst bombs and bullets' spray,*
> *This hero, of countenance black and proud,*
> *Guided the way, through the battle's fray …*

This poem, celebrating the power of the Black warrior and calling its reader to take pride in his valor and sacrifice, likely played a role in the strengthening of the Afro-Creole will to insist on their right to educate their children on equal terms with white New Orleans. Soon after Honoré's poem appeared, in the summer of 1866, Black leadership sought to hold a new constitutional convention in New Orleans with the idea of focusing on the Black right to vote. To launch this convention in full ceremonial splendor, the Native Guard led a procession that began just downriver from the Quarter, wound its way through the streets around Royal, and then emerged onto Canal Street to begin the convention. They never arrived at the convention, however, for as soon as the parade emerged from the Quarter onto Canal Street, it was massacred.

The mayor allegedly coordinated with the police in what was an explicit "attempt to exterminate the n——s."[59] Though the event is often referred to as a riot, only 3 whites were killed, as compared with 34 Blacks, and the whites who were killed were well-known partisans on the side of the Black suffrage; an additional 119 Blacks were wounded in contrast to only 17 whites.[60] At least one son of an elite Afro-Creole family of the sort that defined the Royal Street corridor – Victor LaCroix – was not simply killed but his corpse mutilated and dismembered in the middle of the street.[61]

A long poem on this subject by Camille Naudin called "Ode to the Martyrs" appeared in *La Tribune* a year later that compares Victor LaCroix to Jesus Christ and calls on people on both sides of the racial divide to honor his sacrifice and to recognize the sources of evil among the city's officials: "Policemen and firemen, come! Does calm arise? / No, for atrocities they win the prize." Another poet, Armand Lanusse, wrote about the massacre, "Let There Be Light," which also appeared in *La Tribune*: " … it was a day of rage / Of sinister harvests, of murder and of carnage, / When brothers' blood upon the pavement splashed" and then adds, "The sky concealed itself in solemn shadows." And Joanni Questy wrote a poem for *La Tribune* entitled "To the Conservatives," which refers explicitly to the massacre and to the mayor's collusion with the murderous police in planning it.

Of course, not all Creoles were devoted to the political vanguard as voiced in this poetry. The other sort of Creole held the attention, in particular, of one of the most popular American novelists of the nineteenth century – George Washington Cable. A Confederate veteran of the war, he was an unflinching advocate, as Matthew Smith notes, for racial justice. He was also an enormously popular "local color" writer, who focused on his native New Orleans in the late 1870s and early 1880s, when the city became a favorite focus for efforts in the national press to understand the perennial postwar topic of unity-in-diversity.[62] He first burst onto the national literary scene when *Scribner's Monthly* published his short story "'Sieur George," a subtle tale about a mysterious old recluse and gambler who lived for some fifty years in the squalor and decrepitude of an apartment at 640 Royal Street.[63] The old man had a steamer trunk that his landlord expects is full of gold; George undergoes a series of transformations, always from bad to worse, until in the end he is revealed to have nothing of value at all.

More such stories of exotic New Orleans came from Cable, and he soon became an extraordinary popular success. The first batch was collected under the title *Old Creole Days* in 1879, a volume that sold particularly well to tourists who had begun to use the new railroads in increasing numbers to visit what Cable showed them was a special, exotic city. The first story in the collection, "Madame Delphine," begins with a lengthy description of the experience of stepping off Canal Street to wander down Royal, a transition not simply out of the American sector and into the vastly different Creole world, but out of the West altogether and into what he casts as the mysteries of the Orient. The story was added to the book a few years after the first edition appeared, perhaps signaling Cable's desire to emphasize that walk down Royal as a symbolic entry into the cultural world that was his ultimate subject. Madame Delphine, who lives at 253 Royal Street, says, "My daughter is seven parts white. The law did not stop her from being that; but now that she wants to be a white man's good and honest wife, shall that law stop her?"[64] To cancel the wedding, the white groom is made to seem insane and thus not a viable husband for her daughter, but Madame Delphine has a superior, though more heartbreaking strategy to make the ceremony happen: she claims that she is not her daughter's mother and shows a photograph of a white woman, claiming that this woman, instead, is the young woman's true mother; the marriage thus goes forward. But when Madame Delphine confesses this sin of deception to her priest, the telling of it breaks her heart and she dies.

Cable carries this critique of the racial logic of New Orleans farther in his masterpiece, *The Grandissimes*. Set at the dawn of the nineteenth century, it follows a man from Philadelphia who opens an apothecary on Royal Street at the corner of Conti as he struggles to understand the nuances of racial etiquette in New Orleans. He has two friends, both named Honoré Grandissime, one white, the other a free man of color, half-brothers who share a father. The book made Cable hated in New Orleans, for it foregrounded bitter ironies that white Creole elites preferred to keep quiet – having children by women they enslaved and lynching those who would threaten this social order. Cable left New Orleans soon after its publication to spend most of the rest of his life in Massachusetts, foreshadowing a larger exodus that would soon be underway from those blocks along Royal Street.

The 1920s: A Post-Creole Bohemia
After the Civil War, the inner core of New Orleans became less appealing to elite families. Increasingly crowded and industrialized, the neighborhood was also easily escaped via the new streetcar line. The elite could return to the gritty urban hub when necessary, but spend the rest of their time in the lovelier, quieter world, for example, out Esplanade Avenue. Their former homes, those sumptuous Creole townhouses, were carved up into small apartments that were soon crowded with Sicilian immigrants.

Italy had recently unified but continued to look down on Sicilians, prompting many of them to seek better opportunities elsewhere at precisely the same time that elites in the American South were searching for a new labor force to revive the decimated plantation economy. Given the old shipping lines between the Mediterranean and the Caribbean, significant immigration to Louisiana soon began, the peak coming between 1890 and 1908, when at least 42,000 Sicilians came to Louisiana,[65] part of a larger population shift that brought, in the first four decades of the twentieth century, roughly 100,000 in all.[66] A significant enclave soon formed in the downriver half of the Quarter, particularly along Decatur Street between St. Ann and Esplanade, which became known as Little Palermo. By 1905, between one-third and one-half of the Quarter's population of 30,000 was Sicilian-American, transforming the Royal Street corridor into a thoroughfare of what seemed a Mediterranean port city. Living conditions in the adjacent Little Palermo were quite poor, as overcrowding and sanitation problems led to considerable disease as well as the desperation that, in turn, bred crime. Almost as soon as this community took shape, the local press in New Orleans started reporting evidence that this group was organizing itself into crime syndicates, with nearly two-thirds of the articles about this community between 1849 and 1963 related to criminal activity.[67]

The primary literary artifact that marks the end of the elite Creole era along Royal Street and the transition into its decades of squalor and violence is Rodolphe Desdunes's *Nos hommes et notre histoire* (*Our Men and Our Story*, 1911). A descendant of free people of color in Haiti, Desdunes fought in the Civil War against the Confederacy and was injured in one of the Reconstruction-era street battles; he had written for *L'Union*, helped to found the group that initiated the historic *Plessy v Ferguson* Supreme Court case, and even lived to see one of his daughters become a celebrated blues pianist associated with early Jazz pioneers Jelly Roll Morton and Bunk Johnson. His literary and political history of the Afro-Creole community, however, voiced a deeply disillusioned vision of the community's prospects for surviving in the US. He offered the book, nonetheless, as a long-shot attempt to revitalize this proud people, but only five years later, the French language would be banned from public schools in New Orleans, and Desdunes himself would go blind and move to Nebraska, where, not long after, he died.

Only a few years after this final work of the elite Creole period, a new literary bohemia would emerge along Royal Street. As John Shelton Reed explains, in his classic study of this scene, *Dixie Bohemia: A French Quarter Circle in the 1920s*, the Vieux Carré would follow the same pattern as San Francisco's North Beach and New York's Greenwich Village, whereby a neighborhood first becomes identified as a "shady" Italian-American enclave, and then the low rents, the "exotic" and "passionate" atmosphere, and the live-and-let-live Sicilian cultural style would combine to attract certain Anglos who were inclined to understand themselves, vis-à-vis the mainstream US, as adventurous outsiders in search of exciting material from which to make art.

The first trace of this new and fully national literary bohemia appears in the career of O. Henry, who lived in the same blocks where Cable set *The Grandissimes*. The most widely read writer of short stories the US has ever known, he was also a supreme master of irony. He likely learned a lot about irony from reading Cable and from witnessing the extraordinary changes to that neighborhood that were at their dizzying peak in the years that he lived there.

Born William Sydney Porter, O. Henry was working in a bank in Austin, Texas, when certain "irregularities" were found in his accounts amounting to a little under a thousand dollars; he was fired and went to Houston to work for the newspaper there. In February of 1896, he was indicted for embezzlement, then hopped a train for New Orleans a few months later, sleeping on a bench in Lafayette Square his first few nights in town before taking a room at 238 Bourbon Street across from the Old Absinthe House. He began to write for local newspapers. According to one legend, he took on the pseudonym O. Henry soon after settling in New Orleans during a night of drinking at a place called the Tobacco Plant Saloon, where the bartender was named Henry and the patrons would call out for another drink by saying "Oh Henry, another of the same."[68] According to another legend, he concocted the pen name from a list of guests at a Mardi Gras ball. Whatever its origin, the pseudonym was essential to his life on the lam.

After a handful of months of drinking in the Quarter and writing for newspapers, he left for Honduras; when his wife fell ill, however, he returned to Austin to stay with her, and soon faced prosecution. Sentenced to five years in a federal penitentiary in Ohio in 1898, he served a little over three years, and, during this time, he began to write fiction in earnest. Released in 1901, he made his way to New York City and quickly became a celebrity. Some have suggested that his time in prison scarred him deeply, leading him to withdraw into reclusive, eccentric patterns. As his fame skyrocketed in New York and as more and more of his stories began to appear, he drank and gambled more and more recklessly. In less than a decade after his release from prison, after becoming among the most widely read writers of his time, he died.

O. Henry wrote four stories that are based on his experiences of New Orleans, each of them rooted in ironic moments of loss, recovery, and double identity. "Blind Man's Holiday" is about a "shady skulker on the ragged edges of respectability" who falls in love with a girl he encounters in a cheap restaurant on Chartres Street – "that street of ghosts" where "each doorway [has] its untold tale of gallant promise and slow decay." He suspects the girl might be a sex worker and starts tailing her in the hopes of uncovering her secret, but he finds out instead that she works a second job making Mardi Gras costumes to support her family. In "Cherchez La Femme," two friends who work as reporters for different newspapers are sitting in a Dumaine Street café, when they learn that a jeweler, who is also a descendant of a prominent Creole family, has been found dead in his Royal Street apartment. He was holding someone else's money for safekeeping when he died, and that money is now presumed lost, but then it turns out to have been hiding in plain sight all along. "The Renaissance of Charleroi" begins with a young man sitting in a Royal Street café, trying to figure out how to win the love of a certain young woman; this eventually involves contacting her long-lost brother, who, it turns out, has been living as a vagabond in the swampy outskirts of the city, too proud to reappear back in the French Quarter. "Whistling Dick's Christmas Stocking" is another story of a vagabond, this one exposing a burglary plot and winning a significant reward, but in the end choosing to slip away from the luxurious home where his moral character has earned him such high praise and a small fortune to return to vagabondage.

The bohemian circles in which O. Henry moved in the French Quarter before going to prison would eventually expand to transform the neighborhood as much as the Sicilian influx had, and, for that matter, the Domingan influx of a century prior. A key moment in this process came with the 1926 publication of a short book, *Sherwood Anderson and Other Famous Creoles*, by William Spratling and a young William Faulkner. The book can be thought of as an indirect spoof on Desdunes's work, a tongue-in-cheek portrait of a community of artists who were taking over a place where, in contrast to Desdunes, they knew they didn't belong, having no history there nor any clear path to any sort of social relevance beyond their own drinking binges and masked balls.

The book was brought forth by Pelican Publishing, which was based at the Pelican Bookshop on an upper block of Royal Street, a hub for the new literary bohemia. The press seems to have been born, initially, for the sole purpose of publishing Faulkner and Spratling's satire of the community centered around Sherwood Anderson, whose apartment in the Pontalba was the other hub of the community's socializing and drinking.[69] As John Shelton Reed notes, most of the famous Creoles in Faulkner and Spratling's book were not in fact Creoles in any sense, many of them not even native New Orleanians; nor were they particularly famous, but rather, as the old joke has it, were widely recognized for being well known and internationally famous locally. They were not an especially tight knit group, but were rather held together, if at all, by the shared institutions by which they earned a living – most of them worked either for Tulane University, Newcomb Art School, or one of the city's newspapers.

They hatched in turn a number of important institutions. In late 1916, Le Petit Théâtre was born in a former flophouse in the Lower Pontalba and was instantly a roaring success – by 1928, it had 3,500 subscribing members, and *The New York Times* was calling it the greatest cultural force in the community, for it staged plays by many of the most important playwrights of the era, and also offered experimental workshop productions.[70] Perhaps yet more important was the founding in 1921 of the Arts and Crafts Club in the old Bank of Louisiana building at 520 Royal Street, a co-ed institution, and the only place in the region where men could get formal training in the visual arts (women had the additional option of studying at Newcomb). In the mid 1920s, the Club had nearly 500 active members, and its enrollment jumped from roughly 70 to nearly 150 students. The Arts and Crafts Club played a major role in introducing New Orleans to Modernism, and also to the artistic culture of Central America.[71] And it would surely have been, in particular, an institution where a readership was incubated for *El Mercurio*, a monthly magazine that featured important Spanish-language writers of the era, used cutting-edge full-color printing technologies, and emphasized New Orleans as a hemispheric hub perfectly positioned to lead the world forward in the aftermath of World War I.[72]

But the most important literary development of this Modernist moment in New Orleans was the appearance of the "little magazine" known as *The Double Dealer*. Founded in the spring of 1921 by Basil Thompson, Julius Weiss Friend, Albert Goldstein, and John McClure, they housed the journal in a vacant floor at 204 Baronne Street, just across Canal Street from the French Quarter, where the bohemia with which they identified was beginning to thrive. They named the magazine after a 1693 play by English dramatist William Congreve, explaining that Congreve's play reflected what they saw as a Modernist commitment to "the raw stuff," adding that "We mean to deal double, to show the other side."[73] The office became a natural destination for drifting poets and thinkers, many of them extraordinary characters themselves, as described in Frances Jean Bowen's history of the magazine, most of them sharing a boredom with antebellum nostalgia and an excitement about the turn toward an aesthetic radically new.[74] Although it published well-known writers associated with the Modernist movement like Sherwood Anderson, Hart Crane, Ezra Pound, and Thornton Wilder, it also discovered some writers who, though unknown, would soon become international luminaries, namely Ernest Hemingway and William Faulkner.

Despite the magazine's devotion to a new aesthetic, most of its issues seemed altogether uninterested in notions of racial progress. Particularly odd is that the group seemed to have no interest whatsoever in Jazz.[75] Born only blocks from the apartments and bars up and down Royal Street and around Jackson Square where these artists and writers were drinking and talking far into the night, Jazz was sweeping all of the other cultural capitals of the US and Europe. This new, forward-looking music would have seemed the perfect fulfillment not only of the potentials of the Creole/Freedmen alliance yearned for in *L'Union* and *La Tribune* a half-dozen decades earlier; and not only an answer to the implicit call for renewal in Desdunes's *Nos hommes et notre histoire* in 1911. Beyond these, Jazz was precisely the radically new cultural practice and form that the Modernist literary figures were pushing themselves to deliver, flowering without them and right under their noses, apparently without their noticing.

Of this entire literary community, only William Faulkner produced work of lasting and widespread interest, but the significance of the ten-year fit of inspiration and productivity that followed his sixteen months in New Orleans is hard to overstate. It probably helped to spark, in large measure, the generations of literary bohemia that continued to thrive in the neighborhood through the 1980s. Surely no writer has had a more fertile ten years than Faulkner had immediately after he left New Orleans. When he first arrived in the city in early 1925, he was a kind of late-Victorian poet in the manner of Swinburne. But then, while living a few steps off Royal on Pirate's Alley, just behind Jackson Square, he began to fabricate a new identity, wildly exaggerating his record of valor and the wounds he suffered during World War I (he falsely claimed to have a silver plate in his skull and walked with a cane, though he had no actual need for one), and claiming too a background as a planter aristocrat. But his identity changed in other ways too, as he shifted from poet to fiction-writer, composing his first novel there – *Soldier's Pay* – and, in addition to *Famous Creoles*, a series of short stories and sketches for *The Double Dealer*, as well as another novel, *Mosquitoes*.

After a trip of a few months in Italy, he was back in New Orleans, but then gone for good in 1926, whereupon he underwent a creative explosion that catapulted him to the heights of the international literary vanguard. He published eight novels in ten years, including all of his most celebrated masterpieces – *The Sound and the Fury* (1929), *As I Lay Dying* (1930), *Light in August* (1932), and *Absalom, Absalom!* (1936). He also published his two New Orleans novels in this early burst – *Pylon* (1935) and *Wild Palms* (1939), the only works of his post-New Orleans career that did not take place in his fictional north Mississippi county named Yoknapatawpha. Ten years later, in 1949, this staggering run would land him the Nobel Prize.

Absalom, Absalom! is routinely cited as among the highest achievements in US fiction. Set mostly in the nineteenth century, it hinges explicitly on the way a mythic New Orleans figures as a symbol in the US imagination. An allegory about the fate of the American South, and perhaps about America as a whole, it ultimately suggests *Paradise Lost* as a vision of the fall of a rebel, a "demon" by the name of Thomas Sutpen. This doomed protagonist is a Kaintuck, who seeks to forge a new identity by marrying the daughter of a churchgoing family in northern Mississippi and by using his mysterious fortune to fill a dazzling new mansion there with treasures purchased in New Orleans. He is brought low, however, precisely by this striving, for he articulates his upward ascent into the realm of honor (and away from the social death that is the hallmark of the enslaved) by insulting people, especially women and people of color, and these insults incite vengeance.

The possibility of redemption in *Absalom, Absalom!* is associated with endless repetitions of lore and ritualized storytelling, and through form in the broadest sense. As such, redemptive storytelling requires an immersion in history, whereas Sutpen is wholly devoted to erasing his past and suppressing certain particulars that would oppose his plan to pass himself off as a gentleman. As the novel progresses, spiraling backward into the past, Sutpen's links to people of color are revealed, and in particular a son in New Orleans who lives according to a cosmopolitan racial logic entirely at odds with north Mississippi, where Sutpen seeks to establish his kingdom. At the center of the novel is a chapter in which this New Orleans son unveils the full range of what his New Orleans life means – racially and sexually – and, as such, sets up a kind of alternative universe, one that, from the point of view of the north Mississippi frontier, is defined by impossible sophistication and worldliness, a savvy about life's possibilities that flows directly back to the Old World and even to that oldest world, Africa. Ultimately, the New Orleanian becomes the apotheosis of love, not as an airy, abstract, moral imperative, of the sort that might drive the Mississippian, but rather as rooted in the human body, both as eroticism and the blood-ties of family, the body taking on supreme value, given its fleeting temporality. This territory is entirely beyond the white Mississippian's grasp, capable as he is only of insult and consumed exclusively by the singular goal of social ascent.[76]

In profoundest contrast to Faulkner's Sutpen, another body of writing that emerged through New Orleans to astounding heights in this same period is today largely forgotten: the work of Dorothy Dix. She was born Elizabeth Meriweather at the border between Kentucky and Tennessee and was riding horses before she could walk.[77] A few years into her marriage, she suffered a nervous breakdown and went to a cottage on the Gulf Coast to recover, where she became friends with the woman in the cabin next door who happened to be the owner of the *New Orleans Daily Picayune*.[78] She soon had a job in New Orleans, writing up otherwise unreported births and deaths for the "vital statistics" page. She fell in love with the work, and was soon asked to write an advice column for women, most pointedly about how to find a husband and how to endure having one. More generally, she wrote, as Christine Vella notes, to assuage the average woes of average people.[79] She continued to do this without interruption for fifty-five years, until her death at age 90, in 1951. Her syndicated column had more readers around the world than any other writer of her day: 60 million people – a figure nearly half the population of the US at the time – read her work *on a daily basis*.[80]

Preservationists The lasting legacy of this bohemian community in the Quarter, aside from the institutions they founded and Faulkner's career, is in the preservationist movement. The very existence of the Quarter as we know it today owes a great deal to their activism in safeguarding the historic architecture. Their work in the 1940s and 50s paved the way for the classic series of books *New Orleans Architecture* that appeared in the 1970s and 80s, and, in our own time, for Richard Campanella's considerable – and indispensable – body of work on the what, where, and why of the city's built environment.

She had been living just across Canal from the Quarter during those years when her career took off, and it was in the Quarter that she cultivated her social circle. Though she left New Orleans in 1900, when she was hired away by the *New York Journal*, she formed there a close friendship with O. Henry, and they surely talked of their fondness for those blocks along Royal Street, where newspaper writers met to eat and drink.[81] After seventeen years in New York, she moved back to New Orleans, where the readers of her advice column assumed she had been

All Marriage Is a Leap Into the Dark

Marrying a Person You Never Have Seen Is No More Risky Than the Chances We All Take in Picking a Husband or Wife, Says Dorothy Dix; Golden Rule? There Is None.

By DOROTHY DIX

The top of a typical Dorothy Dix column. Wikimedia Commons – Public Domain.

the whole time. In the 1920s, she associated regularly with a number of people who appeared in the Faulkner–Spratling spoof on the Quarter's bohemia, and was well acquainted with Sherwood Anderson, the founders of *The Double Dealer*, and Faulkner himself. She had no particular interest, however, in the themes of New Orleans or even of the South, for, as Vella observes, she belonged to the whole of America, and for that matter the world.[82] Her close friend, Harnett Kane, published a year after her death a gorgeous and loving biography of her that runs a few hundred pages called *Dear Dorothy Dix: The Story of a Compassionate Woman.*

1940s: The Stars at Home

The post-Creole literary scene along Royal Street that had crackled to life around Sherwood Anderson and *The Double Dealer* in the 1920s inspired such an influx of writerly talent that a second wave of major literary history began to unfold there by the late 1930s and continued into the early 50s. This second wave probably peaked in the mid 1940s with Tennessee Williams's *A Streetcar Named Desire*, but another half-dozen or so major careers flourished in the French Quarter in the 40s, so much so that it would be wrong to think of that cohort as a bohemia, for they share, in nearly all cases, a fame that is properly understood as superstardom.

Moreover, they were, in most cases, citizens of the world who chose the blocks around Royal Street as a place where they might settle relatively late in life or use as a base to circle back to between their far-reaching and widely followed travels. In short, so famous had the French Quarter become by the middle of the twentieth century that a number of these literary celebrities of the 1940s chose to call it – despite its swarms of transients of various kinds, its reputation for exotic "otherness," and its utter raucousness – home.

In addition to their radical cosmopolitanism, they shared as well an interest in the sensual delights of the French Quarter, particularly those associated with libation and libido. Aside from the openly queer Tennessee Williams, two other key writers in America's queer literary legacy, William March and Truman Capote, are closely associated with Royal Street in this period. And two others – W. Adolphe Roberts and Katherine Anne Porter – lived, though heterosexually, at a distance from the traditional, still-dominant norm of long-term monogamous relationships. And, as with earlier and later Royal Street writers, the irony implicit in double identities crops up all through the lives and major works of most of the figures associated with the blocks along Royal in the 1940s.

The story of this second, post-Creole cohort properly begins and ends with Robert Penn Warren, who moved to Baton Rouge to join the English Department at Louisiana State University in the fall of 1934 and, for weekend getaways with his wife, took a small apartment in New Orleans, on Royal Street.[83] During the years that Warren kept his Royal Street apartment, he finished *Understanding Poetry* with his LSU colleague Cleanth Brooks, the book that birthed the New Criticism and entrenched a particular way of reading and teaching literature that would dominate US high schools and colleges for nearly half a century. In the same years, Warren was the editor of *The Southern Review*, and there he often published the work of the eminent short-story writer, Katherine Anne Porter. His friendship with Porter was crucial to his intellectual and social life during his Royal Street weekends, for in the late 1930s she rented an attic room in the Lower Pontalba with a view of Jackson Square, around the corner from Warren's apartment, where she embarked upon a romance with Albert Erskine, then Warren's managing editor at *The Southern Review*.

Porter had come to New Orleans in the hope of living quietly and finishing the trio of short novels that would appear under the single title, *Pale Horse, Pale Rider*. She was 50, and her life, particularly its first few decades, had been tumultuous, even harrowing. Perhaps she viewed her move to Jackson Square as a kind of homecoming, for, briefly, as a young girl, she had been enrolled at the boarding school next door that was attached to St. Louis Cathedral and may have remembered those years as a relatively pleasant and settled time. A direct descendant of Daniel Boone (the original Kaintuck) and a relative of O. Henry, Porter lost her mother when she was two months old, and then her grandmother, who was raising her, died when she was 11; at 16, she married the son of a wealthy ranching family, but he beat her and eventually threw her down a flight of stairs, breaking her ankle; she divorced him and worked as an actress and singer on the small-town entertainment circuit for some years, but was then diagnosed with tuberculosis and spent two years in a sanitorium, where she began to write; soon thereafter she nearly died in the 1918 flu pandemic, all of her hair falling out, and, when it grew back, it was white and remained so for the rest of her life. This is the subject of the trilogy, *Pale Horse, Pale Rider* which takes its sardonic title from the Book of Revelations and which she came to the attic of Pontalba in the French Quarter to finish. Perhaps she was circling back, in midlife, to the only stable, trauma-free environment she had known in her girlhood, to write about her closest brush with death as a young woman, imagining Jackson Square as the closest thing to a home she had ever known.

While finishing that work, she divorced her third husband in order to marry Albert Erskine, despite the fact that she was the same age as his mother. The ceremony took place on Royal Street at the Palace of Justice with Robert Penn Warren and his wife standing as witnesses. However, Porter was soon travelling constantly on the instant and extraordinary success of *Pale Horse, Pale Rider*, putting considerable strain on her marriage to Erskine, which, eighteen months after it began, ended.

Erskine would soon join Random House as an editor and work closely with William Faulkner, Eudora Welty, Ralph Ellison, Malcolm Lowry, and Cormac McCarthy, among many others.[84] In fact, when working with Lowry on *Under the Volcano* (1947), he urged Lowry to leave Vancouver and finish the work in New Orleans, which Lowry did, taking rooms at 622 St. Anne, between Royal Street and the Pontalba. The book is now commonly cited as the definitive masterpiece of the horrors of alcoholic disintegration.[85]

After divorcing Erskine, Katherine Anne Porter continued producing short stories that, when they were collected in a single volume in

1966, won both the National Book Award and the Pulitzer Prize. When Porter left New Orleans in 1940, she went to Yaddo, the legendary writers' retreat in Saratoga Springs, New York, where, during another stay a few years later, she would befriend one of Royal Street's most extraordinary literary phenomena, Truman Capote.[86]

Capote claimed to have been born on Royal Street in the Hotel Monteleone, where his mother, then 17, was staying (she was in fact staying there, but she arrived at the nearby Touro Infirmary in time to deliver him). Capote left New Orleans as a child, but he returned and took an apartment at 711 Royal Street in early 1945, when he was 21, to work on what would be his debut novel, *Other Voices, Other Rooms*. The novel is centered around Joel Harrison Knox, an effeminate 13-year-old-boy in New Orleans who is sent away to a plantation in a remote part of Mississippi to live with his father. The boy soon discovers a queer dandy named Randolph living at his father's mansion and learns that Randolph shot his father, reducing his father to a mute quadriplegic. The boy soon learns of a strange lady who is also living in the mansion, who he assumes for most of the novel is a ghost, but the final paragraph implies that the lady is really Randolph in drag. The boy, who at several points in the novel has had the experience of failing to recognize himself in the mirror, then moves toward Randolph in acceptance of his own feminine identity.

Published in 1948, when Capote was 24 years old, *Other Voices, Other Rooms* was on *The New York Times* best-seller list for nine weeks. Among the first novels openly to engage queer themes in US literature, it imme-diately made him a celebrity. Capote would visit New Orleans many times, writing about the French Quarter again near the end of his life in *Music for Chameleons* (1980), having become the epitome of the high-art celebrity, associating regularly with Andy Warhol and countless movie stars and travelling with the Rolling Stones during their infamous 1972 tour of the US. In addition to the classic crime narrative, *In Cold Blood*, he also wrote *Breakfast at Tiffany's*, the main character of which is modeled on a Tulane alumna (then Newcomb College) from Monroe, Louisiana, named Marguerite Littman, the book itself prompting Norman Mailer to call Capote "the most perfect writer" of his generation.

Perhaps inspired by *Other Voices, Other Rooms*, William March moved to New Orleans soon after that book appeared. Born William Campbell, he grew up in poverty outside Mobile, joined the Marines, and fought with such valor and distinction in World War I that both the French and US military decorated him with highest medals. After the war, he returned to Alabama and became a great financial success. He began to write in his late thirties, and, in his late fifties, walked away from his business and settled into an apartment at 906 Royal Street. According to his biography, *The Two Worlds of William March* by Roy S. Simmonds, he never married but fell in love with New Orleans, feeling more at home in the French Quarter than anywhere else, for he felt he could observe human nature there most directly, without the cloak of puritanical modesty.[87]

He began to write his most admired work, *The Bad Seed*, soon after he settled into New Orleans in January of 1952, which tells the story of a mother's realization that her 8-year-old daughter, an otherwise sweet and ordinary child, is in actuality a serial killer. A month after it was published to favorable reviews, March died of a heart attack at age 60, never living to see the novel's extraordinary success. Nominated for a National Book Award, it became a popular Broadway play, and, by 1956, an Oscar-nominated movie. It was made into a film twice more, in 1985 and 2018, taking its place in the canon of high-camp classics, a particular favorite with queer audiences.

Though Capote might have inspired March to start a new life in New Orleans at nearly age 60, the towering success of Tennessee Williams in the years before March arrived is likely the greater influence, for, as popular as Capote became in the late 1940s, few American writers of any generation can match the stature that Williams enjoyed in the middle years of that decade, when his masterpiece, *A Streetcar Named Desire*, was first performed. The presence of New Orleans in Williams's creative life, especially his beloved French Quarter, is hard to overstate. In addition to *Streetcar* and *Suddenly Last Summer*, more than a dozen of his works are set in New Orleans, and he estimated that 50 percent of his entire corpus was composed while living in the French Quarter.[88]

Williams gave himself the name "Tennessee" while travelling on a bus in 1938 en route to New Orleans for the first time, and, among his first uses of that name came when, upon arriving in the city, he registered at the boardinghouse at 722 Toulouse Street, a half-block off Royal. The French Quarter, he later said, was the place he "was made for." For he learned to embrace his sexual identity among those blocks along Royal, where, in turn, he found his spiritual home, and, as Gore Vidal notes, created a literature that "changed the concept of sex in

America."[89] Signaling the importance of this neighborhood to the arc of his development and his achievement, he began writing a play when he first arrived in the late 1930s that he would continue to revise for the next forty years, only finishing it a few years before he died. The play was based on his experiences at the boardinghouse on Toulouse Street and is called *Vieux Carré*. He was perhaps too close to the subject, too personally invested in it, for, having tinkered with the play off and on for forty years, its first production in 1979 closed after only five performances.

The Royal Street corridor of the 1940s seems in hindsight fairly crowded with literary celebrities who, like Williams, March, and Capote, considered it the sort of home that could spark their creative energies the way no other place could. Consider the example of Frances Parkinson Keyes: she came to New Orleans at age 55 for the Mardi Gras of 1940, having already written some fourteen books, and was immediately in love with the city, producing the novel *Crescent Carnival* two years later, and then another seven books that would be set in Louisiana. But her most famous is *Dinner at Antoine's*, which its book jacket hails as a "multi-million best-seller of 1948". A novel of manners structured as a murder mystery, it hinges on how Keyes's Catholic faith, which she adopted late in life, understood the sacrament of the funeral mass as akin to a question of honor, which was particularly important to the Creoles of the French Quarter among whom the novel is set. Keyes was keen to capture the historic atmosphere of New Orleans, and so bought a mansion on Chartres Street that had been the home of Confederate General P. G. T. Beauregard, who started the Civil War when he fired on Fort Sumter in 1861. But her novels weren't the only ones written just off Royal Street in the 1940s that were saturated with a sense of the past.

The first novel in W. Adolphe Roberts's trilogy of historical fictions is called, of course, *Royal Street* (1944). The other two are *Brave Mardi Gras* (1946) and *Creole Dusk* (1948). *Royal Street*, set in the 1840s, is woven of scenes depicting the Creole culture of fencing and duelling, gambling, and the meetings of political groups as the region begins to move toward secession, and the other two follow this community through the years of the Civil War and Reconstruction. Roberts's life, as detailed in his autobiography, *These Many Years*, gives an idea of what a presence he must have been in the Quarter of that period. Born and raised in Kingston, Jamaica, he left in his teens seeking newspaper work, living in the roaring bohemia of New York City, as well as in San Francisco,

Paris, and Havana, becoming a good friend of Jack London and likely a lover to Edna Saint Vincent Millay. By the late 1930s, around the age of 50, he published a tract advocating for the independence of Jamaica, founded the Jamaican Progressive League, and became a leader in the movement to throw off British rule. Around the time World War II broke out, however, he angered the regime then directing affairs in Jamaica and knew he would now be cut off from any possibility of visiting for a long time; he then settled into New Orleans as an exile to devote himself to writing.[90] He lived in a small house on Dumaine Street near the corner of Royal for most of the 1940s, producing there not only the fictional trilogy about nineteenth-century Creoles, but also the monumental history called *The Caribbean: The Story of the Sea of our Destiny*, as well as a book called *Lake Ponchartrain*, a history of New Orleans from the viewpoint of its swampy back end, as opposed to the glamorous front-facing French Quarter. Deeply contented during his ten-year stay in New Orleans, he said that he wished that he had landed there as a young man after first leaving Jamaica. He might never have left, nor might his decade-long stay in the 1940s have ended, had not the course of history in Jamaica finally called him away to take a leading role in the independence movement.

This mid twentieth-century period of Royal Street's literary history properly ends with the publication in 1954 of Robert Penn Warren's *Band of Angels*, exactly twenty years after Warren leased that Royal Street apartment in 1934. As William Bedford Clark claims, there is probably no US novelist more consumed with the nation's history than Robert Penn Warren, and none of Warren's novels realize this historical vision more deeply than *Band of Angels*.[91] Though most remembered for his other Louisiana novel, the iconic *All the King's Men* (1946), it is *Band of Angels* that reckons most directly with the history of New Orleans. As Clark notes, at the center of this novel set in the years just before, during, and after the Civil War is the familiar plight of the girl who appears to be white but who is technically African American and is thus plunged into the horrors of the slave trade in ways designed to galvanize white outrage against the peculiar institution.[92] Though the novel's plot is at times strained, Warren evokes mid nineteenth century New Orleans in rich and convincing detail, featuring several iconic situations, from the downriver steamboat journey to the auctions of the enslaved to early jubilation about secession to the growing sense of dread as the city prepares for the Union army to seize it to the horrifying massacre of Civil Rights advocates in the summer of 1866.

In the French Quarter of the 1940s, the sheer social reach of these writers – Robert Penn Warren, Katherine Anne Porter, Frances Parkinson Keyes, and Adolphe Roberts – combined with the millions of young soldiers passing through the city to serve in World War II cleared the way for Tennessee Williams, Truman Capote, and perhaps William March to articulate to increasingly wide audiences a new dimension of the city's long-standing reputation for being particularly sexually permissive for white men. No longer restricted to the slave markets or to the nearby red-light district that is an obvious descendant of the slave market, the long-standing sexual privileges of monied white men probably made possible, by the 1940s, the sexual candor discernible in the queer literature that sprang up around and about Royal Street in that period. This literature in turn gave the French Quarter a new foothold in the larger and more repressive American imagination of the mid twentieth century, from which it would play a substantial role in the massive social transformations that characterized the second half of the twentieth century: a recognition, in short, of how many otherwise ordinary homes were doubling as masks.

1960s: Multiple Undergrounds

Sherwood Anderson, so important to the 1920s, would play a key role in another generation of Royal Street's literary stars as the 1940s began, but his work on this count didn't bear fruit until the 1960s. He was the person John and Gypsy Lou Webb contacted when they arrived in town in 1940 and to whom they looked to get their bearings.[93] John had robbed a jewelry store in Ohio as a young man, but his scheme, though ingenious, failed and he went to prison for a few years, where he began to write – at first, mostly detective stories for pulp magazines. Shortly after his release, however, he drifted with his wife to Saint Louis and then to New Orleans, where they took an apartment at 648 Royal Street and stayed for twenty years.[94] Within a few years of their arrival in the Quarter, they met John Steinbeck, Tennessee Williams, and Ernest Hemingway, and, in 1948, John published a serious memoir of his prison experience called *Four Steps to the Wall*.[95] A bit later, Lawrence Ferlinghetti, an important role model for the careers they would soon launch, visited their Royal Street apartment on his way back to San Francisco from his famous visit to revolutionary Cuba in 1960, the year the Webbs founded their magazine, *The Outsider*.

The magazine's first issue had a print run of three thousand, and was typeset, collated, and bound in their tiny Royal Street apartment, where for months they worked sixteen hours a day, seven days a week to bring it out. They stopped drinking for a year to create the financial nest egg they needed to launch it; he was 55, she 44, and this was to be their shot at taking a place in literary history.[96] The first issue featured new work by Gregory Corso, Diane Di Prima, Allen Ginsberg, William S. Burroughs, and Gary Snyder. The second would feature new work from Jack Kerouac, Jean Genet, Howard Nemerov, Henry Miller, William Burroughs, and Charles Bukowski.[97]

When in 1957 tensions in Tulane's Theater Department led *The Tulane Drama Review* to decamp to Yale and become *The Drama Review*, the Webbs were able to buy the journal's production equipment.[98] With that machinery in their cramped Royal Street rooms, they founded Loujon Press and used it to publish Charles Bukowski first book of poetry, *It Clutches My Heart in Its Hands*, which got a favorable review in *The New York Times*. They then brought forth Bukowski's second

Charles Bukowski and Gypsy Lou Webb. Courtesy of the Historic New Orleans Collection.

book, called *Crucifix in a Deathhand*, which was nominated for a Pulitzer Prize. The Webbs left New Orleans in the mid 1960s, drifting around the southwest, publishing a Henry Miller manuscript, and then settling briefly in Nashville, where John died suddenly in 1971.

After John's death, Gypsy Lou Webb made her way back to New Orleans. She was certainly well known by then, as Bob Dylan named his song, "Gypsy Lou," for her, probably after meeting her and John during his Mardi Gras visit of 1964 that also inspired "Mister Tambourine Man." In the ensuing years, she lived in an apartment above a bar on Bourbon Street and supported herself by working in a t-shirt shop. She sometimes shocked visitors by reaching into a locket she wore around her neck that contained ashes and bone fragments from her late husband's remains and also from the remains of a child they had together but lost when they first moved to New Orleans. She would pull out little fragments of bone and pop them into her mouth, crunching them up with her teeth and swallowing them. Their close friend, the celebrated painter Noel Rockmore, witnessed this first hand, as did Liza Williams, a one-time girlfriend of Bukowski's. Gypsy Lou finally passed away in mid December of 2020, at the age of 104, having outlived the love of her life by a half century.[99]

John and Gypsy Lou's magazine, *The Outsider*, united high literary seriousness with gritty, down-and-out urban experience in ways that recall the stated mission of *The Double Dealer* some forty years prior. But no figure surpasses, in these terms, the achievement of John Rechy, whose *City of Night* (1963) climaxes in the French Quarter during Mardi Gras and is now a benchmark in the history of queer literature. The book's narrator is a gay male sex worker, based closely on Rechy's own life-experiences, and it portrays a catalogue of other, similar men and their customers, as well as male drag artists of various kinds, all of whom, as Charles Casillo notes, crafted artificial personas to camouflage and protect the vulnerable inner selves that the dominant social reality of that era would have destroyed.[100] This novel of what was then called "the homosexual underground" embodies the beatnik aesthetic of having been written on the fly, but in fact went through seven drafts of meticulous revision. The first lines of Rechy's introduction to the 1984 edition read, "*City of Night* began as a letter to a friend in Evanston, Illinois. It

> **Bukowski** Charles Bukowski would drift in and out of New Orleans many times over the course of his life, sometimes staying for months. His poem "Young in New Orleans" captures what he loved most about his life in a rat-infested garret in the French Quarter: the anonymity it afforded him. An excerpt: "being lost / being crazy maybe / is not so bad / if you can be / that way / undisturbed. // New Orleans gave me / that / nobody ever called / my name."

was written in El Paso the day following my return to my hometown in Texas after an eternity in New Orleans." He then turned this letter into a short story called "Mardi Gras," inspired by an epiphany he had in New Orleans that hinged on an experience of silence on Ash Wednesday. The story appeared in the sixth issue of *Evergreen Review*, which was then publishing Artaud, Beckett, Camus, Kerouac, and Sartre, but, as Rechy's story began to grow into a novel, he had trouble finding publishers willing to risk such a project. He returned to hitchhiking and working the streets for a time, but then settled back at the home of his Mexican-American parents in El Paso to finish the book. He considered different titles, including *Shrove Tuesday* and *Masquerade*, but finally settled on *City of Night*. It was the publishing event of 1963, quickly arriving at the top of the *Times* best-seller list, making Rechy rich.

The year 1963 was very important in other parts of the New Orleans underground, for that November, of course, President John F. Kennedy was assassinated in Dallas, allegedly, by a young New Orleanian named Lee Harvey Oswald. A vast literature has arisen around that event. Some works that conjure the French Quarter underworld of that period provide essential context and a useful starting point for contemplating the killing of the president and all that has been written about it.

Christine Wiltz's *The Last Madam: A Life in the New Orleans Underworld* tells the true story of Norma Wallace, whose career properly began when she stepped off Royal Street through the ladies' entrance to the Cosmopolitan Hotel (the massive structure's other entrance was a block away on Bourbon) and understood instantly that many of the ladies she saw in the lobby were sex workers. She was probably 15 years old, but later in life she admitted that she had lied about her age so many times and for so long that she had lost track of her actual birth date. The women in the lobby of the Cosmopolitan told her to learn the trade elsewhere, recommending that she go to Bertha Anderson's house at 335 Dauphine, a madame who had worked in Storyville, under the legendary Josie Arlington. One night, when she was running the house in the absence of the madam, a man died in bed with one of the women who worked there – Wallace had to handle the dead body and the cops, make sure no one got arrested, and, on top of that, keep the madame's husband from dipping into the till. After she managed that night with success, she knew she was ready to have her own brothel.[101] Though Wallace had no education beyond a year or two of grade school, she was shrewd enough to have survived, in her teens, her first husband shooting her and to have developed two personas that profited off each other enormously: "one that operated in the respectable world ... and the other that was equally comfortable in the underworld."[102]

Her establishment was the longest continuously running operation of its kind on record in the history of the city. She ran it for forty years, and for most of those years it was housed at 1026 Conti, in a building that had once been owned by Ernest J. Bellocq, who figures centrally in the literary legacy of nearby Storyville. She finally moved her operation out of the French Quarter when she was in her sixties, around the time she married a 25-year-old.[103] By then, her house on Conti had become an underground institution: John Wayne and Don Ameche visited, and Marjorie Rambeau once spent 30,000 dollars there in a single night. In the spring of 1936, Alvin Karpis, then at the top of the FBI's most-wanted list as a key member of Ma Barker's infamous gang of bank-robbers, appeared at Wallace's bordello; she recognized him and notified the police, who soon arrested him; Karpis would spend the next twenty-six years at the island prison in San Francisco Bay known as Alcatraz,[104] eventually becoming a mentor and guitar-teacher to his young cell-mate, Charles Manson, in the years before the latter was loosed on the psychedelic streets of the Bay Area in the mid 1960s.

A particular sign of Wallace's power: when she decided to get a police dog and name it Vidalia, after a small country town upriver from New Orleans, the women who lived and worked in her house soon began to use the name Vidalia as code for rural men who seemed never to have been in a big-city brothel before. The term soon caught on and spread widely, even among cab-drivers and bellhops, always to refer to male tourists who seemed unsophisticated in their obvious search for a sex worker. The term is still in wide use in New Orleans today to refer to naïve-seeming outsiders and new-comers.

One of Wallace's most illustrious protégés, Frenchy Brouillette, must have seemed a Vidalia when he first arrived in the French Quarter, but he didn't stay that way long. He had left the small Cajun town of Marksville at age 17 in 1950 on his older brother's Harley Davidson and a few hours later was on the street in New Orleans in a world that, as he put it, was "cooler than rock and roll." His memoir, *Mr. New Orleans: The Life of a Big Easy Underworld Legend*, offers some 400 pages of wisecracks and gossip, uproarious tales of human moral frailty and daring, and no little philosophic wisdom, all delivered in the lyrical gangster lingo of that era, but it climaxes when Brouillette slips into a forty-page tell-all about how his friends and colleagues in the criminal underworld of New Orleans assassinated President Kennedy and got away with it.

Brouillette was first taken under the wing by one of Wallace's husbands, Blind Pete Gulotta, the world bantamweight champion of 1917 who had been badly thumbed in the eye during a fight, but kept fighting until well after his sight was nearly gone (he called it "boxing by Braille"). Brouillette says that Wallace, in the middle decades of the twentieth century, was the most powerful woman in New Orleans, and that he was proud to know her as his lifelong guardian, mentor, and friend.[105] Just as Wallace and Gulotta educated him in how to succeed in managing a prostitution ring, he was educated in illegal gambling rackets and initiated into the New Orleans Mafia more generally by Dutz Murret, whose wife was a sister of Lee Harvey Oswald's mother. Brouillette met Dutz's historic nephew several times in the summer of 1963, and had long-running friendships with a number of Oswald's close associates.

Oswald lived for a while as a teen with his mother a half-block off Royal Street in the Quarter at 126 Exchange Place, in a small apartment above a pool hall.[106] Oswald also lived with his favorite uncle, Brouillette's mentor Dutz Murret, when he returned from the Soviet Union, and again in the summer of 1963, a few months before the assassination; Oswald otherwise is famously hard to know, for, as many have noted, he himself had very little idea of whom he worked for or, more to the point, who was assembling his identity. He could never have defected to the Soviet Union and then returned to the US without significant sponsorship. Could that sponsorship have come from anywhere but the CIA? His favorite television show as a child had been *I Led Three Lives*, about a Boston man who secretly befriended communists at the height of the Cold War, but did so, yet more secretly, as an FBI informant.[107] His short life may have followed a version of that logic.

Mafia The earliest traces of organized crime among Sicilian-Americans in New Orleans reaches back to the 1860s, the first Mafia in the US. In 1947, Carlos Marcello became the local boss, and grew so wealthy so quickly that he soon drew the attention of federal investigators, particularly John and Robert Kennedy. Less than three months after John's inauguration and appointment of Robert as Attorney General, they had Marcello deported. Dumped in Guatemala with no chance to prepare, Marcello finagled his way back into the US in less than two months and swore a vendetta against them.

Much more central than Oswald to the story Brouillette tells is Mafia-kingpin Carlos Marcello. A product of Little Palermo in the lower half of the French Quarter, Marcello, during the early decades of the twentieth century, rose to become the ruler of a shadow government that stretched from Tampa to Dallas, and dominated the Gulf Coast and the deep South from the immediate aftermath of World War II until the early 1980s, when Marcello was arrested as part of a sting operation on a massive, long-running bribery machine. As Brouillette and most observers of the New Orleans underworld of that period proclaim, perhaps with a trace of hyperbole, Marcello owned every card game, dope deal, and whorehouse in the region, which allowed him, rather quickly, to amass sufficient financial resources to start buying up, in turn, numerous judges and jails and entire police departments. Marcello himself always insisted that he was just a humble salesman for his Pelican Tomato Company.

To delineate his precise maneuvers over the middle decades of the twentieth century is difficult, for obvious reasons. Nonetheless, the best starting point for sorting out Marcello's extraordinary career is *Mafia Kingfish* by John L. Davis (1989). Davis was a cousin to Jacqueline

Carlos Marcello, the Mafia kingpin who was based in New Orleans, seen here at a 1959 Senate Hearing. Wikimedia Commons.

Kennedy Onassis. His book traces the history of the Mafia in New Orleans and the particular details of how Marcello rose from a petty hoodlum in the French Quarter to the chief money-launderer for New York slot-machine magnates and mob-bosses, Frank Costello and Lucky Luciano. From there, the book explains how Marcello began to pressure politicians, killing, for example the newly elected Attorney General of Alabama in 1954, Albert Patterson, for having campaigned and won on a pledge to crackdown on a mob-run, vice-ridden town near the Georgia border. Davis then ultimately explains how and why J. Edgar Hoover steered investigators away from the Mafia's role in the assassination of Kennedy and toward the framework, more easily sold at the height of the Cold War, that casts Oswald as an isolated "communist wacko."

Another essential book on Marcello's role in the assassination is Lamar Waldron's *The Hidden History of the JFK Assassination*, which hinges on a set of secret recordings that were made in Marcello's prison cell in the mid 1980s at the federal penitentiary in Texarkana, in which Marcello can be heard explaining how and why he had Kennedy killed. The story of these extraordinary tapes actually begins a decade earlier, in the summer of 1975, when the relationship between the Mafia and the CIA, particularly in efforts to assassinate Fidel Castro in the early 1960s, were becoming front-page news.[108] Questions began to arise about the possibility of that same partnership having killed Kennedy, setting off a chain of no fewer than nine gruesome slayings that silenced those leading figures who were set to cooperate with the investigation then underway by the House Select Committee on Assassinations.

In 1979, that Committee declared that the killing of President Kennedy likely proceeded by conspiracy, and that Marcello (along with Tampa/Havana crime boss Santo Trafficante) had the motive, the means, and the opportunity to have led it. In the absence of hard evidence against Marcello, however, no additional action was taken – until two years later, when Marcello was arrested and sent to the federal prison in Texarkana on bribery charges; soon, a clock-radio was given to his cell-mate, Jack Van Laningham, that concealed a recording device.

As the aging kingpin began to talk about the events in Dallas in November of 1963, the sound of his voice was relayed in real time all the way up to the then Attorney General of the United States, Edwin Meese. These tapes hung the killing of Kennedy on Marcello, but because they also implicated the FBI and the CIA, to whom Meese was loyal, he never acted upon them.

Marcello's relationship with the CIA is the most difficult dimension to nail down. Was the CIA using Marcello the same way it used Oswald, a second layer of patsy in case the "lone communist wacko" framework fell apart? Or was Marcello leveraging what he knew of CIA plots to kill Castro to force the CIA to cover up his killing of Kennedy as only they could? Either way, one thing is certain: in the early 1960s, when Marcello had been ascendant in New Orleans for a solid fifteen years, the city, as a gateway to Latin America, was also a primary hub of CIA activity. *JFK and the Unspeakable* (2010) by James W. Douglas and *The Devil's Chessboard* (2016) by David Talbot explore in depth the possibility of the CIA's role in Kennedy's death and the subsequent cover-up that climaxed in the mid 1970s with the nine murders of those slated to meet with Congressional investigators. Within the particular context of New Orleans, Joan Mellen's *A Farewell to Justice: Jim Garrison, JFK's Assassination, and the Case That Should Have Changed History* (2005) explains how much of this was nearly exposed a mere half-decade after the assassination.

Set in the same year as the assassination and Rechy's rise to fame, yet another underground provides the backdrop for the finest novel of the French Quarter in the 1960s, Robert Stone's *A Hall of Mirrors* (1967), a book that unfolds amidst political extremists, conspiracies, and con-games in a New Orleans cast in the most noir-ish of tones. At 23, Stone moved with his wife Janice to New Orleans in January of 1960 and settled into the French Quarter on St. Philip Street, between Royal and Bourbon, in a furnished apartment with a balcony overlooking the street, replete with iron lace. Stone nearly took a job performing in a travelling Passion Play, but, rather than leave his pregnant wife alone in New Orleans while he travelled the region, he got a job with the census, recording information about households as he went door to door. He worked too for a time in a soap-factory downriver from the city. All of this would be folded into *A Hall of Mirrors*. A year or so later, the young family would be back in New York, but would decamp soon to Stanford, where Stone had a Wallace Stegner creative writing fellowship, and where he would write his New Orleans novel, finally publishing it on his thirtieth birthday in August of 1967.

The novel brings together three lives: Rheinhardt, a young man who is already succumbing to

> **Occultists** In 1967, a splinter group from the Church of Scientology called the Process Church of the Final Judgement set up a base on Royal Street, as Alison Fensterstock explains, from which, in purple and black robes with large pendants, acolytes sold the cult's magazines, books, and newsletters. Their publications were noted for their stunning graphics, a sample reissued by Feral House in 2011. Well into the 1970s, they offered a psychotherapeutic technique for both people and pets, as well as courses in hypnotism, nutrition, and t'ai chi, but several books cast them in the most sinister terms.

devastating alcoholism; Geraldine, a down-on-her-luck latter-day Kaintuck who has recently lost both her husband and baby, and is fleeing a violent pimp in Galveston; and Rainey, an idealistic misfit who yearns for the moral improvement of the world. Rheinhardt is at the center of the book, and it begins and ends focused upon him. He is of the beatnik generation, and, in spite of his alcohol problem, he is a study in sardonic self-possession and supreme "cool." Embarking on a short-lived romance with Geraldine, he presents himself as the diametric opposite of Rainey, with not a trace of the uncouth naïf or do-gooder about him. Though an intellectual, he takes a job at a right-wing talk-radio station, and soon becomes a featured presence, pretending to embrace the role of the fear-mongering racist who serves up the rhetoric that drives the backlash against the Civil Rights Movement. But, just as he fools the people for whom he works, they in turn have sinister ambitions to manipulate a "patriotic rally" into a miniature riot by way of galvanizing a white mob. In the end, Rheinhardt becomes a supremely ironic figure, wholly disconnected from himself and his surroundings, the perfect reversal of the "cool" that has characterized him through most of the novel, every bit as lost as his buffoonish doppelganger, Rainey; his inability to know himself, to see a mirror image of himself in the others upon whom the illusion of his power is based, undergirds the novel's ending in an apotheosis of ironic self-disconnection, a double identity in which the right hand has no knowledge of the left.

The novel ends in the months just before the Kennedy assassination and makes no mention of that event. But it offers in its final sections a perfect distillation of noir irony, a vision of New Orleans in the early 1960s as an impenetrable shadow that may, at last, be as close as we can ever come to the truth of what happened in Dallas.

Since the 1960s: A Mythological French Quarter

As the 1960s and the era of the Kennedy assassination began to recede into the past, New Orleans, after nearly a century of being celebrated in the American literary imagination for its exotic charm, its otherness, and its power to inspire revolutions, aesthetic, political, and sexual, perhaps began to sag under the weight of its extraordinary meaningfulness. The arc of every bohemia is much the same: as soon as artists and writers begin to "discover" a place where rent is cheap and the neighbors tolerant, they start fixing up the decaying spaces, eventually opening cafés and galleries, and the "revitalized" neighborhood starts to draw less serious people, gawkers and poseurs, and then, hard on their heels, outright tourists, as long-term residents soon complain that the place just isn't what it used to be, as still more properties get even more fixed up, and the real-estate values skyrocket to the point that artists are driven out altogether.[109] Thus, compared to the immediately prior generations, far fewer works of lasting interest began to invoke the Royal Street corridor after 1970, and most of those that did were only self-consciously engaging the setting more for its mythic resonance, rather than to conjure any contemporary verisimilitude or historical complexity.

This new, mythological vision of the French Quarter begins with what remains its most successful iteration: Ishmael Reed's *Mumbo Jumbo* (1972), a visionary Afro-centric rendering of the Jazz Age, in which the music born in New Orleans is really the expression of a spirit-god known as Jes Grew; though white people understand its spread in terms of plague, it is actually a sacred force, dancing forth across the American landscape, in search of its sacred text, the Book of Thoth, which will codify and anchor it as a religious institution for all time. Though Reed's novel begins in the French Quarter at St. Louis Cathedral in Jackson Square, it follows the "plague" to Harlem and then spirals back to cosmic battles in ancient Egypt. A similar move shapes Anne Rice's *Interview with the Vampire* (1976), which uses the house at 1132 Royal Street as the model for the home of Lestat, who would become a central character in her multi-volume mythology as he ranges across continents and centuries.[110] In tones similar to Reed's comic masterpiece, Tom Robbins's *Jitterbug Perfume* (1984) tells the story of a pagan king in pre-Christian antiquity who has embarked upon a quest for immortality. Along the way, he and his lover meet the god Pan and, to conceal Pan's highly sexualized stench, they create a perfume for him to wear that comes to be known as the most enchanting of scents, a supreme trigger to memory and desire, and, in turn, the mystic power of immortality. The novel leaps back and forth between Paris, New Orleans, and Seattle, and from one century to another, as the sacred bottle of perfume gets lost and ends up in New Orleans, with a family that runs a perfume shop on Royal Street. In a more folksy vein, Harry Crews's *The Knockout Artist* (1988) would seem the most recent installment in the nearly 200-year tradition of stories about Kaintucks running amok in the French Quarter, bringing the folklore and mythology that characterizes the major French Quarter novels of the 1970s and 1980s back to their roots in the lore of the "alligator horses" of the flatboat era. The titular character of Crews's novel is Eugene Talmadge Biggs, a failed boxer and denizen of the New Orleans Athletic Club at the edge of the Tango Belt in the Quarter, who discovers that he can punch himself in the face hard enough to knock himself out, and thus becomes a kind of circus freak whom the decadent rich of New Orleans hire as entertainment at their parties.

Paula Fox's *The God of Nightmares* (1990) suggests in its title an interest in some of the same territory as *Jitterbug Perfume* and *Mumbo Jumbo*, but undertakes none of the comical, cartoonish allegory of those works. It is set mostly in the late 1930s and early 1940s, when a young woman, new to the city, comes to rescue her aging, deeply alcoholic aunt, who is living in a decaying mansion on Royal Street. She falls in with the French Quarter bohemia of the era, and then interprets her experiences among them some twenty years later in terms of her having first come to know, through them, fierce romantic attachment and also mortality, a kind of initiation into adulthood through the cocktail parties of the Royal Street artists and intellectuals of the 1940s. This world comes to embody the mythic forces of Eros and Thanatos for her, shaping her experience along explicitly allegorical lines and looming most boldly into view when, right after being caught in a torrential downpour on Royal Street, she learns of the murder of a close friend, likely killed for having a gay relationship with the son of a powerful smuggler. The same noir-ish fatalism appears in Elise Blackwell's *The Lower Quarter* (2015), a highly literary thriller set in the immediate aftermath of Hurricane Katrina, in which the city is conjured, as one reviewer notes, as "seething, wounded, garish, and unstoppable" and where, as Blackwell herself puts it, New Orleans is still what she always has been: "a receiver of outsiders and immigrants, a blender, a granter of new identities, a place where you could disappear and then resurface under new terms."[111] Recalling some of the wistful nostalgia and mourning that characterizes Fox's novel, Blackwell ultimately invokes this myth-tinged, French Quarter atmosphere to let the final emphasis land on the unkillable energy of desire. Yet another novel that works this same well-tilled ground is C. W. Cannon's *French Quarter Beautification Project* (2016), a comic romp in the manner of Robbins, with traces of Rice, that is narrated by the god Dionysius as he bar-hops around the Quarter with his bumbling sidekick, a failed music composer. And, most recently, the Guggenheim-award-winning novelist, Louis Edwards, who lives in the Quarter, published the highly praised *Ramadan Ramsey*, about a boy of that name growing up in twenty-first-century New Orleans who, after losing his mother, learns that his relatives are trying to kill him to prevent him from getting his inheritance and sets out to find his father in Syria. Ramadan is one of the names of God for Muslims, and the name of the holiday that commemorates Muhammad's first revelation; and Ramesses is the name of ancient Egypt's most venerated pharoah, the titular character's name thus giving Edwards's excellent novel a keen mythic resonance.

This mythic inclination in major French Quarter writing of recent decades surfaces in other ways too. For example, the well-known musician and writer, Ed Sanders, published just after Hurricane Katrina *Poems for New Orleans*, a boldly whimsical set of notes in verse on key turns in the city's much storied history. And the essayist and humorist Roy Blount Jr., who has kept a home in the Quarter for many years, and has been a regular guest on public radio's *Wait, Wait, Don't Tell Me* and *A Prairie Home Companion*, gathered together, just before Katrina, a gorgeous fabric of riffs about the neighborhood's legends and lore under the title *Feet on the Street: Rambles Around New Orleans* (2005). And another public radio regular, Andrei Codrescu, collected his short pieces about his New Orleans experiences, mostly in the French Quarter, into *New Orleans: Mon Amour: Twenty Years of Writings from the City* (2006), in which, in contrast to Blount, he seems bent on creating a lore of his own out of the eccentrics who pop up around him or by ruminating in personal ways on his encounters in New Orleans with primordial forces. Codrescu also published in 1999 a novel in the Tom Robbins vein called *Messiah*, which unfolds during the first carnival season of the twenty-first century and tells the story of a pair of women who decide that they are two severed halves of a single entity.

No one, however, conjures a more mythological French Quarter with more deftness or charm than Dalt Wonk in *French Quarter Fables, Vol. I and II*. Each volume offers nearly twenty intricately rhymed fables, each with a vibrant, highly skilled illustration and each accompanied by a single-sentence moral that also gets its own full-page illustration. The characters these fables are built upon are never people; one, for example, is about a flower, another an insect, another a rodent, and so on, all of them native to the French Quarter, where nearly all of the pieces take place. The struggles and passions that unfold among these non-human characters echo all sorts of timeless dynamics between people, but these characters are never merely disguised people: as Wonk notes, they retain their animal nature, reflecting perhaps a trait of those who live along the Royal Street corridor, where appetites are given freer rein to amplify than they are in most other places. A cat plays the saxophone to lure a swallow away from its children, who rush to her room to find it empty of all but moonlight and as still as a tomb; a rabbit falls for a poodle's cabaret routine, and, after getting drunk by buying round after round of drinks (the poodle's are secretly water), discovers that his wallet is empty and the poodle is gone; an ant, working as a waiter, growing exasperated with an aristocratic and impossible-to-please customer, puts a knife in his throat; a lizard and a frog fall in love and marry, but when the lizard tries to show her love by getting into the frog's beloved courtyard lily pond, she drowns. There are nearly forty of these across Wonk's two beautifully illustrated volumes of rhyme and moral wit, and they land with a quirkiness, even gorgeousness, entirely worthy of their setting.

Coda: Valerie Martin's *Property*

Apart from these works of myth, fable, and folklore stands the very best novel about the French Quarter in at least the half-century since Stone's *A Hall of Mirrors*. In this novel – Valerie Martin's *Property* (2004) – the French Quarter is a vividly conjured hellscape, its much-promoted magic being nothing positive but rather simply an effect of the blind superstition, delineated with razor-sharp psychological accuracy, at the center of the myth that is white supremacism.

Property is a first-person narrative from the point of view of a deeply unhappy white woman who, as the novel begins, is living in the early decades of the nineteenth century on a plantation on the outskirts of town but then decamps to her mother's house on St. Ann Street in the Quarter. Her husband is, at best, the consummate bore, but, more to the point, he is a predatory womanizer who cannot keep his hands off the people whom he enslaves. His special favorite is a young, light-skinned woman named Sarah, with whom he has already sired a child. Martin's research into the details of plantation life and the epidemics that ravaged the Quarter in that period is impeccable. The voice of the narrator, suffused with a mix of boredom and bitter rage, delivers something quite rare in fiction about the old South: the psychological toxicity of slavery not simply for those who are enslaved, but for the slave-owners, who, through the dark logic of the institution, often become ever more perverse and sadistic until they are finally broken by their own absurdity.

The planter's financial problems, the constant worry about the prospect of a maroon-led insurrection of the enslaved that, at any time, could roar over them from the thick swamps that surround them, and the horror of the epidemics of that era: all of this is woven into Martin's portrait of a society hovering, always, on the brink of inevitable annihilation and fabricated, moment to moment, out of the lies that extend from the original myth of white supremacy.

When her husband's mistress, Sarah, escapes and begins to move, disguised as an elderly, ailing white man, up the eastern seaboard, the narrator, rather than being relieved by her departure, is utterly livid – and consumed by the goal of returning this "property" to its rightful owner on St. Ann Street. For Sarah, on the move, has come to know a freedom that she herself will never know, for her identity depends entirely on the untenable myth that she can own Sarah, leaving her trapped, in turn, beneath what she thinks the mask of her whiteness means, and the fatal suspicion that what is underneath her mask is, in the end, nothing at all.

The particular power of Martin's novel hinges on the thinness of this fabricated identity – the word "lies" is at the center of the book – an identity finally as mythological as those in Reed, Rice, Robbins, and Crews, but here developed as a direct expression of the literal details of a very real history. The narrator, for example, summarizes the character of her father – the only entity standing between her and absolute chaos – in a single word, "imposter."[112] When the masquerade is followed to such an extreme, as in Stone's *A Hall of Mirrors*, the right hand knowing nothing of the left, the potential for tragic irony becomes boundless.

1. Kalamu Ya Salaam's boyhood home – 2517 St. Maurice
2. Marcus B. Christian's home – 1438 St. Maurice
3. Mother Catherine Seals's Temple – 2400 Charbonnet
4. Fats Domino's birthplace – 1937 Jourdain
5. Fats Domino's home – 1208 Caffin / Fats Domino Ave
6. The Club Desire 3319 Law Street
7. Frantz Elementary School – 3811 N. Galvez St
8. Black Panthers' Headquarters – 3544 Piety
9. Wharf where Algren's fictional Dove Linkhorn enters the city
   – Desire at Chartres

10. Lombard Plantation – 3933 Chartres
11. Latrobe's cottage – between Louisa and Clouet on Chartres
12. The Olympic Club – SE corner of Royal and Press
13. Homer Plessy's arrest – NW corner of Royal and Press
14. St. Roch Cemetery – 1725 St. Roch Avenue
15. Tennessee Williams's fictional home in Streetcar for
    Stanley and Stella – 632 Elysian Fields
16. House where John Waters lived

Map of the St. Claude corridor: Lower 9th Ward to Elysian Fields.

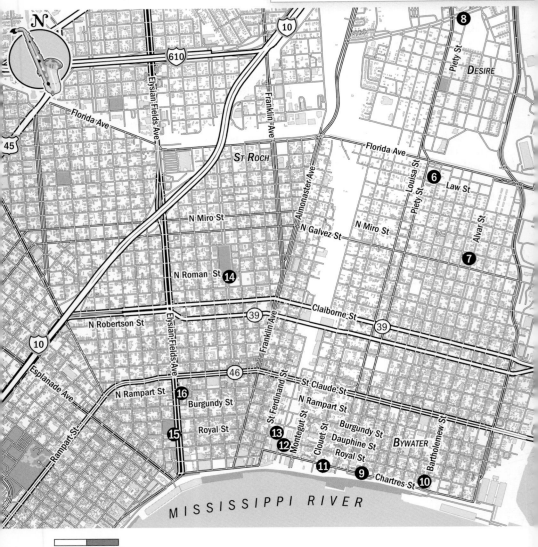

St. Claude Avenue – Hard Times and Good Children

The Lower 9th Ward – Desire – St. Roch – Bywater

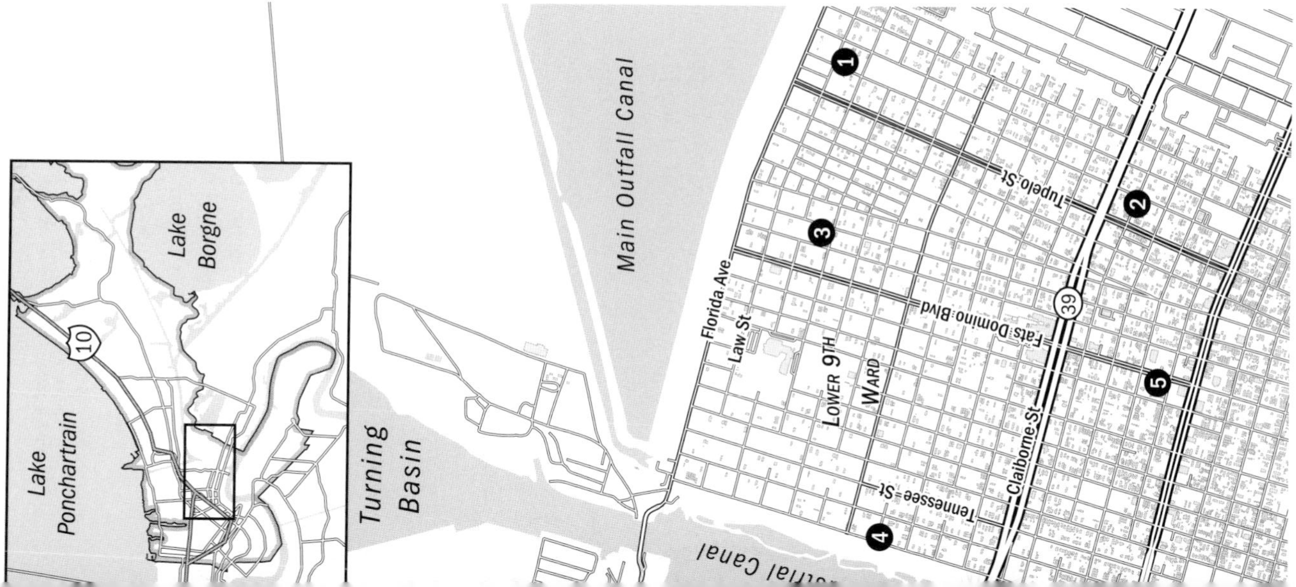

2

Lake Ponchartrain

10

Lake Borgne

Turning Basin

Main Outfall Canal

Outfall Canal

Florida Ave

Law St

LOWER 9TH WARD

Tennessee St

Fats Domino Blvd

Tupelo St

Claiborne St

39

① ② ③ ④ ⑤

"One must go straight out Saint Claude, below the Industrial Canal," wrote Zora Neale Hurston in the opening words of her 1934 portrait of Mother Catherine Seals. That first sentence continues by directing the reader to turn onto "Flood Street and go almost to the Florida Walk," for there one would find something that "no ordinary person created."[1] To reach it, one would walk through a marsh to a large, high-walled enclosure that occupied an entire block, over which flew a variety of flags. The place was called Bethlehem, and inside were two main structures – the Manger and the Temple of the Innocent Blood. When one was invited to enter what was in effect a single vast altar, one encountered several hundred lamps, countless statues and images, as well as many different animals – a goat, a sheep, a donkey, some dogs and parrots, a few canaries. All of the people present wore her insignia (the women wore veils, the men armbands), emblazoned with the letters M. C. S., which meant "Mother Catherine's Saints." There would be a great many small children on the premises, for the most immediate, material purpose of Mother Catherine's compound was to shelter unwed mothers, and any other mothers with small children who needed her, and, for that matter, anyone at all who turned to her healing powers in the absence of other resources or options.

Hurston explains that "it would take a volume to describe in detail all of the things in and about this chapel," adding that Mother Catherine's bed was on a raised platform in the tent where she held court, surrounded by many musical instruments and within easy reach of a large coffee urn.[2] When Hurston first encountered Mother Catherine, she reported, "It seemed perfectly natural for me to go to my knees upon the gravel floor, and when she signaled me to extend my right hand, palm up for the dab of blessed salt, I hurried to obey because she made me feel that way."[3]

Hurston spent two weeks with Mother Catherine during her 1927 research trip for what would become her classic study of Black folklore and hoodoo called *Mules and Men* (1935), a work that prepared her to write, two years later, her masterpiece, *Their Eyes Were Watching God.* Her essay, "Mother Catherine," appeared the year before the first book in *Negro: An Anthology* (1934), and it surely helped to establish Hurston as a powerful new voice on – and within – African-American culture, as one who, throughout *Mules and Men*, could depend on her upbringing in a small Black community in south Florida to do what most scholars of Black culture and folklore could not: enter the scene as a trusted insider.

Mother Catherine's compound flourished for a little under a decade, from 1922 until her death at age 43 in 1930. She had been born in the south-central Kentucky town of Hustonville, but came to New Orleans at age 16, where, as she had in Kentucky, she suffered significant physical abuse from men.[4] In her early thirties, she took a vow of celibacy and founded her ministry.[5] She refused to follow the segregationist protocols of the Jim Crow era, and, with many thousands of devoted followers of both races, her compound was sometimes attacked by outsiders as a scene of race-mixing – attacked, too, because she was a woman.[6] She was, however, uncowed, and told Zora Neale Hurston, "It is right that a woman should lead. A womb was what God made in the beginning, and out of that womb was born Time and all that fills up space."[7] So great was Mother Catherine's devotion to the sacred character of small children – "the blood of the innocents" – that, according to legend, after she was initially lifted over the 12-foot wall onto the grounds, she chose never to leave it again until she died.[8] When she passed away, the

Mother Catherine Seals. Courtesy of Xavier University of Louisiana, Archives & Special Collections.

Mother Catherine's followers at the Temple of the Innocent Blood. Courtesy of the Historic New Orleans Collection.

funeral parade that made its way up St. Claude Avenue was among the largest then known in the city's history. She was buried under a large statue at St. Vincent de Paul Cemetery just off St. Claude on Louisa Street.[9] Her devotion to small children, particularly those born into poverty, is a quintessential iteration of a motif that defines the literary legacy of the St. Claude corridor.

Background: The Built Environment and Its Cultural History

St. Claude Avenue, the primary thoroughfare that links Mother Catherine's neighborhood in the Lower 9th Ward to the center of New Orleans, was originally named Rue Des Bons Enfants, then later given the same name in English: Good Children Street. The name came from Bernard de Marigny, an extraordinarily wealthy and engaged citizen, but also something of a colorful wastrel who introduced the game of Craps to the US, and, through it, lost most of his fortune. As he sold off his plantation's grounds just downriver from the French Quarter in the first decade of the nineteenth century, he chose to call that particular street Good Children, because, as the boundary between the vast swamp and the newly developing area along the river, it became the place where a great many children would play, catching frogs and crawfish, chasing each other through the underbrush. Many of these children, incidentally, were produced by liaisons between the wealthy white men who lived in the Quarter and the women of color who were their mistresses and lived in the cottages along what Bernard de Marigny chose to name Love Street. Later, Love was renamed Rampart, though it was not exactly a continuation of the part of Rampart that forms the rear border of the Quarter; the actual continuation of that part of Rampart took the name Good Children as it passed downriver at Elysian Fields. Good Children was eventually renamed St. Claude to honor Claude Tremé, whose name was also given to the neighborhood immediately behind the French Quarter.

St. Claude Avenue stands in stark contrast to those blocks of Royal Street discussed in the last chapter, for St. Claude has never known the opulence and institutional power of the latter, but rather has been always the primary thoroughfare of the relatively hard-scrabble 8th and 9th Wards. The literature that has emerged along this strip and about it, however, is considerable, and, given the relative financial strain that has historically defined this area, much of it emphasizes, as Mother Catherine did, children – specifically, a faith in their redemptive innocence and the hope that they will have better lives than those who bore them. In fact, though the St. Claude corridor is defined by four distinct neighborhoods, each with its own literary significance – first, the Lower 9th Ward, and then, in the Upper 9th Ward, Desire and St. Roch, and finally, Bywater – these neighborhoods share not only the common artery of St. Claude Avenue but a literary legacy that often hinges on this same faith in the innate goodness of the very young to uplift what is otherwise a world of hard times.

Times were not always hard in this part of New Orleans, not for the people who originally owned it. In the decades just before the War of 1812, some twenty-one plantations operated along the river on that 5-mile stretch between the French Quarter and the Chalmette Battlefield, where that war essentially ended. The rear of these properties stretched far back into the cypress swamps toward Lake Pontchartrain into an uninhabitable territory called La Cyperie – the Cypress Swamp – and which was probably the inspiration for the gloomy piano étude by nineteenth-century New Orleans composer, Louis Moreau Gottschalk, called "La Savane."[10] This string of mansions that faced the river is the setting for a short story of 1880 by George Washington Cable called "Belles Demoiselles Plantation," about a wealthy man who is doted upon by his beautiful daughters (*belles demoiselles* is French for "beautiful young ladies"). The story ends in disaster when the Mississippi River floods the area and wipes out the plantation.[11] Cable's short story was prescient, for, in 1899, the river flooded precisely this area, destroying everything along the street closest to the river (North Peters), even dissolving the ground over which the street itself ran, making Chartres Street suddenly and precariously the road closest to the newly established riverbank.[12]

Only one of the original plantation houses from that era is still standing: the Lombard mansion, at the corner of Chartres and Bartholomew, which was beautifully restored in the 1990s by renowned clarinetist and scholar, S. Frederick Starr, whose book, *Une Belle Maison*, is an invaluable guide to the early history and architecture of this part of the city. This house, though, is hardly representative of how the entire waterfront would have looked throughout the antebellum era, for the next plantation upriver from this one, the DeClouet mansion, was converted in 1816 into an amusement park for the city's children. The next house upriver, between what is now Clouet and Louisa, was where Benjamin Henry Latrobe, commonly identified as the father of American architecture, settled into a relatively modest cottage in 1819. Latrobe had designed the US Capitol, and, after his son had come to New Orleans to build the city's waterworks but quickly died of yellow fever, he followed his son to the city to finish the project, only to succumb within a few years to the same fate – leaving behind, however, a valuable record of his short time in the city under the title, *Impressions Respecting New Orleans: Diary and Sketches, 1818–1820.*[13]

> **Epidemics** A classic film-noir of 1950, *Panic in the Streets*, offers scenes of the downriver waterfront of that era as officials struggle to arrest a killer who is known to be carrying a dangerous virus before he can start a deadly epidemic. The movie touches on what was then a century-old worry about the city as a well spring of mass death, for, between 1820 and 1910, as the population grew to 300,00, cholera and yellow fever killed some 40,000 New Orleanians, in a succession of waves that constituted the hardest of hard times.

A short walk back down the riverfront was the site where, some twenty years after the senior Latrobe's death, the Catholic Orphanages Association, led by a fledgling French religious group known as the Congregation of the Holy Cross, created St. Mary's Orphanage. It would ultimately house up to 300 children, becoming the principal orphanage for boys in south Louisiana. Two years later, the same group would found Notre Dame University in South Bend, Indiana. A little further downriver from this orphanage, the Ursuline order of nuns built a vast convent and school in 1823, which flourished for nearly a hundred years before being torn down to make way for the Industrial Canal. The building dwarfed the neighboring plantations and signaled that this all-female community, with its commitment to educating girls, would be a permanent and considerable power in the city.[14] Having relocated within the city, Ursuline Academy today enjoys the distinction of being the oldest continuously operating Catholic school – as well as oldest girls' school – in the US.

The dawn of the twentieth century brought other extraordinary changes to the built environment of this part of New Orleans. The vast cypress swamp to the north of what would become St. Claude Avenue was drained when a young man named Albert Baldwin Wood devised bold improvements to the existing system of drainage pumps, and the area soon filled with houses.[15] The Wood Screw Pumps were adopted in the ensuing decades all over the US, as well as in Egypt, India, and China; some of those he installed in New Orleans have been in continuous use for over a century now, without need of repair; and new ones continue to be built that are based directly on his designs.[16]

By the time Baldwin's technology began to drain the area on the lakeside of St. Claude, the neighborhood on the other side of this street, closer to the river, had won a place in the history of the country's popular culture through the Olympic Club. This building, which occupied the block bounded by Press, Montegut, Royal, and Chartres, became a boxing mecca in the final decade of the nineteenth century. Four stories tall in French Renaissance style, with a mansard roof and galleries, it had, inside, a swimming pool, multiple parlors for billiards, a bowling alley, a shooting range, a reading room where literary clubs met, and, in the rear, one of the largest amphitheaters in the US, where, with seating for 10,000, a string of championship boxing matches were held in the 1890s.[17] The Olympic Club's fame reached its peak on September 7, 1892, when the club hosted the world's first modern boxing match. This heavyweight championship bout between the two Irish-American superstars, Jim Corbett and John L. Sullivan, was the first to proceed according to Queensberry rules,[18] which meant using gloves rather than proceeding in the traditional "bare knuckle" style, and structuring the match as a series of three-minute rounds that would end when one of the contestants took more than ten seconds to stand up after a knockdown. Sullivan had been the heavyweight champion for ten years, and was enormously wealthy and well-known; thus, all over the country, people gathered in theaters, newspaper offices, and sports clubs where telegraphed updates were announced after each round.[19] Ultimately, he failed to handle the newcomer, who knocked him out in the twenty-first round by using what were hailed as his new "scientific" methods.

Three months before the legendary Corbett–Sullivan fight and diagonally across the intersection of Royal and Press from the Olympic Club is the site where a far more important fight was begun. On June 7, 1892, a young man named Homer Plessy, who appeared white but had one-eighth African ancestry, was removed from a train and arrested after announcing to the ticket-taker that he was, in fact, not entirely white and that he refused to leave the "whites only" train car. Plessy's arrest is just one moment in a long and proud tradition of Creole activism against racial injustice, beginning with *L'Union* and *La Tribune* and the Native Guard's valiant campaigns against the Confederate army, to say nothing of the scores of benevolent associations that organized for philanthropic causes and Civil Rights in the decades that followed. But Plessy's case is the most widely remembered, for it went all the way to the US Supreme Court, which, four years later, ruled against him and thereby instituted the "separate but equal" policy that launched what came to be known as the Jim Crow era, which is second only to slavery itself in defining the history of race in the US.

Roughly a half-century later, a key force in ending this agonizing and shameful chapter in US history was a youth movement that sprang from the other side of St. Claude Avenue, downriver, near the Industrial Canal, not far from the spot where, a few decades earlier, Mother Catherine Seals ran her Temple of the Innocent Blood. That force that helped to end Jim Crow would come to be known all over the world as rock'n'roll.

In 1956, when an interviewer asked Antoine "Fats" Domino about the origins of the new music that was sweeping American youth, Domino explained that "what they call rock'n'roll is really rhythm and blues, and I've been playing it in New Orleans for fifteen years."[20] Some context: the first rock'n'roll recording was made on Rampart Street, just beyond the upriver end of the St. Claude corridor in the French Quarter, when Roy Brown recorded "Good Rockin' Tonight" in June 1947 and thereby established the template for rock'n'roll singing; a little over two years later, in the same studio, in December of 1949, Domino, who was born and raised at the other end of the St. Claude corridor in the Lower 9th Ward, recorded "The Fat Man," which added the other crucial element of what would later be known as a rock'n'roll – "the big backbeat … the big, big beat."[21] Though that sound was essentially unknown in mainstream pop music at the time, Domino's heavily percussive music – the big backbeat – would grow quickly in popularity toward a 1955 climax, when, with "Ain't That a Shame," he became the first African American to cross over from the R & B charts to the pop top-ten. That heavily percussive style became the dominant, even signature feature of the pop music of that era, as it still is today.[22] Other pioneers of this music – Little Richard, Chuck Berry, and Elvis Presley – were all Domino fans well before they became stars themselves.[23] Around the same time that "Ain't That a Shame" rocketed up the pop charts, Martin Luther King pronounced that school integration would be easier now that youth of both races shared a love for the same music.[24]

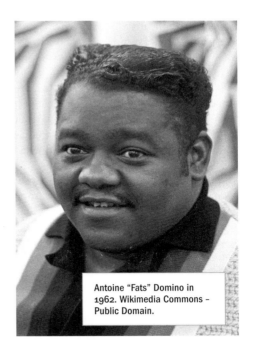

Antoine "Fats" Domino in 1962. Wikimedia Commons – Public Domain.

Domino's last name likely derived from Domingo, or Saint-Domingue, which, as discussed in the last chapter, was the scene of the slave uprising that created the nation of Haiti; Domino's ancestors had been taken from there in the early nineteenth century to work on a sugar plantation some 50 miles upriver from New Orleans. A little over a century later, following the historic flood of 1927, Domino's father moved with his brothers to the Lower 9th Ward, and they all bought houses very close to each other that directly abutted the downriver levee of the Industrial Canal, about halfway between St. Claude Avenue and Mother Catherine's temple complex. Domino was born in his parents' house at 1937 Jourdan Avenue, the household language being Creole French, and was delivered by his grandmother, who had been born into slavery.[25]

In his teens, Domino began to play the piano at the nearby Cousin's Bar (pronounced Coo-*zan*'s) at the corner of Forestall and Derbigny, a half-dozen blocks north of St. Claude.[26] He entertained too at Sunday afternoon backyard parties at the homes of his older siblings and uncles and aunts, all of whom lived in the surrounding blocks. Well-known around the downriver end of the St. Claude corridor by 1948, he accepted that year, at age 20, another weekly gig at the Hideaway Club, a ramshackle juke-joint on the other side of the Industrial Canal in the Desire neighborhood. Here, his style came into full bloom, and his local notoriety widened significantly. Soon, the patrons of the nearby and upscale Club Desire began to step across the railroad tracks during set breaks to hear the "wild" pianist known to everyone simply as "Fats." His signature tune was the "Junker's Blues," a pun on those who collected scrap metal for a living, loading it onto wagons, and the heroin addicts, who were "loaded all the time."[27] When the president of Imperial Records, who was visiting from Los Angeles, came to hear him at the Hideaway in the autumn of 1949, a deal was struck, and Domino was in the studio that December to record "The Fat Man" – an instant, local hit, based on "The Junker's Blues."

Domino didn't have a record player, so every day he would walk up to St. Claude Avenue to a grocery store that had a jukebox so he could listen to his song.[28] With his first paycheck for "The Fat Man," he went to a small music shop called Valon's, also on St. Claude Avenue, and bought a new sixty-six-key piano.[29] A deeply private and shy young man, Domino found it hard to travel away from home, where he was related to so many of his neighbors, into worlds that would have looked and felt so different from what he knew. Nonetheless, despite minimal touring to support the record, he soon had another paycheck – this one for the unimaginable sum of 20,000 dollars; he and his wife Rosemary bought a house on Caffin Avenue, only blocks from the one he was born in. He would make his home there for the next five decades, until Hurricane Katrina.

Around the same time that Domino was emerging as a local star, the energy that would soon coalesce as the Civil Rights Movement flashed into view for white people when the popular entertainer Louis Jordan announced at a 1948 concert in Municipal Auditorium in New Orleans that he would never again perform before a segregated audience. Barely more than five years later, white teenagers' demand for Domino's Lower 9th Ward sound – "the big, big backbeat" – had reached such a fever pitch around the country that riots routinely broke out at the end of Domino's performances, as the kids simply couldn't bear for him to stop. Touring in that period eleven months per year behind a string of hits, he sometimes played through injuries sustained in the riots of the preceding nights.

Ultimately, the thundering piano of Fats Domino became a primary force in the broader momentum that would tear down the Jim Crow system of separate-but-equal that had begun some half-dozen decades earlier and about two dozen blocks up St. Claude Avenue from his house.

A climactic moment in this history occurred near Domino's home when, on November 14, 1960, a group of four 6-year-old girls desegregated the area's schools. Three of them marched up the front steps of the McDonough 19 Elementary School at 5909 St. Claude Avenue, in the Lower 9th Ward – Leona Tate, Tessie Prevost, and Gail Etienne. On the other side of the Industrial Canal, the fourth girl, Ruby Bridges, walked into Frantz Elementary School at 3811 North Galvez in the Desire neighborhood, despite being surrounded by a screaming mob of segregationist whites. The event is a milestone in the history of the Civil Rights Movement, and became the subject of *The Problem We All Live With*, an iconic 1964 Norman Rockwell painting that has hung in the White House.

An account of Ruby Bridge's heroic steps into that school building serves as the grand finale to John Steinbeck's *Travels with Charley* (1962). The last book Steinbeck would write, *Travels* went to the top of *The New York Times* best-seller list, and a few months later, he won the Nobel Prize. In this final chapter of his final book, Steinbeck writes of the 6-year-old hero: "The little girl did not look at the howling crowd but from the side the whites of her eyes showed like those of a frightened fawn."[30] Steinbeck describes at length a "group of stout middle-aged women, who by some curious definition of the word 'mother,' gathered every day to scream invectives at children." He adds, "A small group of them had become so expert that they were known as the Cheerleaders, and a crowd gathered every day to enjoy and applaud their performance."[31] The Cheerleaders took turns in the role of lead screamer, and the words of each of them in turn were "carefully and selectedly filthy," making a kind of "frightening witches' Sabbath," particularly as they "simpered in happy, almost innocent triumph when they were applauded," showing at last that "These were not mothers, not even women. They were crazy actors playing to a crazy audience … for these speeches were not spontaneous," but rather "memorized and carefully rehearsed."[32] After the little girl was safely inside the school building, "the crowd rushed home to watch themselves on television, and what they saw went out all over the world."[33]

Steinbeck's writing about this scene perhaps influenced the film-maker John Waters, who lived near the corner of St. Claude and Elysian Fields some ten years later, just before the 1972 release of his breakthrough movie, *Pink Flamingos*. During Waters's time in New Orleans, he later said, he was the poorest he had ever been in his life. He shared a small apartment with Mary Vivian Pearce and Danny Mills, who played the

Ruby Bridges descending the steps in front of her school. Wikimedia Commons – Public Domain.

characters Cotton and Crackers in *Pink Flamingos*, names that resonate in obvious ways with the American South.[34] The movie is a surreal, campy race-to-the-bottom that calls to mind the theatrics described by John Steinbeck as Waters's main characters compete for the distinction of being the "filthiest person alive."

The ghoulish but ultimately comedic pathos conjured by Steinbeck and Waters pales, however, in comparison to the terror and grief that were delivered in late summer of 2005 to the St. Claude corridor, particularly to its overwhelmingly Black blocks just to the north and east, when Hurricane Katrina overwhelmed the federal levees. The experience of that historic disaster in this part of the city comes to life in Dan Baum's *Nine Lives: Mystery, Magic, Death, and Life in New Orleans* (2010), which profiles, among others, JoAnn Guidos, the transgender owner of Kajun's Pub on St. Claude, which never quite closed as the disaster ensued, and Ronald Lewis, a working-class African-American man who ran a cultural museum out of his house in the Lower 9th Ward, a block off St. Claude.

In the decade or so that followed Hurricane Katrina, as the novelist Maurice Carlos Ruffin notes in his essay "Saint Claude Avenue" in

Rebecca Solnit and Rebecca Snedeker's *Unfathomable City: A New Orleans Atlas*, the recovery of the area was, more than anything else, a grossly imbalanced process in which the high ground closest to the river gentrified at a dizzying pace while the area on the lakeside of St. Claude has never regained its vast and dense cluster of African-American communities. In more recent years, the latter area has become a patchwork of grassy lots where flooded houses have been bulldozed and given way to freshly painted and landscaped homes.

Long-term residents of the area had been devastated by Hurricane Betsy in 1965, and thus were, in 2005, no strangers to hard times. That earlier storm was a central memory of their childhood. Not surprisingly, the major writing of the neighborhoods along the St. Claude corridor has emphasized the redemptive power of children, their ability to spur hopes for a better future and to preserve the glories of the cultural past against the forces – cataclysmic weather and unchecked gentrification – that threaten to erase it.

The Lower 9th Ward

In the 1950s, on St. Maurice Street, which intersects St. Claude and marks the downriver flank of the Lower 9th Ward, there lived a middle-aged man named Marcus B. Christian and, nine blocks further north, on the same street, a talented, bookish boy named Valerie Ferdinand. Both loved to read and write, but they would never meet until many years later, after the boy had changed his name to Kalamu Ya Salaam (which means "pen of peace"). As a boy, Salaam had been absorbed in the novels of Frank Yerby, the most famous of which, *The Foxes of Harrow*, was the first novel written by an African American to sell more than a million copies and to be optioned as a movie. Its plot, Christian always maintained, had been stolen from him. He never saw a penny from this historic blockbuster, but the young reader up the street helped to reward Christian in another way several decades later.

Some background: Christian lived an extraordinary and highly literary life. He wrote *The Negro Ironworkers of Louisiana, 1718–1900*, as noted in the first chapter. He also wrote a thousand-page history of Black people in Louisiana, which has never been published, as well as several hundred poems. He exchanged letters with Langston Hughes, W. E. B. Du Bois, Sterling Brown, and Arna Bontemps,[35] and co-directed the Negro division of the Louisiana chapter of the Federal Writers Project. Otherwise, he lived a very isolated life. His childhood had been hard. He lost both his parents and his twin sister by the time he was 13; at

17, he began to work as a chauffeur and then, at 26, he opened a dry cleaners. In his forties, he got a job in the library at Dillard University, which he lost when someone noticed that he had no college degree, and, in the ensuing years, he withdrew into extreme solitude, sank into dire poverty, even delivering a paper route in his fifties. When Hurricane Betsy flooded his neighborhood in 1965, he struggled to rescue his manuscripts and rare books, only to be arrested as a looter. A few years after this arrest, however, he was hired as a poet in residence at the University of New Orleans, where his papers are now archived. Less than ten years after starting work at UNO, he passed away. In a beautiful and detailed reminiscence of Christian that appeared nearly a decade after his death, Tom Dent notes that the Black literature of New Orleans, as he defined it, properly begins with Christian. For, unlike the Creoles who were publishing in the nineteenth century, who either didn't identify as Black at all or did so only as a relatively abstract choice, motivated by the complicated political currents of the moment, Christian, on the other hand, engaged the social terrain of those who had known the experience of slavery and its aftermath from the inside.[36]

A high point in Christian's career came when, in 1968, *The New Orleans Times-Picayune* published his poem "I Am New Orleans," on the occasion of the 250th anniversary of the city's founding. This poem was reprinted in 2020 by Kalamu Ya Salaam in a book of the same title that gathers some four dozen Black poets of New Orleans to commemorate Christian's achievements through poems of their own about what New Orleans means to them. They are all, in a sense, Christian's devoted offspring, particularly Salaam. A central line of Christian's poem – "Sing, O my children, sing! / Sing of a day that long was / And, fondly remembered, still is" – is answered throughout the collection, as Christian's literary descendants do precisely what he asked them to do in those lines. The second poem in the book, appearing right after Christian's, was written by a 13-year-old named Nia Gates: entitled "My Neighborhood is Changing," it eloquently laments gentrification and the loss of a connection to the past; the next one, Karen Celestan's "Blood Nativity," ends thus: "Ancestors touching my face through searing sunlight, / Holding this young spirit aloft in preparation and solicitation to battle / every strata of plantation mentality." Many of the poems hinge on the experience of Hurricane Katrina and the struggle to hold on to a treasured cultural history while hemmed in on all sides by extraordinary devastation and loss.

Salaam's exceptional work on this volume is characteristic of a lifetime devoted to Black culture and the cause of social justice. Growing up down the street from Marcus B. Christian, though almost two full generations Christian's junior, Salaam's career since his graduation from high school in the mid 1960s is impossible to summarize. He has been writing, speaking, and performing continuously for five decades. He has worked in support of the Sandinistas in Nicaragua, faced off against the Ku Klux Klan in Tupelo, Mississippi and in New Orleans, been involved in theater, in political conferences, in cultural productions, and in a variety of music and arts festivals in Havana, Rio de Janeiro, Munich, London, Suriname, Zanzibar, and throughout the Caribbean. His impact on the cultural institutions of New Orleans continues to be extraordinary.

In the late 1960s, he became involved in the Free Southern Theater, co-founded *The Black Collegian* magazine, and struck up what would be a decades-long literary friendship with Tom Dent, through whom he would come to communicate directly with James Baldwin, Toni Morrison, Alice Walker, Amiri Baraka, Ishmael Reed, and Toni Cade Bambara, among many others, and, in turn, become inspired to produce hundreds of poems and essays.[37] Perhaps most importantly, within months of meeting Dent in the summer of 1968, they produced together the first issue of a literary journal called *Nkombo* that would, over the next six years, yield a total of nine issues that stand today as a primary literary expression of the Black Power and Black Arts era in the American South. In the following years, Salaam's activism would inspire generations. He led a takeover in 1981 of the mayor's office and occupied it by way of protesting the racist murderousness of the New Orleans Police. In the ensuing years, Salaam served at a community health center in the Lower 9th Ward, became a local radio personality, and, all the while, has been mentoring young writers with workshops and organizing tutoring programs. In recent decades, he has been a far-reaching, indefatigable force on social media, a sort of literary father to numerous writers who would follow the trail he blazed, as well as a powerful inspiration to the well-known children of his father's sister: Branford, Wynton, Delfeayo, and Jason Marsalis, and especially to Wynton's son, the novelist Simeon Marsalis.

Salaam's younger cousins aren't the only musicians he may have inspired. From the same Lower 9th Ward neighborhood where he grew up, there emerged in the summer of 2021 a hit record by Dawn Richard – the daughter of the frontman of the iconic 1970s funk band Chocolate

Milk. Her album, called *Second Line*, is a blend of Afro-futurist electronic dance music, Hip Hop, oral history and cultural preservation – precisely the sort of work that Salaam has championed for decades, a mission he may have learned, if only indirectly, from the older neighbor of his childhood on St. Maurice, Marcus B. Christian.

Desire and St. Roch

On the other side of the Industrial Canal and north of St. Claude is the upriver counterpart to the Lower 9th Ward, an area that has two distinct neighborhoods, Desire and St. Roch.

Desire is most commonly associated with the Desire Street Housing Development, a place that has loomed large in the moral imagination of New Orleans and has often been cast as the poorest neighborhood in the poorest city in the US. Problems with the buildings themselves, as many have noted, became evident a full six weeks before the complex's grand opening in the spring of 1956, when it was declared unsafe for human habitation. Built on what had been a flood-prone cypress swamp and near a dump site for industrial and residential waste, it was the largest and most cheaply built of the city's public housing projects.[38] It was, crucially, the only housing project built without concrete beneath its floors and steps, so it began to sink as soon as it was built – walls cracking and pulling apart, porches and steps leaning away from their buildings, sections of sidewalk separating, even sewer lines twisting until they snapped. There were other problems: piles of garbage, for whatever reason, went uncollected for days, even weeks; a local foodstore that failed to meet health standards but remained in business anyway would jack up prices for several days after welfare checks arrived. As if all of this were not enough, the neighborhood was bordered on two sides by railroad tracks and on a third by the Industrial Canal, a configuration that could delay ambulances and thereby kill residents who would have survived had they received timely treatment.[39]

A report to the mayor in 1970 noted that there were approximately 10,600 people living in the Desire Public Housing Project, and roughly 8,300 of them were under the age of 21. This, in a 100-acre area, only 12 blocks long and 3 blocks wide. There weren't enough schools in the

Black Power's Aftermath Right after the battle in Desire between Panthers and police, Geronimo Pratt would be arrested for murder and serve twenty-seven years in prison, eight of them in solitary confinement. He was released when prosecutors were discovered to have concealed evidence that would have acquitted him. H. "Rap" Brown, working to break up a heroin-trafficking ring in Harlem in early 1971, was charged with robbery and sent to Attica a year after prisoners there were massacred, where he converted to Islam and took the name Jamil Abdullah al-Amin. In 2000, he was given a life-sentence for killing two policemen and sent to a "supermax" in Colorado.

area, so students had to attend classes in shifts. The same report noted that, given the lack of recreation facilities, children swam in clogged sewers. People in such circumstances, as Civil Rights attorney Lolis Elie noted, tend to feel too ashamed of their situation to talk to each other about it, much less organize to improve it.[40]

Into this situation, in the summer of 1970, stepped a group of young men and women known as the Black Panthers – a story told in Orissa Arend's 2010 *Showdown in Desire*. The Panthers immediately started a free breakfast and clothing program for kids, led workshops on community responsibility, self-respect, and self-defense, and became a significant presence in the community. They soon drew the attention of the police, for tensions were already quite high between law enforcement and activist youth movements from the killing, only months earlier, of four students at Kent State University, and more pointedly, of two at an historically Black university, Jackson State, in nearby Mississippi. In fact, barely two months after the Panthers settled into the Desire Projects, they would find themselves in a stand-off with police that would make national headlines.

The idea to start a New Orleans chapter of the Panthers came from Geronimo Pratt, who was born in 1947 and raised in Morgan City, Louisiana. The subject of a biography by Jack Olsen called *Last Man Standing*, Pratt did two tours of Vietnam, where he engaged the enemy nearly daily. By the time he was 20 years old, his stunning record of valor under fire had earned him no fewer than eighteen combat decorations. Between the two tours, his unit was deployed to Detroit to confront the riots there in the summer of 1967, and thus began his political awakening. A little less than a year later, while sitting in a foxhole during the historic siege of Hue City, he first heard the news crackling over a transistor radio of the murder of Martin Luther King. Returning to Louisiana that summer, he agreed to drive his sister to Los Angeles, where she would become a college student. Upon arriving in LA, Pratt decided to hang around too, for, through family friends, he connected with Louisiana-born Alprentice "Bunchy" Carter, the founder and the first president of the Los Angeles chapter of the Panthers.

Pratt became Bunchy Carter's bodyguard, and began to teach classes at the Panther headquarters on the guerilla strategies he had learned in Vietnam. Since returning to the US, Pratt had come to feel that he had merely changed one war zone for another, that the war had followed him home, and that there was no escaping it. When his Louisiana friend and

Panther president was killed by a rival faction on UCLA's campus over the direction of the newly emerging Black studies program in January of 1969, Pratt ascended to the role of the leader of the Los Angeles chapter. When his counterpart in Chicago, Fred Hampton, was murdered by police that December, Pratt assumed he would likely soon meet the same fate, so, embracing the guerilla strategy he had learned by watching the Viet Cong, he began to move around: guerillas, he knew, could only function offensively, in hit-and-run tactics, because to fight defensively – that is, from a fixed location – is to make oneself vulnerable to the enemy's vastly superior numbers and firepower. Pratt visited New York, New Haven, Newark, Birmingham, and Atlanta, teaching Black activists in those underground communities how to organize patrols, how to handle various kinds of guns, how to use sandbags to fortify bunkers, and how to dig tunnels for escaping those bunkers. In the midsummer of 1970, he visited the newly arrived Panthers in the Desire, and helped them to prepare for the inevitable police raid.

> **Labor Strife** In 1895, several hundred white dockworkers who were union members attacked African-American non-union longshoremen as they were loading a ship, killing six, in what is remembered as the Dockworkers Riot. The governor of Louisiana had to call in the National Guard to restore peace. The event forms the backdrop to a short story by Alice Dunbar-Nelson called "Mr. Baptiste" and is essential context for understanding other events of the moment – *Plessy v Ferguson*, the Corbett–Sullivan match, Storyville's opening, and the white riots that targeted Robert Charles.

That raid came on the morning of September 15, 1970, the seventh anniversary of the infamous church bombing in Birmingham, Alabama. Soon after police arrived, gunfire began and lasted for thirty minutes. Miraculously, there were no deaths. The police came back a second time on November 18 for another battle. In the end, a little over a dozen Panthers were arrested and jailed in the same facility where, only two years earlier, H. Rap Brown, the native Louisianan who succeeded Stokely Carmichael as Chair of SNCC, had penned his famous "Letter from Orleans Parish Prison."

H. Rap Brown, known today as Jamil Al-Amin. Wikimedia Commons – Public Domain.

That letter, in which Brown intoned, "No slave should die a natural death," can be read as the proper beginning of the literary legacy of the Desire Public Housing Project, for, as the Panthers took their stand there in the autumn of 1970 against the New Orleans Police Department, they often spoke explicitly of "revolutionary suicide."[41] Brown's letter, written during a hunger strike of several weeks in the spring of 1968, ends thus:

> America: if it takes my death to organize my people against you, and to organize your jails against you, and to organize your troops against you, and to organize your children, your God, your poor, your country, and to organize mankind to rejoice in your destruction and ruin, then here is my life!

The phrase "revolutionary suicide" became the title of Huey P. Newton's 1973 memoir, in which he notes being born in Louisiana and named after its most famous governor, then going on to found the original chapter of the Black Panthers by way of responding to the police harassment he had endured only a few years earlier as an Oakland teen. Thus, when the Panthers battled the New Orleans police in the autumn of 1970, a Louisiana story was coming full circle via California and four Louisiana natives, Huey Newton, Bunchy Carter, Rap Brown, and Geronimo Pratt.

After the Panthers left the Desire in the final weeks of 1970, conditions there deteriorated quickly.[42] What the neighborhood became in the 1970s and 80s is discussed to powerful effect in Jed Horne's true-crime courtroom procedural, *Desire Street*, the characters and setting of which are so richly drawn, as many have noted, that the book reads like a novel. Horne's narrative follows, through a grim institutional wasteland of police and judicial corruption, the random 1984 murder of a white middle-aged housewife in a grocery store parking lot just north of the Desire projects. Horne's horrifying vision of the depravity of the cops and courts is juxtaposed with a detailed vision of the hopelessness of life in Desire in that period. A local drug dealer named Curtis Kyles was soon arrested for the murder and quickly sent to death row, where he would spend fourteen years while his case went to trial five separate times. Eventually, new evidence emerged of gross incompetence and corruption among the police who initially arrested Kyles, evidence that suggested that the man's romantic rival, Beanie Wallace, had actually carried out the killing and then framed Kyles so as to have Kyles's wife to himself. Wallace had been raised by Kyles's mother-in-law, who had once managed to talk Kyles out of killing Wallace over a 150-dollar drug deal, though Kyles admitted that he never wanted to kill Wallace but only felt obligated to do so in order to save face within the social codes of the neighborhood. Horne's book is especially valuable in detailing these codes and the wider social fabric of the Desire, for the public housing project was demolished in the late 1990s, dispersing this community to other parts of the city.

An invaluable counternarrative to Horne can be found in Clarence Nero's *Cheekie*. Based on Nero's own childhood in the 1970s and 80s in the Desire, *Cheekie* was published in 1998, in the midst of the demolition of the Desire, when its author was only 27 years old, and was named one of the best first novels of the year by *Library Journal.* Told from the point of view of an especially innocent child, the novel offers only a few glimpses into the dimensions of the neighborhood that Jed Horne discussed. In this social world, adults beat children, men beat women, and women sometimes menace men with handguns, but Cheekie's essential sweetness remains intact, and he sees none of the other troubles that came to define the area in this period. He loves going to church with his grandmother and prefers to skip rope with the girls than play football with the boys – a preference Nero repeats in the final lines of the book. Nero himself agrees with reviewers who praise his young hero for refusing to succumb to despair and for striving instead to do well, Cheekie being the paragon of the human power of hope. At the novel's end, Cheekie earns a scholarship to a good high school far from the Desire. In reality, however, three of Nero's brothers were murdered in its surrounding streets.[43]

Nero's tale of a young and innocent heart that triumphs over adversity continues a local tradition of the St. Claude corridor that began one hundred years earlier in an older neighborhood a few blocks upriver, with Alice Dunbar-Nelson's *The Goodness of Saint Rocque.* Though Dunbar-Nelson never lived in the St. Roch neighborhood (no one today spells it the way she did), this collection of short fiction, named after the lead-off story in the book, takes up the themes of hard times and good children more explicitly than any other work associated with the St. Claude corridor.

The St. Roch neighborhood takes its name from the street that runs through the middle of it and from the cemetery that faces onto that street. Saint Roch, according to James Nagel, was a priest in fourteenth-century France and Italy who seemed to have the power to cure people of the plagues then decimating Europe. A small cult of followers sprang up around him as he was canonized as a saint, and it eventually spread to nineteenth-century Louisiana, where epidemics sometimes killed thousands of New Orleanians in a single summer. In the immediate aftermath of the Civil War, a priest in the area named Father Thevis proclaimed that, if none of his parishioners died from yellow fever for a year, he would construct a shrine to honor Saint Roch. This came to pass, and the chapel was built in 1871 in the cemetery that was then named after him.[44]

Dunbar-Nelson's short story "The Goodness of Saint Rocque" draws attention to the ways European Catholicism, in this downriver, working-class neighborhood of New Orleans, melds fully with the Caribbean traditions of voodoo, not as an exotic, dramatic force, but as a standard practice of everyday life.[45] The story focuses, as nearly half the pieces in this collection of fourteen do, on young love, and more generally on the ways various adversities test the "true heart" and its specific power to rebound and re-instate itself in triumph. In the next story, "The Fisherman of Pass Christian," the young girl at the center of the story doesn't get what she wants (an opera career in Paris) but is happy to have discovered how untrustworthy the people of that world are and to stay home, a case of innocence rewarded with and preserved by the promise of a much more wholesome future than the one she nearly pursued. Similarly, in "Sister Josepha," a young girl living in an orphanage thinks about leaving to follow a pair of brown eyes that has enthralled her, but in the end she turns away from secular pleasures to commit to life in a convent. In "By Bayou Saint John," two lovers are sitting on the bank of the waterway, having a final conversation by way of breaking up, while a great many happy street urchins play nearby; a dangerous snake is discovered near the water, but in the end the bayou "gathers into its bosom" this newly "broken hearted romance," as if washing away the serpent-like force of grief and returning the lovers to the innocent state of the playing children. The final story, "Titee," delivers the book's theme most explicitly: an undernourished child who has been skipping school to roam the streets turns out to have been secretly sharing his meager lunch with an elderly man, who is hiding on the edge of the swamp. In an earlier version of the story, published in *Violet and Other Tales*, the angelic boy breaks his leg, dies, and is buried in St. Roch cemetery.

Most of the other stories in *The Goodness of Saint Rocque*, when not focused on the goodness of the young, explicitly situate themselves in the context of deep financial strain. And although these stories nearly always make explicit reference to particular New Orleans streets, the race of particular characters, as many have noted, is almost never identified. This feature of these early stories perhaps arises from particular aspects of Dunbar-Nelson's own childhood in uptown New Orleans. A light-skinned Black woman, born in 1875 to a laundry woman who had been enslaved in Opelousas, Louisiana and a man about whom little is known, she spent her girlhood at 56½ Palmyra Street, but gravitated toward the descendants of those who in the preceding decades had been identified as free people of color, particularly when she enrolled at Straight University on Esplanade Avenue to be trained as a teacher. In an unpublished story called "Brass Ankles Speaks," she writes of "growing up white enough to pass for white, but with a darker family background, a real love for the mother race, and no desire to be numbered among the white race."[46] Her complexion thus isolated her from both the dominant races in the city, almost as if she had no racial affiliation at all, at least not within the Jim Crow binary that informed the larger US context. At 20, she published *Violets and Other Tales* about the Creole culture of New Orleans, and just a few years later published *The Goodness of Saint Rocque*, leaving New Orleans permanently the year after it came out to live in New York City.

She had been corresponding, for a few years, with Paul Laurence Dunbar, the most famous African-American literary figure of that era.[47] Soon after they met in person, he raped her, but five months afterward they married, only to separate four years later when he got drunk and beat her. Soon after leaving Dunbar, she moved to Baltimore, began teaching high school, and started a relationship with a much older woman who was the principal of the school where she taught.[48] She began to contribute regularly to W. E. B. Du Bois's *The Crisis* on the suffragette movement and was soon immersed in the Harlem Renaissance, publishing poetry, much of it written when she was much younger, and a great deal of political journalism. She took teaching very seriously. She married twice

Alice Dunbar-Nelson. Wikimedia Commons – Public Domain.

more but also had serious romances with women, and most importantly wrote her way into a life quite different from her mother's and the horror she herself had known in that first marriage. Her life, thus, presents a kind of testimony to the power of youthful hope to triumph over hard times.

The Bywater

On the river side of St. Claude Avenue, between that street and the river, and between the Industrial Canal and the railroad tracks, lies a neighborhood that originally had been a string of some twenty-one plantations, and that for most of the twentieth century was home to a mostly white working-class community that was brilliantly depicted in the cartoons of the late Bunny Matthews. Today, its concentration of writers is surely among the most dense of any neighborhood in the city, and if we stretch what is technically the upriver border of the Bywater a little farther upriver from the railroad tracks to its more logical border at Elysian Fields, there are even more. This neighborhood also provides the setting for three major works – first, Tennessee Williams's *A Streetcar Named Desire* (1947), then Nelson Algren's *A Walk on the Wild Side* (1956), and finally Valerie Martin's *A Recent Martyr* (1987). These major works and the preponderance of writers living in the area today suggest that perhaps Bywater is itself the good child, as it were, of the vibrant bohemia that roared through the French Quarter from the 1920s through the 1960s.

The case of Seth Morgan suggests an early, tragic, and quite extreme iteration of what has become the dominant, negative stereotype of the Bywater *hipster* in the decades that followed his death there. According to Mike Capuzzo's harrowing profile and elegy published in *Esquire* in 1991, Morgan was born in 1949 to wealthy, literary parents who lived on Park Avenue in Manhattan, was shuffled through a succession of elite boarding schools as a kid, and then enrolled at UC-Berkeley, from which he dropped out in 1970 to move in with Janis Joplin, as the two had fallen in love when he was selling her cocaine. They planned to marry, but soon after meeting Morgan, she died. He then began to work as a barker for a San Francisco strip club, continued to sell narcotics, worked sometimes as a pimp, and pulled at least one armed robbery, landing in prison for two and a half years. After his release, he continued to muddle along in San Francisco this way until, in 1986, as he told an interviewer, "I hied down to New Orleans to quietly drink myself to death, and nearly did, but something awoke in me and I wrote a book instead."

Specifically, in four months, he produced a manuscript of over a thousand pages that Jason Epstein, a Random House editor and friend of his father's, trimmed to a readable length and published in 1990 as an autobiographical novel called *Homeboy*. The critical response could hardly have been splashier, as he was hailed as the heir to William Burroughs and Ken Kesey, praised by Norman Mailer and William Styron, and began to negotiate a lucrative deal for a movie that would star Johnny Depp. He immediately began work on a second novel, which would be called *Mambo Mephisto* and set in New Orleans; however, less than six months after *Homeboy* had appeared to such acclaim, Morgan was speeding down St. Claude Avenue on his motorcycle with a girlfriend when he hit the abutment in the median on the bridge over the Industrial Canal. He and the woman died instantly.

Though Morgan had bought a house in the Lower Garden District at 1232 Camp Street,[49] Morgan likely knew well the bars near where he was killed. BJ's Lounge, for example, at the corner of Burgundy and Lesseps, was owned by the poet Lee Meitzen Grue for decades until her death in 2021, and Morgan likely would have spent many evenings there. Grue created the Backyard Poetry Theater behind her home on Lesseps Street. She also founded the New Orleans Poetry Forum and ran it until 1990, and served as writer in residence at Tulane from 1993 to 1998. She published more than a half-dozen books of poetry, as well as a novel. One of her former tenants, Jim Gabour, who now lives in the upriver end of the neighborhood on Marigny Street, has worked extensively in the film and music industries, and been a featured writer for *The Guardian* since 2008. Gabour's comic novel, *Unimportant People*, which he wrote over several years in the 1990s and published in 2018, follows the misadventures of a child-like mystic who lives with his dog in a cardboard box under a New Orleans expressway and who becomes involved in local politics as a champion of misfits, derelicts, and outlaws. In his perfect innocence, he seems poised to save New Orleans from itself. Gabour's most recent book is a set of stories about various cats who have shared his home and become something like his spiritual children or his muse. He wrote them to entertain his dying, 100-year-old father, and then, after his father's passing, he published them with Pelican Press.

Gabour's neighbor on Marigny Street, Glen Pitre, made the classic film *Belizaire the Cajun* in the mid 1980s, among many other works about the Cajun culture of southwest Louisiana. His most recent novel is *Advice from the Wicked*, an historical novel set in the 1890s that ranges from sugar plantations to Storyville, and centers around a son who will do anything for his mother. Another story of a remarkable son, this one with a Bywater setting and focused on a mother who will go to any lengths to defend that son, was written by Jean Stafford under the title, *A Mother in History*. It recounts the days Stafford spent talking with Marguerite Oswald about her son, Lee Harvey Oswald – who, in Marguerite's view, was heroically doing all he could to prevent the assassination, an interpretation advanced most recently by James Douglas. Oswald, as a young boy, lived with his mother in the neighborhood around BJ's Lounge on Alvar, Pauline, Congress, and Bartholomew, and was born on Alvar directly across from Frantz Elementary, which Ruby Bridges desegregated three years before the Kennedy assassination.

In the middle part of the Bywater, halfway between BJ's Lounge and the Marigny Street of Gabour and Pitre, runs Clouet Street, which has been home to a disproportionate number of writers. Chris Lawson, for example, who is most known as a visual artist, and who has lived and shown his work in Northern Ireland, Haiti, and Cambodia, as well as throughout the American South and New York City, now lives a few steps off Clouet; he has begun publishing poems and essays regularly and to write plays. Anne Gisleson, who has lived on Clouet for two decades and in New Orleans her entire life, regularly publishes essays in national magazines, and her memoir, *The Futilitarians*, details the role of great books in her struggle to process family tragedies. A few blocks north on Clouet, Ed Skoog made his home for nearly a decade in the years before Hurricane Katrina, and, since then, has published four books of poetry with the elite Copper Canyon Press that call to mind John Ashbery in conjuring a bewitching verbal music that hovers at the horizon of interpretable meaning. And close to the corner where Clouet meets St. Claude is the home of Jami Attenberg, who has published several skillfull and highly praised novels about contemporary romance and family, set mostly in New York, though her most recent novel, *All This Could Be Yours*, takes place in New Orleans and focuses on the struggles of the adult offspring of a deeply toxic man to sort out what his life means for theirs. Also, just a few blocks closer to the river, near the corner of Piety and Burgundy, Matthew Griffin lives. He is the author of the award-winning novel *Hide* (2016), about the final phase of a sixty-year relationship between two men in a small Southern town.

A few blocks farther downriver on St. Claude, the artist known only as Otter hosts her Backyard Ballroom, which presents live theater

BJ's Lounge. Photo by the author.

of various kinds fairly regularly, and, on Piety, near the corner of St. Claude, is the home of the novelist Yuri Herrera, a towering figure in contemporary Mexican literature. Piety Street was also the home a few decades ago of the celebrated, Louisiana-born poet Yusef Komunyaaka. A few blocks upriver from Piety is where the Grammy-winning vocalist and composer, Rickie Lee Jones, lives, and where she wrote her stunning memoir, *Last Chance Texaco*. Nearby, too, is where the novelist, C. W. Cannon grew up and still lives, and the journalist and historian,

Rien Fertel, also makes his home. The city's premier music writer in this era, Alison Fensterstock, has lived in the area for nearly two decades. And the New Orleans Center for Creative Arts, where virtually all of the city's most famous musicians of recent decades have gone to high school, is in the heart of the neighborhood, where the railroad tracks meet the river.

The Bywater is not only home to an unusually high number of writers – it has also served as the setting for three major achievements of the latter half of the twentieth century. The latest is Valerie Martin's *A Recent Martyr* (1987), which traces a love triangle in the 1980s against the backdrop of an epidemic that has led to the sealing-off of the area between Claiborne and the river, and between Canal Street and the Industrial Canal. Though this quarantine zone includes all of the French Quarter, some of Tremé, and much of the Upper 9th Ward, the narrator announces in the book's opening lines that she makes her home in the Bywater, and nearly all of the action in the book unfolds within a demographic that is unmistakably the Bywater. She is cheating on her husband with a cynical, sadistic man named Pascal, who, in turn, seems to flirt in a bullying way with a very young woman named Claire, who has decided to take a year away from the convent where she has been living to confirm that she has no interest in worldly pleasures. The young novice becomes friends with the narrator in the weeks just before the plague settles over much of the St. Claude corridor, a plague that, given the novel's late 1980s setting, evokes HIV, but is also, more broadly, a metaphor for erotic love. The novice begins to work in the makeshift hospitals inside the quarantine zone, and, at the novel's end, decides to return to the convent, as rumors spread that she has been performing miracles. After an horrific twist of fate, however, the narrator is left to ruminate on the girl's life and how, when we die, we are not released from this "gorgeous planet," but simply from the miseries of our sexual bonds to each other, as figured in the dystopia brought on by the plague. The miracles Claire may have been performing in this context mark her as perhaps the supreme exemplar of the good child transcending hard times.

A radically different novel that ultimately engages these same themes, Nelson Algren's *A Walk on the Wild Side* (1956), is set during especially hard times, the Great Depression. Though much of the novel's action takes place some distance from Bywater on Perdido Street, which during the Depression was a seedy red-light district, the main character – Dove Linkhorn – enters the city from the wharves of the

Bywater, at Desire Street, spending his first night in the city in a flop-house there. Later in the novel, he circles back to this part of town as a door-to-door salesman, making his way up Spain Street to the wharves. Dove is essentially illiterate and homeless, ultimately performing live sex shows in order to eat. He ends up spending most of 1931 in New Orleans, but, for nearly half of this time, he is in jail. Upon Dove's release from jail, a legless strongman who has discovered that Dove was having an affair with his wife beats Dove until he is permanently blind. The novel ends focused on Dove, more down on his luck than ever, but eternally good-humored, returning to his hardscrabble Texas hometown to reconnect with the young sweetheart who had been try-ing to teach him to read and who he assumes will take care of him now.

The author of the novel had drifted through New Orleans much the same way, in the same period, doing some of the same kinds of work, but Algren ultimately differs from his protagonist. As Russell Banks points out, Algren is among the most important writers of his genera-tion, with *A Walk on the Wild Side*, his greatest work, being compara-ble to Twain's *Huckleberry Finn* and Wright's *Native Son*. The novel's style and tone is a miracle of sardonic lyricism. Incidentally, the other-wise marginal movie version of *A Walk on the Wild Side* (1962) begins with Saul Bass's celebrated title-credit sequence, all three minutes of which are focused on a cat slinking through an urban nightscape to fight another cat; it likely inspired a mid 1970s movie, set among boxers and gamblers in the Bywater during the Great Depression, called *Hard Times*. At the end of the latter movie, a cat performs the function of the vulnerable innocent that the tough boxer wants to make sure is well cared for before he departs, a gesture which redeems the hardboiled fighter, making him seem sweetly human, even tender. The cat in short fulfills the "good child" function and thereby turns the brutal, aging boxer into one too. Likewise, in *A Walk on the Wild Side*, if Dove too is to be well cared for in the end, then the brutal horror of the world of that novel does, on balance, resolve into the comedic, as its richly playful and witty language suggests it will.

Coda: Stella's Baby
A version of the same tension arises at the very end of the most iconic work set in the Bywater, arguably the most iconic work in the his-tory of the American stage, Tennessee Williams's *A Streetcar Named Desire* (1947). The address of the apartment where *Streetcar* takes place is identified early in the play when Blanche is asking for directions: 632 Elysian Fields. Technically, the house, now a bicycle shop, is in the

Marigny, but Stanley and Stella's household is culturally and socially of the St. Claude corridor.

Many have focused on the fact that Williams began the play as a study of Stanley, who functions as an avatar of the New South, urbanized and crowded with immigrants, but ended up creating a far more complex and interesting figure in Blanche, who is drowning in hard times as the plantation society that is all she has ever known crumbles out from underneath her; and many too have focused on how Blanche herself is transformed over the course of the play from a vapid, obnoxious snob to a savvy operator for whom prostitution and careful lighting are the keys to her survival, until in the end she becomes a tragic, destroyed relic of all that civilization and humanity once might have meant. At the end of the play, the horror of Stanley's raping Blanche while his wife, Stella (Blanche's sister), is at the hospital giving birth often overshadows the fact that the play does end with the birth of a child.

A commonplace of traditional approaches to literature holds that a story that ends with a birth or a marriage is comedy, whereas one that ends in a death is tragedy. *Streetcar* a comedy?! Surely, no one has ever found the psychological annihilation of Blanche at the end of *Streetcar* to be funny. However, Stella's commitment to her baby means, moreover, a commitment to Stanley, and as such a denial of the fact that he has recently raped her sister, a commitment, at last, to the realm of make-believe, a sort of "organized innocence" that, at least in these circumstances, must pass for redemption. This commitment to strategic fiction is the signature survival strategy of Blanche, who has been, with varying degrees of success throughout the play, the voice of civilization against Stanley's savagery. The child is the linchpin to the entire fictional edifice of Stanley and Stella's marriage – the marriage being a microcosm of the artful fabrication that, in this play, is humanity. And that illusion in turn is probably all we have in a world of hard times.

1. The Colored Waifs Home – 801 Rosedale Drive
2. Dueling Oaks – City Park, across from 900 City Park Ave.
3. Spanish Fort – 6400 Beauregard Avenue, near the mouth of Bayou St. John, between Lake Pontchartrain and Allan Toussaint Blvd.
4. Edgar Degas' cousin's home – 2306 Esplanade
5. Bob Kaufman's boyhood home – 1660 N. Tonti
6. Bob Kaufman's other boyhood home – 1565 N. Miro
7. Campus of Straight University from 1868–1877

8. Jelly Roll Morton's boyhood home – 1443 Frenchmen St.
9. Sidney Bechet's boyhood home – 1716 Marais St.
10. Barney Birgard's boyhood home – 1726 N. Villere
11. Birthplace of Louis Moreau Gottschalk – 640 Esplanade
12. The Couvent School – 1947 Dauphine St.
13. Slave Market where Solomon Northup was trafficked – on Chartres, running the entire block between Esplanade and Kerlerec.
14. The Quroum – 611 Esplanade
15. John Dos Passos's apartment – 525 Esplanade

Map of
Esplanade
corridor fro
the Mississ
River to Ba
St. John.

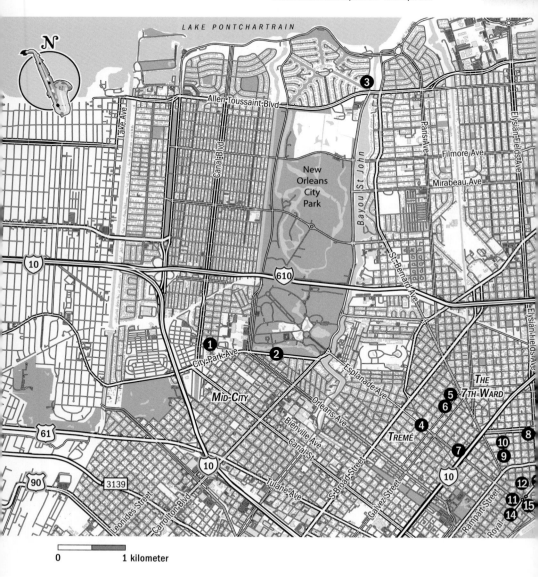

Esplanade Avenue – Escape Routes

The Marigny – 7th Ward – Bayou St. John

3

In the spring of 1925, in the 7th Ward of New Orleans, between the oak-canopied boulevards of Esplanade Avenue and St. Bernard Avenue, a poet was born. Though not widely remembered around his hometown today, his name was recently given to a street in San Francisco, where he spent the latter half of his life: through the heart of the bohemian enclave of North Beach, there runs Bob Kaufman Alley, so named in 2015, nearly thirty years after his death. In Paris, he is known as the Black Rimbaud.[1]

In 1959, he was jailed at least thirty-nine times, targeted by police, many assume, because many of those who adored him and crowded together at his performances were white women, as was his lover, and, moreover, beatniks were, in the eyes of the police, a problem in general, he being particularly so. A paragon of the ethos and the aesthetic of the Beats, he is widely credited with having coined the term; he was also a devoted Buddhist, so much so that, after President Kennedy was murdered in 1963, he took a vow of silence by way of cultivating a peace within himself that, he believed, could spread through the people around him and into the world. According to legend, he did not speak again until the Vietnam War ended, some twelve years later.

A leading scholar of Kaufman's work, Mona Lisa Saloy (a native-born and long-time resident of the same 7th Ward blocks where Kaufman grew up, and about whom, more shortly) notes that Kaufman's poetry is a crossroads where major currents in the poetic thought of the first half of the twentieth century merge and give way to those of the latter half of the century. While his work grew out of the Harlem Renaissance and was loved by Langston Hughes, his interest in Jazz, especially be-bop, made him loved, in turn, by the mostly white beatniks who, in the 1950s, tried to emulate what they understood of that art form; he thereby helped to set the stage for the Black Arts Movement that Amiri Baraka spearheaded in the aftermath of the murder of Malcolm X in the mid 1960s. More broadly, in his defiance of the past, he was a Modernist in the manner of 1920s and 30s but, more specifically, an arch Surrealist, for his poems are laced with phrases that defy conventional logic, to say nothing of cliché, and thereby open onto the always idiosyncratic dreamwork of the unconscious. This feature of his writing was met with a warm reception in the Bay Area of the psychedelic era, and, in recent decades, among those poetic descendants of John Ashbery who relish the well-timed burst of obscurity. Ultimately, when Kaufman presented his work to the public, he drew on oral-performance traditions that reach back to the African-American pulpit of the antebellum era – and through which he anticipated, in turn, the hip hop of the late twentieth century.[2]

He was the seventh of thirteen children, born to a German-Jewish father who waited tables and a mother who had grown up in the French Quarter and become a highly accomplished pianist, and who was so light-skinned she could pass for white.[3] According to family lore, she would go to estate sales to buy up entire personal libraries to fill the 7th Ward houses at 1660 N. Tonti and 1565 N. Miro where Kaufman grew up. Everyone in the house was reading and talking about what they read, all the time. After high school, Kaufman joined the Merchant Marine and worked in the boats' kitchens. Sailing to New York and San Francisco, Calcutta and Ceylon, he soon became prominent in the labor movement among the seamen and honed, in that setting, his skills in oratory. In these years, he became friends with the visual artist Joe Overstreet, and, after he left the Merchant Marine, the two met up in Manhattan and took an apartment.

From there, the legend of his life took off. Some say that the parties he and Overstreet threw were attended by Billie Holiday and Charlie Parker, and that he was in the car for some of Jack Kerouac's cross-country road trips of the sort immortalized in *On the Road*.[4] Everyone in the New York arts scene seemed to know him or know about him. By 1953, he was making his home and performing his poetry in San Francisco, in the North Beach bars and coffeehouses that were ground zero for the West Coast wing of the beatnik movement.

In the latter half of the 1950s, he suffered horrific abuse at the hands of the police – arrested and beaten, released, then, within days, arrested and beaten again. He finally went back to New York, where, in 1960, he was arrested for walking on the grass in Washington Square Park; this arrest landed him in Bellevue, where he was forced to undergo electroshock therapy. By most accounts, while at Bellevue, Kaufman seemed to lose faith in humanity, withdrawing thereafter into an ever-thicker haze of marijuana and alcohol that alternated with Buddhist devotion. In 1965, his first book appeared, *Solitudes Crowded with Loneliness* from City Lights Press, and it contains a section called "Jail Poems," all of them written in cell #3 of the San Francisco City Jail. A short sample of some of the lines in this five-page sequence gives a sense of his verse:

I am sitting in a cell with a view of evil parallels
A golden sardine is swimming in my head

My past has turned its back on me
Cities should be built on one side of the street
There, Jesus, that didn't hurt a bit, did it?

By the time Kaufman died in the mid 1980s, he was a legendary "street poet," known to shout his poems at random strangers from the sidewalk as they struggled to park their cars. Hardly a mere madman, Kaufman, in the end, was a kind of escape artist: he pursued Surrealism to escape cliché; be-bop, to escape mass-culture commercialism; drugs, to escape the traumatic memory of police beatings; oral performance, to escape the fixity of the printed page; and even silence, to escape the cataclysmic political violence of his era.

Kaufman's boyhood neighborhood, which he left in his teens, never to return, is in the heart of the 7th Ward, an area bordered by the river to the south and Bayou St. John to the north; its downriver border is Elysian Fields, and its upriver border is Esplanade – a street that perhaps surpasses all others in its geographical importance to the city. That sliver of high ground, stretching between the river and the bayou, is the reason the city itself was built where it was.[5] At 2 feet above sea level, in an area that is generally lower, it was the natural, original, and literal highway into and out of town.

The poet Cassie Pruyn explains that, historically, boats that sought to go up the river from the Gulf of Mexico faced the extraordinary challenge of navigating the river's mouth: that mouth has always been "notoriously tricky to discern, hidden among a mesh of streams and bayous … hurtling refuse, shifting sandbars, varying winds … [demarcated in no way by the land that is] so fluid it can barely hold a man's weight," being nothing more than a drifting assemblage of "drowned meadows."[6] However, by sailing from the Gulf into Chandeleur

Bob Kaufman, 1959, by Jerry Stoll. Courtesy of Casey Stoll.

Sound, from there into Lake Borgne and onward into Lake Pontchartrain, the boats could then enter Bayou St. John and thereby reach a point that offered a short portage of 3½ miles to a point fully 95 miles above the mouth, from which they could make their way into remote reaches of the hinterlands. This portage between the bayou and the river, the back-door entrance to the city that long preceded the front and that opened up such wide possibilities of movement, eventually became Bayou Road; around 1830, however, the function of that gently curving thoroughfare was usurped by Esplanade Avenue, when that downriver border of the Quarter was "ploughed through" by surveyors and engineers in a straight line all the way to Bayou St. John.[7]

What made this pathway possible was itself a sort of escape. Pruyn draws from the magisterial *Gateway to New Orleans: Bayou St. John 1708–2018* by Hilary Somerville Irvin, R. Stephanie Bruno, Heather Veneziano, S. Frederick Starr, and Richard Campanella, to explain how some 2,000 years ago, about a half-dozen miles upriver from the French Quarter near what is presently Armstrong International Airport, the river burst its banks. It created a distributary down what is now Metairie Road to the present-day routes of Gentilly Boulevard and Chef Menteur Highway to empty into Lake Borgne. This secondary river was at some points 1,000 feet wide and 50 feet deep; it carried sediment, which it threw up around its sides for roughly 1,300 years, layer upon layer. The berms and ridges that formed grew tall enough to trap part of the sea and thus create Lake Pontchartrain; and, as water sought to escape that bowl, it did so in a long, crooked finger between two ridges that poked their way back in the direction of the river. This became Bayou St. John.[8]

The River The city sits on sediment delivered by the river, much of the highest ground having arrived well under a thousand years ago. As Lawrence Powell explains, between southern Illinois and southern Louisiana, the land only slopes about 285 feet, and downriver from Baton Rouge, the slope flattens still further to a mere 7 inches per mile. Such rivers are prone to meander, and the Mississippi might be, as Powell notes, the crookedest in the world – and the most unstable. It has changed its path many times. The levee system that holds it in place now prevents new sedimentation and thus contributes to coastal erosion.

At the point where the bayou was closest to the river, a particular berm rose that, for indigenous groups who migrated seasonally around the region, was the natural choice for a portage. Over time, as Pruyn notes, the path was "worn smooth by dragging canoes" and would figure prominently on the maps the indigenous made for early European settlers, who were eager to figure out how to move in and out of the area as they developed commercial networks. What would become New Orleans – a city, in Pruyn's words, perched on an "ever shifting slab of river-spewed land"[9] – soon began to spring up at what is now the intersection of Esplanade Avenue and Bayou St. John. And then, at the other end of this path – at the bank of the river – it boomed.

The sheer precariousness of the city, the persistent, creeping sense that one must always be ready to run – or swim – for one's life, shapes the contemporary English essayist Geoff Dyer's account of the few months in early 1991 that he lived on Esplanade near the intersection with Royal. He mulls the fact that the city, being built on mud, is steadily sinking, a worrisome vertical process complicated by the phenomenon of "horizontal drift" (his essay's title), by which the vast masses of sediment flowing down the river cause the landmass under the city to travel in a lateral way. The upshot: Dyer's apartment was no longer as close to the river as it had been in the nineteenth century, and the river itself seemed to him "so old and heavy it had long ago lost all interest in making its way to the Gulf of Mexico or wherever."[10]

Dyer amplifies this dour tone at the end of his essay as he reflects on the fact that his only friend in this famously friendly city has been talking about suicide. In the end, Dyer drifts out of town to seek new adventures in the West, loses contact with his friend, and in the final lines of his essay wonders whether the guy carried out this ultimate escape. This same theme marks the ending of the best-known work associated with Esplanade Avenue – Kate Chopin's *The Awakening* – the ending of which is marked by ambiguities that are themselves an escape from any firm and obvious endpoint.

The main character of *The Awakening* is defined by an ever-present dream of slipping off and stealing away to some elsewhere, a dream that defines moreover the literary legacy of Esplanade Avenue and the 7th Ward, from Chopin to Kaufman to the present day, and it reaches back much earlier. To move back and forth between the two ends of Esplanade, from the bayou to the river and back, to track the way these two areas developed and the major writing associated with these processes is to see again and again in that writing the same dream of flight, sometimes actualized and sometimes not, sometimes as nightmare and sometimes as salvation.

Bayou to River: Settlement to Civil War

Among the first wave of settlers at that spot where Esplanade Avenue intersects Bayou St. John was a 23-year-old named Antoine-Simon Le Page du Pratz,[11] who set up his plantation near there in 1718. Some forty years later, he published his *History of Louisiana*. The first such account, it reports on the Natchez people in such rich detail and with so much sympathy and insight (Le Page became fluent in their language), that, a half-century later, when Lewis and Clark set out to explore the full range of the Louisiana Purchase all the way into the Pacific Northwest, Le Page's book was one of the few they carried with them.[12]

Soon after getting established near Bayou St. John, Le Page du Pratz moved to the settlement at Natchez, where he lived for most of the 1720s, leaving just prior to the massacre of November 28, 1729, in which, in less than two hours, that indigenous group shot and axed to death 145 white men and more than 90 white women and children.[13] Le Page du Pratz discussed that event at length, for it struck such horror into the hearts of the colonial bureaucracy of the region that, along with failure of the tobacco crop, it compelled the French to scale back their plans and, in essence, leave the settlement downriver at New Orleans largely to its own devices. The subsequent neglect, as Lawrence Powell explains, enabled the city to develop, for the next thirty years, as a relatively independent Creole society, until the Spanish took over – though they too would give up the hope of controlling and profiting from it after a few decades.[14]

The mass bloodshed at Natchez in 1729 and the colonial reaction to it also loom large in the memoir of a French bookkeeping clerk named Marc Antoine Caillot, who worked in New Orleans for only two years, beginning in 1729. Caillot's departure, so soon after arriving, was spurred in part by the massacre, and is thus a sort of microcosm of the original French project in the area. In counterpoint to Le Page's sober anthropological record of indigenous folkways (dress, medicine, government, marriage, child-rearing, and funerals), Caillot's *Relation du Voyage de la Louisianne* touches on some of the same subjects but also offers bawdy entertainment. Caillot's is the first written account of a Mardi Gras celebration in the city, as Caillot – dressed up in drag, led by enslaved torch bearers – hiked with friends late one night out the portage path that would become Esplanade Avenue to Bayou St. John to drink and dance till nearly dawn. They travelled back out to Bayou St. John the next day to continue their revelry, for Caillot had fallen in love, though only briefly, with a young woman there.[15] Caillot's narrative, as Erin Greenwald notes, is a remarkable artefact of the various ways people travelled in that period – on foot, horseback, and boat.

In addition to cutting Caillot's stay short, the Natchez event shaped the opposite end of this thoroughfare – especially where it meets the river – in the construction of a fort on the site that is now the US Mint and that was meant to defend against the same sort of attack. The settlers began to dig a moat at this spot that was supposed to wrap all the way around the developing town, but, as the panic over Natchez faded, the project was abandoned without nearing completion. This same pattern would reappear a little over a half-century later, when Spanish colonial administrators, fearing an attack from Kaintucks, tried to wall the city in, beginning at this spot, but that project too fell apart before being finished.[16] The area then became a park in 1821 to honor Andrew Jackson, but less than fifteen years later, it was demolished on the orders of Jackson himself to make way for the US Mint, from which would flow US currency for a few decades, and, far more briefly, Confederate currency.

The man who designed that building, William Strickland, a student of Latrobe, never visited the area, and so made no provisions for the loose deltaic soil. Thus, as soon as it was built, the US Mint began to sink and develop structural problems.[17] Though these were addressed, the building became notorious in other ways, as one of its key officials who lived inside the building, John Leonard Riddell, began to claim, falsely, that he had been elected governor of Louisiana and was accused of murdering his wife in their Mint apartment. Riddell also published, in 1847, science fiction about a voyage to the moon.[18]

A movement far more profound than Riddell's lunar-expedition fantasy defines those 7th Ward blocks across Esplanade from the Mint. As this area that stretches back from the river – known as the Marigny – filled with many hundreds of Creole cottages in the early decades of the nineteenth century, the dominant presence in the newly developing area became free people of color, particularly after the influx of those fleeing the revolution in Haiti in 1809.[19] By the time of the Civil War, three-fourths of the properties in the Marigny had been owned by free people of color, a great many of them women.[20]

How did so many women of color come to own houses in the Marigny in the early nineteenth century? As Powell explains, the racial codes of New Orleans differed from those of the Chesapeake, another major hub of the US slave trade, and, in fact, from the rest of the US South,[21] for a white man in New Orleans lost no social status for forming an intimate bond with someone whom he enslaved. Without the stigma attached to such relationships, these white men were more likely to sustain these liaisons for much greater durations, and to acknowledge them publicly and the children born of them. What's more, as Powell adds, this acknowledgement often took a material form, when white men would give their partner of color money, either while the white men were alive or as a dying gift in their will. They also often granted these women their freedom.

This practice, fairly unique within the US, was made possible by the Spanish slave codes, which were far less restrictive than the Anglo and the French, and redefined, at least in part, the racial dynamics of the city while the Spanish ruled it from the 1760s through the 1790s. During this period, nearly twice as many women as men were freed, and nearly half of those were explicitly granted freedom for "meritorious service."[22] As Powell notes, in that period, the number of free people of color in the city jumped *a full sixteenfold*.[23] The Creole cottages of the Marigny are a kind of memorial to the practice of escaping slavery and ascending to property.

But, as Emily Clark has argued, this phenomenon has been widely misunderstood, even mythologized, a fantasy retrofitted onto a paucity of hard evidence. First, over the middle decades of the eighteenth century, when the French colonial project floundered, the enslaved could, in whatever spare time they had, make a little money by hiring themselves out or selling extra food they might cultivate in small gardens. When the Spanish took over the colony in the latter half of that century, their slave codes included a key difference from those of the French who preceded them and the Americans who would follow: the right of the enslaved to purchase their own freedom. Radically incentivized to develop skills and save money, the enslaved were soon becoming free people of color in large numbers in the final decades of the eighteenth century. Clark further notes that the practice of *plaçage*, by which a wealthy white man would "place" a mistress of color in a household of her own by formal contract, seems not to be supported by any archive where such contracts can be found.[24] On the other hand, the presence of wills wherein white men bequeathed a portion of their wealth and real estate to long-term, intimate partners would seem partly to explain the preponderance in the Marigny of home-ownership by women of color.

The fantasy of white male control over Black female bodies and of women so skilled in the erotic arts that they could use the bedroom to transition from owned to ownership has been mythologized in major literature and pervasive lore about the city, a topic that will be enlarged upon in Chapter 4. An important example is the way it figures at the heart of William Faulkner's masterpiece, *Abasalom, Absalom!*, wherein one of the characters cautions a newcomer to New Orleans against ever misunderstanding this sort of woman: she is not a "whore," nor even a "courtesan," for she "reigns, wise supine and all-powerful, from the sunless and silken bed which is her throne."[25]

Faulkner's extravagant language aside, these women had an extraordinary impact on the city, as illustrated in the story of Marie Couvent. Born in Africa around 1757, enslaved in Saint-Domingue (soon to become Haiti) until the revolution in the 1790s, she was able to purchase, by means not in the historical record, two pieces of land on Dauphine Street a few blocks downriver from Esplanade Avenue at the corner of Touro in 1806; when she died in 1837, her will declared that her fortune be used to create a school for Black children, which would be situated on her property; the Couvent School opened about a decade later, emphasizing an education in the ideals of equality that were advanced during her girlhood through the revolutions in France and Haiti, and that would sweep Europe again the year after her school opened. The Couvent School would either graduate or hire as teachers many who would become the most illustrious Afro-Creole writers of the nineteenth century, particularly the poets who would publish regularly in *L'Union* and *La Tribune*, as discussed in Chapter 1: Desdunes, Questy, Lanusse, and Duhart, among others, were all affiliated with the Couvent School. In fact, this school was the starting point when, in the summer of 1866, the Native Guard rallied to march through the Quarter to advocate for equal rights, only to be massacred near Canal Street by white supremacists. The Couvent School was an epicenter for the Afro-Creole literary, intellectual, and political elite of the middle decades of the nineteenth century, and, in its emphasis on the revolutionary ideal of equality, it prepared generations to lead people of color forward through the racial conflicts that would define the city as it grew.

Such conflict would preside over the birth of Esplanade itself in 1810. The Quarter having filled up by the end of the eighteenth century, the competition among the elite to develop, as a sort of spillover, what had been an alley behind the mansions of Barracks Street was so heated that a full twenty-five years of lawsuits delayed the creation of what we now know as that part of Esplanade.[26] At last, with the 1809 arrival of nearly 10,000 refugees from the Haitian Revolution, who doubled the city's population in a matter of months, and right on the heels of that sixteenfold increase in the population of free people of color in the final decades of the preceding century, a continuation of the elite blocks of Royal with their stately, tightly packed Creole townhouses became inevitable. And thus those first half-dozen blocks of Esplanade, near the river.

The legal entanglements that delayed the development of the river-end of Esplanade were a minor squabble compared with what happened at the other end, near Bayou St. John.[27] Almost immediately after founding the city in 1718, plans had been made to cut a canal that would extend Bayou St. John all the way to the doorstep of the city at Rampart Street, stopping at what became Basin Street as the point where the boats would turn around. Just before the Louisiana Purchase in 1803, the canal was finally dug – but this led to elaborate legal disputes that would resurface from time to time and prove very difficult to resolve, causing the area along the bayou to fall into neglect, as no one could agree who had what rights to profit from it, nor what responsibilities to maintain it. Development of the area into something like the river-end of Esplanade was stymied by one particular lawsuit, a conflict that, as Pruyn explains, began in 1811, when Myra Clark Gaines's father passed away; she would sue to prove her legitimacy as sole heir to her late father's large plantation and considerable fortune. The legal battle dragged on for nearly eight decades, one of the longest-running lawsuits in US history.

While ownership of this land around Bayou St. John was contested through much of the nineteenth century, it couldn't be sold or developed. It thus remained a sort of unsettled territory in swampy, symbolic counterpoint to the growing urban hub at the other end of Esplanade. An especially storied function of this area would arise in that century, as just beyond Bayou St. John a particular patch of ground became a favorite spot among Creole gentlemen to settle questions of honor with a duel, either via sword or pistol. Though illegal, the duels held at the area that came to be called Duelling Oaks weren't stopped by police, perhaps because they were conducted here at the outskirts of town and the beginnings of the vast swamp behind it. These events spawned a body of legend and lore, and were central to the social fabric of the city's first century and a half. A short piece by Lafcadio Hearn published in 1885 entitled "Under the Oaks" collects some of these tales, and since then, popular novels set in that period never fail to deliver at least one good duel – Arthur Pindle's novel, *Bayou St. John*, is a recent example. Historically, most of the conflicts originated in the ballrooms in the French Quarter, where rivals for a certain lady's attention would issue challenges that would end with one of them dead. This activity seemed to reach a peak in the ten years between 1834 and 1844, when according to a local newspaper, scarcely a single day passed without a duel, and on one Sunday afternoon in 1839, no fewer than ten were held.[28]

In addition to the countless dramas that were resolved on the far side of Bayou St. John, this same area became a constant frustration for slave-owners, reaching a peak at nearly the exact same time as the crescendo in the culture of duelling. This back-swamp allowed the enslaved to slip away and vanish, to travel secret pathways and, if they chose, to con-nect with south Louisiana's endless

Old Duelling Grounds. Photo by the author.

waterways. Living on fish and game, sleeping in small, well-hidden huts, these people – known as maroons – mostly hovered just beyond the outskirts of the city. Many of them did so for considerable periods of time, participating in a shadow economy, pilfering, and staying in contact with loved ones in town or on nearby plantations through visits in the dead of night, all the while eking out an existence at considerable peril in something close to perfect freedom.[29]

The most legendary of these figures, the one who has been the most consistent spur to New Orleans writers, as Bryan Wagner notes, was originally named Squire and was enslaved by a man who lived on St. Louis Street in the Quarter. After losing an arm in a struggle with police – and then escaping – Squire came to be known as Bras Coupé (French for "severed arm") and to embody what the whites feared the most: though most maroons avoided violent confrontation with whites and preferred to slip in and out of town under cover of darkness, Bras Coupé became the boldest of the bandits; he robbed taverns and stores along the bayou at the outermost end of Esplanade, mingling with other runaways, who were dazzled by his exploits, and making such an impression on them that he earned for himself a permanent place in the city's lore.[30] It was widely believed, as Wagner notes, that his skin could repel bullets and his gaze could turn one to stone; he was said to be the greatest dancer at the Sunday gatherings of the enslaved in Congo Square; he was believed to have been the inventor of Jazz. He was reputed to be able to breathe fire and also to teleport.[31]

He also became a hero in the abolitionist press on both sides of the Atlantic.[32] Predictably, in New Orleans itself, he became the focus of a general worry among white elites that the swamps beyond Bayou St. John were filling with runaways, and that he had the potential to organize them and thereby serve as the leading edge of a revolutionary axe that was poised to swing into the heart of the city. He was finally caught and hanged in 1837. Since then, however, he has turned up, as Wagner notes, in countless newspaper articles, memoirs, city histories, tourist guides, poems, novels, and plays. From George Cable to Kalamu Ya Salaam, Marcus Christian to Herbert Asbury, Robert Penn Warren to Tom Dent, a long list of writers have taken up the legend of Bras Coupé. Most recently, Wagner has collected in a single volume all of the primary materials from which the legend and the considerable body of literature grew.

Bras Coupé's legend, given its wide circulation both internationally and locally, might well have turned up in slave markets at the other end of Esplanade, near the river, where, less than five years after Bras Coupé was hanged, Solomon Northup was brought, after having been kidnapped, as a free man of color, in Washington DC, and brought to New Orleans with a shipment of others to be sold. Northup's dreams of escape would have been spurred mightily by whispered stories of Bras Coupé. To live as Bras Coupé apparently had – the freedom, the power – is to experience the complete fulfillment of human desire. In these terms, Bras Coupé's power to fixate the white imagination is readily understandable, to say nothing of the dreams of those who, like Northup, had come to know the horror of enslavement. In such circumstances, some 3 miles down Esplanade from Bayou St. John, might Bras Coupé's name have entered Northup's ear and passed over his lips as something like a magic charm?

On the boat to New Orleans, Northup had plotted to mutiny with a friend, but the friend fell ill and died before they could carry out the plan.[33] Another friend on the boat, whose

Domestic Slave Trade Between 1790 and 1860, about a million enslaved people, according to Walter Johnson, were marched from the Eastern seaboard to work in what was then the southwest, and for a great many of them this process entailed passage through the auction blocks and pens of New Orleans, just as it did for Solomon Northup. New Orleans, in the first half of the nineteenth century became synonymous with human trafficking, in the same way, a century later, Detroit would be for auto-manufacturing and Hollywood for film-making.

circumstances were similar to Northup's, was set free as soon as the boat docked at New Orleans, as he had arranged for rescuers to meet him there; following that friend's lead, Northup wrote a letter as the boat approached the city, pleading for rescue, and found a friendly sailor who promised to take it to the post office. As the letter made its way off the boat, Northup was chained, beaten, and driven by whip to a pen that adjoined a slave market at the corner of Esplanade and Chartres Street.[34] As his journey into the bowels of antebellum Louisiana paused briefly there, Northup began to wonder if he was dreaming, whether any of what he was experiencing could be real, and then he began to pray to God for mercy and deliverance.[35]

He hoped to be sold to someone who lived in New Orleans, because he assumed that escape from within the city would be easier than from a remote plantation, but he was soon sold some 150 miles up the Red River. The story of his departure from New Orleans centers around a young woman named Eliza and her two children. Northup recounts in heart-wrenching detail the story of her son Randall being sold away from her, and then, only a short time later, another buyer purchasing Eliza herself. She begs him to buy her daughter Emily as well, but the seller refuses to let the little girl go at any price, for, in a few years, she will be the most valuable kind of merchandise, a "fancy gal." The agonies that follow the separating of the mother from her only remaining child were "more than language can portray."[36] Northup reports that Eliza was taken to the same area up the Red River as he was, that she never saw either child again, that her grief was so acute that, over the weeks and months that followed, she became delusional, even talking to her missing offspring as if they were at her side. Too pained to be a productive worker, she was beaten again and again, and finally beaten to death.[37]

Northup was rescued from the Avoyelles Plantation twelve years after he was kidnapped, and in that first year of his regained freedom, he wrote *Twelve Years a Slave*, which sold briskly right away and for a few years that followed. It then fell into obscurity until roughly a hundred years later, when Sue Eakin and Joseph Logsdon reissued it in 1968. Eakin had discovered it as a young girl in 1931, in the library of a large plantation house near where she grew up and where

Spirits Early in *The Awakening*, Edna interprets her exultation in learning to swim by saying "There must be spirits abroad tonight." Her companion, a Creole insider, replies that this happens to be the date – August 29, later historic as the date of Hurricanes Katrina and Ida – when, if the moon is full, "a spirit that has haunted these shores for ages rises up from the gulf. With its own penetrating vision, it seeks ... one mortal worthy to hold him company, worthy of being exalted for a few hours into the realms of the semi celestials." If only she had followed that line of thought into a circle of Laveau acolytes....

Northup had survived his years as a slave. She grew fascinated by the old book, as she recognized the family names of her neighbors in it – but was told that it was worthless fiction. As a young woman, she decided to dedicate her life to proving otherwise.[38] When the film version was released in 2013, it won three Oscars and a Golden Globe. Its popularity is evident too in this fact offered by *The Hollywood Reporter*: the year after it was released, it was among the most often illegally downloaded and pirated films of that year.[39]

River to Bayou: Civil War to Civil Rights
Another narrative of the nineteenth century associated with those river-end blocks of Esplanade underwent an extraordinary revival in the year immediately following the 1968 release of the Eakin–Logsdon edition of *Twelve Years a Slave*. That novel would become one of the primary vehicles by which feminism would arrive and flourish in university departments of English: Kate Chopin's *The Awakening*. Like Northup's narrative, it too is preoccupied with the dream of escape and deliverance; and like Northup's, it too was lost for decades before joining the canon of American literature.

Some background: by the end of the 1890s, Chopin had written roughly a hundred short stories, many of them appearing in the most prestigious magazines in the US. When it appeared in 1899, however, *The Awakening* was panned, considered a pornographic scandal, and dismissed as morbid.[40] Afterwards, she wrote little, and five years later, she passed away. The novel fell into near-total obscurity for several decades, until a Norwegian graduate student at Harvard named Per Seyersted got interested in it and began to work on a biography of Chopin and an edition of her complete works. Both appeared in 1969, the latter with an introduction by the highly esteemed Edmund Wilson.[41] In 1972, *Redbook*, the wide-reaching women's magazine, reprinted the entire novel in one of its issues.[42] Over the next two decades, virtually an entire generation of academic literary stars would publish scholarly exegeses about the novel, from Nina Baym and Harold Bloom to Elaine Showalter and Jane Tompkins, among dozens of others.[43] Today, according to Columbia University's Open Syllabus Project, which tracks some 7 million university syllabi in the US, it is the fifth most frequently assigned American novel, surpassed only by *The Great Gatsby*, *Beloved*, *Their Eyes Were Watching God*, and *Invisible Man*.

The main character – a white lady from Kentucky named Edna Pontellier – lives on Esplanade Avenue with her two young children and her wealthy Creole husband, presumably on those blocks near the river, for she grows fond of slipping out of her house to take long walks in the nearby French Quarter. This inclination for long walks is foreshadowed in the novel's opening lines, when a caged parrot shrieks, "Allez-vous-en! Allez-vous-en! Sapristi!" (Get out! Get out! For Heaven's sake!). That theme of escape steadily builds throughout the novel as Edna learns to swim and comes to enjoy an extended flirtation with a bachelor who is hanging around the coastal resort where she is vacationing with her family. Back on Esplanade after the summer holidays, her spiritual and sexual awakening having begun, she grows increasingly disenchanted with the roles society prescribes for her and finally travels alone back down to the coast, and, nude, swims alone out to sea in an apparent suicide. As Emily Toth observes, however, no dead body is ever mentioned, and so the accent in the end lands on wide-open possibility, even liberation, a grace note in counterpoint to the wider context of likely tragedy.[44]

One of the possibilities evoked in the novel, but never actualized, is that of alliance between white women and African Americans. While the wealthy protagonist is an obvious beneficiary of generations of slavery and is not herself in any literal sense enslaved, the novel hints at a certain structural analogy between her position as a woman and that of the Black workers for whom slavery would be well within living memory. In her first interaction with her husband, in the opening pages of the novel, his first words to her, as he finds her sunbathing on the beach with her male friend, are, "What folly! To bathe at such an hour in such heat ... You are burnt beyond recognition." Chopin then adds that, as he spoke these words, he was "looking at his wife as one looks at a valuable piece of personal property which has suffered some damage."[45] Her darkening skin and, ostensibly, her diminishing value are drawn into greater relief by the fact that the young man with whom she is sunbathing, and who has been teaching her to swim and become a love-interest, is named Robert LeBrun, the evocation of the color brown here further suggesting a slippage out of white society. The analogy between Edna's situation and slavery becomes more explicit later in the novel when, in conversation with LeBrun, she scoffs at his claim that he has been "dreaming wild impossible things, recalling men who had set their wives free." She replies, "I am no longer one of Mr. Pontellier's possessions to dispose of or not. I give myself freely where I choose." She continues, "If he were to say, 'Here Robert, take her and be happy, she's yours,' I should laugh at you both."[46] Soon thereafter, she arrives at her commitment to flight, when she thinks of her children as "antagonists, who had overcome her; who had overpowered and sought to drag her into the soul's slavery for the rest of her days."[47] Earlier, in a conversation with a friend, she said, "I would give my life for my children; but I wouldn't give myself,"[48] reflecting a form of double-consciousness between outward societal expectation and innermost life that, according to W. E. B. Du Bois, defines African-American experience.

Ultimately, however, as Toth argues, Edna's anguish is driven by simple loneliness, for, as a Kentuckian, she is a perennial outsider to Creole society. Despite the subtle suggestions of a potential alliance or at least conversation across racial lines, Edna's imagination, for all its yearning to transgress and self-liberate, cannot conjure such a possibility for beating back her sense of isolation.

Her darker-skinned servants, who are ever present in the novel and nearly always silent, might have been particularly flummoxed by her inability to capitalize on her outsider status, for in the latter decades of the nineteenth century, when the novel is set, they would have held close to their hearts a fund of stories about another outsider-woman well known along Esplanade Avenue, who stood in boldest counterpoint to Edna: the voodoo queen, Marie Laveau. Far from lonely, Laveau was one of the best-known figures in the city during her life. And since her death surely few can rival her status as legend.

Part of what has spurred the growth of the Laveau legend is confusion, first and foremost, over the fact that there were in fact two women named Marie Laveau in the city in the middle decades of the nineteenth century, a mother and a daughter; the mother lived on St. Ann Street, near Rampart, a few blocks upriver from Esplanade, and her daughter lived just below Esplanade in the Marigny, on what are now the first blocks of Rampart after it veers south away from St. Claude. Before settling there, the mother lived adjacent to Esplanade on Bayou Road after her first husband vanished, the same street where the man with whom she spent most of her life had grown up (unless otherwise noted, what follows refers to the older Marie, the mother). Between the homes of the two women named Marie Laveau ran Esplanade Avenue, and mother and daughter, legendary for their beauty and charisma, would have made a stunning spectacle together as they led their followers out Esplanade to Bayou St. John for their spiritual ceremonies. Their heads would have been wrapped in the *tignon* that had once been required by law to signal the status of enslaved women but that the Laveaus continued to wear long after the law was lifted, in a modified, highly decorative version, an adornment that alluded at once to the idea of an enslaved woman and also to a queen, and thus implicitly to the movement from the former to the latter.[49]

Additional confusion arises from the two distinct kinds of writers who have taken up the subject of Marie Laveau. On one hand, during the middle decades of the nineteenth century, the popular press painted her spiritual leadership in the most lurid tones, suggesting nudity, race-mixing, and debauchery, and this same thread continued into the 1940s with Robert Tallant's often ghoulish and sensationalistic books on the subject, which, in turn, probably influence the way the topic is presented to tourists today. On the other hand, a more sober, highly literary, and scholarly tradition has done a great deal to explain Marie Laveau's extraordinary power in the city. The most recent iterations of this latter tradition can be found in the excellent scholarship that both Martha Ward and Carolyn Morrow Long have delivered to general readers, giving us as much as we'll likely ever know about the historical reality of Marie Laveau. And the poet Brenda Marie Osbey's essay, "Why We Can't Talk to You about Voodoo," offers, too, a powerful corrective to anyone who would assume that this spiritual tradition is available in any form to voyeuristic outsiders, even scholars. Another key moment in this arc of understanding came in the 1930s, when Zora Neale Hurston published *Mules and Men*, which narrates a half-dozen experiences in the 1920s of immersion in the worlds of those who would continue Laveau's legacy. The starting point for Laveau's literary afterlife, however, came a half-century before Hurston, when Lafcadio Hearn wrote about the older Marie Laveau's funeral in 1881.

Some background: Hearn spent roughly a decade in New Orleans, exploring the Creole culture that, in the years after the Civil War, was moving out of the increasingly industrialized and immigrant-crowded Quarter, opting for the quieter, more pastoral blocks out Esplanade.[50] Two examples of this movement have already been noted in the case of Bob Kaufman's mother and the Pontellier family in *The Awakening*; Frances Parkinson Keyes captured the process too in her 1947 novel for young adults called *Once on Esplanade*. In fact, when Hearn arrived, just as the actual reign of the two Marie Laveaus was coming to an end, those blocks out Esplanade were fast becoming a kind of "garden suburb" or "streetcar suburb," as a streetcar had been installed up and down its length in 1863 that would run for fifty years.[51] Hearn likely would have used this streetcar to travel out Esplanade to witness the voodoo ceremonies along Bayou St. John on St. John's Eve, the annual spectacle held every June 23, at the center of which was Marie Laveau.

Hearn's takeaway from his observation of Laveau: "It is pretty certain that the strange stories in circulation about Marie Laveau were wholly due to her marvelous skill in the use of native herb medicines."[52] Hearn notes that much of Creole medicine derives from African knowledge of natural remedies;[53] Laveau was regularly visited for decades by Native American women who came to sell her the herbs that they gathered for her.[54] She had been trained as a nurse by her mother at age 14, pressed into service to help tend the wounded in the Battle of New Orleans in 1815, and, during the decades that followed, especially during the epidemics,[55] she was credited with saving many hundreds of lives and thereby became the most famous of the Creole "fever nurses."

While Hearn does his best to quell the hysteria around Laveau by praising her as simply a deeply learned herbalist and gifted healer, the prospect of a woman of color rising to a position of such extraordinary importance – a veritable hero, or, during those deadly epidemics, even a savior – was cause for alarm among white elites. In fact, by the time of her rise, voodoo was a well-established concern among those who presumed to control New Orleans; nearly a hundred years had passed since a 1743 court case had included detailed, first-hand testimony about a group of Black people who had been behaving peculiarly on a slave-ship bound for the city, using symbols to alter social reality in ways that threatened to overturn the power imbalance on board.[56] White anxieties about these potentials inevitably colored perceptions of Laveau's medical prowess, and this anxiety probably added to her power. Laveau was known, moreover, to have had great skill in offering personal advice in ways that perhaps anticipated the psychotherapy of more recent decades. Another twist: she was also known to have an elaborate network of enslaved informants working in the households of white elites, through whom she could have been privy to – and poised to leverage – all sorts of personal secrets. Her power, too, might have derived from the Haitian voodoo practice of ancestor veneration that tapped into that era's increasing enthusiasm for séance and sacred trance. Whatever the precise components of her power, it was considerable.

Hearn notes that Laveau often interceded in courtroom trials and spent a great deal of time counseling prisoners. She first became involved this way through her close friend and mentor, the famous priest at St. Louis Cathedral, Père Antoine.[57] He was the paragon of the revolutionary, spiritual leader, advocating for decades against slavery and for social justice for all people of color. Laveau and Antoine had been, as Hearn notes, the closest of friends. When he died in 1829, she took his place as a spiritual leader and social activist in the city through an array of early benevolent societies, as well as through her legendary beauty and charisma. Hearn notes that she became friends with nearly every Louisiana governor and all the lower-level political figures operating in the city in her lifetime.[58]

Hearn also notes the particular importance to the career of Marie Laveau, both mother and daughter, of the annual celebrations of the feast day of John the Baptist. Both women would lead these ritual ceremonies at the far end of Esplanade at Bayou St. John, and farther out the Bayou toward Lake Pontchartrain. Though Saint John was celebrated for having prophesied the coming of Jesus Christ, the great deliverer, the two Marie Laveaus probably celebrated him as a syncretic figure for the African spirit known as High John the Conqueror, a trickster who in lore was brought to the US as a slave but became a master of the arts of escape. High John the Conqueror was the basis for the Louisiana folktales of Br'er Rabbit and probably, in turn, the Warner Brothers cartoon character known as Bugs Bunny. He is also the titular figure of a story by Zora Neale Hurston, who says, for Black people, he was a "hope bringer." His sign was the confident laughter that "evaded the ears of white people, for they were not supposed to know", a laughter that grew out of the certainty of eventual escape, for "trouble don't last always." She concludes, "There are many tales, and variants of each, of how the Negro got his freedom through High John de Conqueror."[59] As such, Marie Laveau's commitment to celebrating High John in the annual ceremony along Bayou St. John is no surprise.

Perhaps those who thronged to Bayou St. John to witness the ceremonies on St. John's Eve – one year, as many as 12,000 were on hand, creating what one observer described as a midsummer Mardi Gras[60] – were seeking contact with or even possession by this spirit of escape and supreme freedom. Whipped up by the popular press's suggestion of nudity and race-mixing, these crowds drew the attention, if not of High John, then certainly of the police, as raids on these ceremonies reached a peak in the 1850s. By the 1870s, however, Marie Laveau began to stage a kind of cat-and-mouse game, announcing her St. John's Eve celebration in one location only to slip away to hold it, without harassment from crowds, newspapermen, and cops, in another. At one of these summer ceremonies, in the late 1870s, the younger Marie Laveau vanished for good. According to legend, she was swept out into Lake Pontchartrain by a heavy storm during a voodoo celebration of Saint John/High John, finally freed forever, as Edna Pontellier would be, by the open water.

Marie Laveau is not the only nineteenth-century legendary voodoo-ist active along Esplanade whom Lafcadio Hearn wrote about. Another, Jean Montanet, was known by a number of different names, including Dr. John, and was thus an avatar of High John the Conqueror, and became, in turn, the namesake of another Dr. John, the popular R & B composer and performer who burst on the national scene at the end of the 1960s after having grown up near where Bayou St. John ends. The second Dr. John describes his grandmother as a spiritual healer who sometimes exhibited supernatural powers, making a heavy table, for example, float off the floor and across the room. And he first learned music from his Irish grandfather who had performed on the vaudeville and minstrel circuits along the Gulf coast at the dawn of the twentieth century.[61] But this Dr. John's music was hardly the first to arise along Bayou St. John, for those crowds who thronged its banks to catch a glimpse of voodoo would likely have also visited the area to hear the earliest traces of a new music that was distinguished by its freely improvised components and that, within a few decades, would be known as Jazz – and, of course, sweep the world.

Garvey's Farewell Shortly after the white riot in East St. Louis of 1917, Marcus Garvey founded the United Negro Improvement Association (UNIA), which soon became the first mass movement for uplifting African Americans in US history and the model many such movements would follow in the future. By 1927, he had become iconic. Perceived as a threat by the FBI, he was deported, sent back to his home in Jamaica on a steamship from the docks at New Orleans. Thousands of Black New Orleanians gathered to bid him farewell, singing the UNIA anthem and crying. He waved his handkerchief to them while his ship pulled away.

Though Jazz is associated with the red-light district at Basin Street, as discussed in the next chapter, the opportunities for musicians to earn a living along Bayou St. John, in the final decades of the nineteenth century, made the area a primary incubator for what would soon develop. Some context: the bayou had lost its importance to regional commerce by the middle decades of that century after a railroad was built a few miles to the east that connected river and lake, and a newer, bigger canal was dug roughly the same distance to the west. And so the bayou became instead an entertainment corridor. A grand resort and casino complex was built near where the bayou meets the lake, adjacent to the site of the old Spanish fort, and a series of pleasure gardens and aquatic parks, as Pruyn notes, reached from there back toward Esplanade. The casino building that still stands in City Park is the last remnant of what had been a considerable expanse of

Invitation to a ball, hosted at Spanish Fort in 1882 by the Independent Order of the Moon. Wikimedia Commons – Public Domain.

nightlife infrastructure. The area was significant enough to the city's culture that, in the 1880s, Mark Twain would write about it in *Life on the Mississippi*: "Thousands come by rail and carriage to … Spanish Fort every evening and dine, listen to the bands, take strolls in the open air under the electric lights, go sailing on the lake and entertain themselves in various and sundry other ways."[62]

Twain's reference to bands was prescient for, around the same time that he published these words, a child would be born in the 7th Ward who would become a foundational figure in the birth of Jazz. Though the precise year of his birth remains uncertain, as does the spelling of his last name – LeMenthe, Le Mothe, LeMott – he would take the name Jelly Roll Morton and fix it forever in the city's history. He was the first to compose Jazz in written form, which, well before the advent of recording studios and radio stations, codified the music's characteristics and identity and allowed it to travel great distances from its birthplace in New Orleans without losing its essence.

As a 6-month-old child, Morton was jailed when the woman taking care of him was arrested, and he claims to remember the singing of the imprisoned women as his first musical inspiration; growing up in a household at 1443 Frenchmen Street (at the corner with Robertson) that spoke no English, only French, and amidst great concern about the realm of the spirits, he was, by the age of 7, known as "the best guitarist around."[63] After his family disowned him as a disgrace when they discovered he was working as a pianist in the red-light district, he "became a wanderer" for the rest of his life.[64]

He drifted first around the Gulf Coast making money as a pool hustler, then around Texas and up to Chicago, then to Memphis and up and down the Mississippi Delta, where he witnessed lynchings. Living nowhere for very long, he next landed for a time in Jacksonville, then Houston and Saint Louis, till he lost track of how long he had been on the road, eventually going all the way to Los Angeles and Seattle, as the 1920s got underway, and then, as that decade ended, on to Chicago and Kansas City. He moved to Harlem during the Great Depression, where he and his music were dismissed as quaint, corny, and outmoded. Falling into poverty, he linked his misfortune to voodoo, saying that, when he was young, these practitioners "with their underground stuff helped me along. I did not feel grateful and I did not reward them for the help they gave. Now, when everything turned against me, these underground streams were running against me too."[65]

Morton never saw meaningful sums of money, even though he had written much of the standard repertoire of the first wave of Jazz: "King Porter Stomp," which has the distinction of being the music's first published composition, and "Wolverine Blues," "Milneburg Joys," "Mr. Jelly Roll," "Black Bottom Stomp," and "Wild Man Blues," to name only a few. He was the living bridge between ragtime and Jazz, a key figure in the piano's stylistic lineage known in more recent times as "boogie woogie." Nonetheless, in the late 1930s, he was destitute and living in Washington, DC. Around this time, he walked through the doors of the Library of Congress to record his memories for ethno-musicologist and folklorist Alan Lomax.

Lomax let Morton speak for a full month, then had the stories transcribed, edited, and published as *Mister Jelly Roll: The Fortunes of Jelly Roll Morton, New Orleans Creole and Inventor of Jazz.* Lomax knew that he had to produce a book from these sessions, for, in looking at the transcriptions, he saw that Jelly Roll spoke "sentences that wound across the page like rivers and mountain ranges … as graceful and finely tuned as the best of written literature."[66] Morton himself never saw the book, because, less than a year after these recordings were made, he suffered stab wounds during a scuffle in a DC bar, and never recovered his health, dying soon thereafter in Los Angeles.

Perhaps inspired by the Morton book, a similar project was soon undertaken with the first New Orleans reed player to become famous for Jazz – Sidney Bechet, who grew up only a few blocks from Morton in the 7th Ward at 1716 Marais. Born roughly a dozen years after Morton, Bechet seems also to have been a child prodigy, and the unique power of his memoir, *Treat It Gentle: An Autobiography*, arises in his philosophical, psychological, and even mystical reveries on the origins of Jazz. The book begins with the idea of The Road as an extended metaphor for life itself: in order to play Jazz and, in Bechet's view, to live life, you must trust The Road, trust that which is much larger than yourself, exceeding you immeasurably in space and time; if you can trust it, you can move with it, even go anywhere and return as you please; without such trust, you are paralyzed, not really living at all. He describes his music as emanating from a remote source in the distant past, coming, as his own life did, like "water moving around a stone, all silent, waiting for the stone to wear away." He adds, "it's like the Mississippi River – it's got its own story."[67] After spending his childhood working with his older brothers' bands and catching fish in the river, travelling once to Galveston as a hobo, where he was briefly jailed, Bechet received in 1918 a letter from Joe "King" Oliver, the New Orleans trumpeter who was thriving in Chicago. The "King" was summoning him to Chicago to join his band and make a lot more money than he could in New Orleans, just as he would make the same offer to Louis Armstrong and others within a few years.

Soon, Bechet would be performing a private concert for King George V at Buckingham Palace, observing of the experience that it was the first time he had ever recognized someone "from seeing his picture on my money."[68] Bechet ran afoul of the police in London directly thereafter for a romantic liaison with a white woman and was deported back to the US. His arrest and deportation, however, saved his life, for when the band departed without him by boat for performances in Ireland, the boat sank, and they all drowned. Bechet would have trouble with European police again a few years later, this time in France, when he got into a gunfight outside a Paris cabaret, and had to spend nearly a year in jail before being deported again back to the US.[69]

The centrality of travel and, ultimately, the mysticism and magic of The Road that are so important to the Morton and Bechet memoirs undergird the life story of yet another early Jazz pioneer who grew up in that same cluster of 7th Ward blocks as they did – Barney Birgard. Growing up at 1726 N. Villere, he became a star clarinetist in the city in his youth when he landed a job on Bayou St. John near Spanish Fort.[70] Shortly thereafter, he was summoned in 1924 to Chicago, as Bechet and Armstrong had been, by King Oliver. After a few years there, he moved to New York to join what would become the Duke Ellington Orchestra.[71] He travelled with the group continuously for roughly a dozen years, until he quit in 1942. After leaving Ellington's group, Birgard joined Louis Armstrong's band and travelled with that unit – again, almost continuously – for nearly fifteen years, all over the world.[72] His book is essentially a series of portraits of the musical immortals with whom he travelled and performed in this period, the chapter titles conveying the sheer movement that defined daily life for these artists: "The Rigors of the Never-Ending Road," "They Kept Us Running Day and Night," "The Fastest Company in the Whole Wide World," and "They Sent a Rolls Royce."

These 7th Ward musicians created a global phenomenon, but their worldliness was hardly new to Esplanade. In the middle decades of the nineteenth century, Louis Morreau Gottschalk, born on Esplanade Avenue at the corner of Royal, left for Europe in his teens, then travelled widely around the Caribbean and South America, a San Francisco newspaper reporting that he had travelled nearly 100,000 miles by railroad by 1865, when he was not yet 40 years old. And in the early 1870s, the iconic French Impressionist painter, Edgar Degas, spent eighteen months living at the home of his cousins at 2306 Esplanade. Two of his brothers had moved to the city to join their maternal uncle's cotton business, his mother having been born in the city as part of a prominent Creole family that had fled the Haitian Revolution earlier in the nineteenth century. Several of his most iconic works were begun in New Orleans and finished in France, most notably his first masterwork, "A Cotton Office." He was particularly interested in painting dancers and racehorses, as a way to capture movement, and, though he despised the term Impressionism, his name is forever linked to that style, as it spread throughout Europe to influence painting in Egypt, Japan, and Brazil.

The international reach of Esplanade is evidenced too in the fact that John Dos Passos lived in a boardinghouse at 510 Esplanade for a few months in the winter and spring of 1924, when he was working on *Manhattan Transfer*, a book about the fast-paced life of New York City and a set of characters who are fleeing bad relationships of various kinds; inspired by Joyce's *Ulysses* and Eliot's *The Waste Land*, it sought to escape traditional narrative modes by pursuing a principle of montage derived from what was then the new, popular medium known as "motion pictures." After a few months on Esplanade, Dos Passos set out on foot for Florida, ending up just north of Miami.[73]

Less than two decades later, at the other end of Esplanade, the bayou played an important role in hemispheric transformation when it served as a testing area for the Higgins landing craft, as depicted in countless movies, novels, and memoirs about the landing of Allied forces at Normandy on D-Day in World War II. Andrew Higgins originally designed the boat for fishermen who needed to traverse Louisiana's shallow waterways, but modified it so it could "crawl" onto sandy, unfortified beaches and release invading troops. One of the largest plants for producing what came to be called the Higgins Boat was on City Park Avenue, directly adjacent to Bayou St. John and the old duelling ground, where each boat was tested before being sent along to the US military and, in turn, used to turn the tide in the struggle to liberate northern Europe from German fascism.[74] These concerns had a particular, local intensity, as, in 1942, German U-boats were trolling the mouth of the Mississippi River, disrupting the city's commercial activity, and one of them even sank the *Robert E. Lee*, killing twenty-five people, before it was itself destroyed.[75]

Esplanade Avenue, near the river, 1940s. Courtesy of the Historic New Orleans Collection.

Another two decades later, the river-end of Esplanade would erupt as a flashpoint in an analogous battle, the struggle to liberate the US from the Jim Crow system of oppression and terrorism, which had begun, as noted in the preceding chapter, only blocks from there with the arrest of Homer Plessy some seventy years earlier. The ground floor of the Creole townhouse at 611 Esplanade was known as the Quorum, an archetypal bohemian coffeehouse of the period, where poets, folk-singers, actors, and visual artists would mingle and perform their work for each other and for off-duty academics. More importantly, the general mingling at the Quorum also involved people of different races – and on equal terms. The social and creative inspiration that followed drew a number of extraordinary people: the future country music star Jerry Jeff Walker performed there regularly, as did Delta bluesman Dave Stovall and percussionist Alfred "Uganda" Roberts; famed Civil Rights attorney Lolis Elie was a regular, as was celebrated African-American artist John T. Scott. John O'Neal of the Free Southern Theater visited there in 1964 and, directly afterward, decided to relocate his group to New Orleans. Upstairs lived the artist George Dureau, later a close friend, mentor, and primary inspiration to Robert Mapplethorpe. The Quorum was, given the mounting backlash to the Civil Rights Movement, on the vanguard of the transgressive possibilities of the time. And so, on July 24, 1964, the police arrived and arrested over seventy people, charging them with "having conversations that did not arrive at conclusions." In other words, for socializing as equals, rather than strictly doing traditional, hierarchical business.

The 7th Ward in Recent Decades

The cosmopolitan character of Esplanade as both an international and local crossroads persists. Within a few blocks of the Quorum, the pre-mier writer of the foodways of the African diaspora, Jessica B. Harris, maintains one of her homes. At the other end of Esplanade, just across Bayou St. John and near the old duelling grounds, Pia Z. Ehrhardt lives with her family. Her collection *Famous Fathers and Other Stories*, set both across Lake Pontchartrain and in nearby St.Bernard Parish, as well as in the French Quarter and near her home, focus on women who navigate their roles as wives and mothers in ways that can be read as a twenty-first-century updating of Chopin's *The Awakening*. Near this same end of Esplanade, close to Bayou St. John, the novelist Gary Gautier has lived off and on, after having hitchhiked in his twenties some 50,000 miles, and then, in late middle age, reprising the adventure by hitchhiking across a dozen countries. Just across the bayou from Gautier is the headquarters of a small press named Lavender Ink that specializes in literature in translation, and just off the middle blocks of Esplanade was the home for nearly fifteen years for the Neighborhood Story Project, which publishes oral histories of far-flung parts of the city that have too often been voiceless among the city's cultural institutions. (The Neighborhood Story Project was uprooted by Hurricane Ida in 2021 and has not yet resettled.)

The area has been home, as well, to musical icons. The city's most important composer after Jelly Roll Morton, Allen Toussaint, made his home in the 7th Ward near Bayou St. John for decades. In the early 1960s, when Toussaint was barely out of his teens, he was involved as producer, arranger, player, or writer – or, sometimes, as all four – on an extraordinary string of R & B hits, many times writing under his mother's name, Naomi Neville, and helping to make international stars out of several local performers, especially Irma Thomas. His work was performed too by several of the British groups that dominated the charts from the middle part of the 1960s onward. Among his first successes was "Working in a Coal Mine," recorded by another 7th Ward native, Lee Dorsey. There followed a wide range of pop stars – from Patti Labelle to Paul McCartney, Elvis Costello to Glen Campbell to Devo, among dozens of others – who worked with him as a producer and recorded what he wrote. His song "Yes We Can," which was first a hit for the Pointer Sisters in 1970 (and recorded too by well over a dozen others), is a funky rallying cry for social justice, and probably shaped the slogan for Barack Obama's historic 2008 presidential campaign. As Paul Kauppila notes, he had a particular gift for writing songs perfectly tailored to the unique qualities of particular singers.[76] Toussaint was also an astute businessman, making sure contracts were written to suit him, and in the decade or so before he died of a heart attack in Spain in 2015, his powder-blue Rolls Royce was often glimpsed floating along the streets of the 7th Ward, especially along Bayou St. John, with a license plate that read simply, "TUNES." In 2022, the street where he lived – Robert E. Lee Boulevard – was changed, by a unanimous vote of the New Orleans City Council, to Allen Toussaint Boulevard.

Toussaint is not the only important song-writer associated with the area. Bob Dylan's longest-running band-member, the bassist Tony Garnier, has roots there, and has been thought of as Dylan's unofficial musical director for more than thirty years. Garnier's grandfather is the legendary Afro-Creole trumpeter D'Jalma Thomas Garnier, and is said to have been among Louis Armstrong's first music teachers at the

Colored Waifs Home. Also, on Esplanade itself, the iconic Memphis-born songwriter and performer, Alex Chilton, made his home for some fifteen years before moving a few blocks west into Tremé, settling in the area to escape the juggernaut of drugs and alcohol that hounded his youthful rise to fame in the 1960s and 70s.[77]

Today, a number of important songwriters are associated with the area, nearly all of them women known for their social-justice activism. Cole Williams, born and raised in a Jamaican enclave in Brooklyn, lived for several years in the same cluster of blocks where Jelly Roll Morton, Sidney Bechet, and Barney Birgard grew up, and created there her brilliant contemporary R & B albums, *Believe*, *Sin City*, and *Testimony*. She is a well-known leader and organizer on behalf of the city's houseless population. Alynnda Segarra, a native of the Puerta Rican community in the Bronx, from which her mother launched an important career in New York City politics, also lives in the 7th Ward. Segarra started hopping freight trains after running away from home at 17,[78] then settled into New Orleans and began singing in street bands, eventually forming Hurray for the Riff Raff, which has toured widely. Paris Achenbach, a gifted songwriter, performer, and multi-instrumentalist living near the end of Bayou St. John, lived for several years just off Esplanade, where she recorded the album *Voice Memos from N. Rocheblave*, after living on a biodynamic agrarian cooperative in central Florida. The album offers some dozen songs that contemplate the value of freedom in the form of cross-country drives, escapes from dead-end relationships, the wind rattling her windows, and the power of dreaming itself, all played and sung by Achenbach, whose voice is instantly captivating. Yet another popular songwriter and vocalist, Alexandra Scott, lives on Esplanade. Defining herself as a "neo-country surrealist," some of her works, like "O, Leona," fit in the protest tradition. And nearby, Denise Frazier, composer, violinist, and scholar of Afro-Cuban and Afro-Brazilian street performance and Hip Hop, makes her home. Frazier's ensemble, Les Cenelles, has collaborated with the activist organization Rise St. James to protest the building of large oil refineries on the burial grounds of the formerly enslaved. Finally, Mia X, sometimes called the Mother of Southern Gangsta Rap, grew up in the 7th Ward and blazed new trails for women entering the hip-hop scene in New Orleans in the late 1990s, her albums *Unladylike* and *Mama Drama* selling more than a half-million and more than 2 million copies respectively.

Other women associated with the worlds along Esplanade Avenue have made careers as singers, namely Lillian Boutte, Sister Teedy, and

Esther Rose, among others. Those first two have a brother named John Boutte, who is among the most beloved vocalists in contemporary New Orleans, his version of "Louisiana 1927," captured live at the 2006 Jazz Fest and available on YouTube, having become the unofficial anthem for those who have struggled to cope with Hurricane Katrina. And Mannie Fresh, another 7th Ward native, served as producer on no fewer than seventeen multi-platinum or gold albums for the New Orleans-based rap label Cash Money Records around the turn of the twenty-first century.

While Mia X and Mannie Fresh were making Hip Hop history from the 7th Ward, a youngster in the same neighborhood named Lonnie Breaux was sitting quietly behind his mother while she attended class at the University of New Orleans (UNO). Abandoned by his father at a young age, Lonnie was a solitary and bookish child; he enrolled at UNO himself as a freshman, intent on majoring in English, in August of 2005, the week before Hurricane Katrina hit. In the immediate aftermath, he started doing sheetrock work in flooded homes, saved up a little over a thousand dollars, and then drove to Los Angeles where a friend had offered him some discounted time in his recording studio. He planned to return to the 7th Ward within six weeks to continue the sheetrock work. However, a chance encounter with an informal songwriters' collective garnered him some attention, and, two years later, having written songs for Justin Bieber and John Legend, he was wealthy. By 2010, inspired by Frank Sinatra and the *Ocean's Eleven* films, he changed his name to Frank Ocean,[79] and released his debut album, *Channel Orange* – through which he took his place among the most important R & B visionaries of the twenty-first century. Ocean's sexual identity, like Mia X's feminism, has opened the way for a far more inclusive music industry that, traditionally, has defaulted to the norms of toxic masculinity.

> **The New Quorum** Testimony to the significance of the Quorum, a mansion several blocks farther out Esplanade toward the bayou took on the name the New Quorum about a half-century after the earlier venue closed. It hosts an artist residency program, whereby writers and musicians from around the world come to stay for an extended span of time to collaborate with local and regional artists. The venue also presents live performances and a range of cultural programs, and has become an anchor for the local arts community.

A comical and highly racialized critique of a particularly white form of masculinity, Jim Jarmusch's 1986 film, *Down by Law*, was filmed in large part in the 7th Ward along Esplanade Avenue and The Marigny in the year before Frank Ocean was born. The look of this area in the 1980s is captured exquisitely through Robbie Muller's cinematography. The film is focused on two young white men, both of them hipsters, doing their despairing best to mimic, as white bohemians have been known to do, what they perceive as Black "cool," one of them a disc jockey and the other a pimp. But at the movie's outset, the pimp is laughed at, long and loud, by a Black sex worker as she lies on a bed and aims a gun at his back. And the disc jockey, in his first scene, is rejected by his girl-friend, as she throws him out of the apartment they share, even tossing his beloved record collection out the window. The disc jockey and the pimp soon meet when they are arrested and assigned to the same cell in Orleans Parish Prison, which they will share with an Italian tourist.

Their foreign cellmate comes to function as what Spike Lee calls a "Magical Negro,"[80] for soon after he appears, the strict narrative logic of realism slips away as he leads them through a miraculous escape from the prison via the city's elaborate network of subterranean drain-age pipes; after they emerge from the pipes into the swamps, the Italian yet more miraculously finds love in an isolated, roadside Italian restau-rant, and the two buffoons agree, as the movie ends, to find their sepa-rate ways, one to Los Angeles and the other to New York, on foot. The upshot: these two low characters are living charmed lives, charmed by the fact that, though they are immersed in what they imagine of Black culture, they'll never fully lose their whiteness and thus face no seri-ous obstacles or lasting trauma; they'll just haplessly shuffle along, it seems, for eternity. As Sarah Guggemos notes, the opening scene of the movie signals this theme, when the disc jockey is gazing at some lines that have been scrawled on the wall of his apartment: "Life is a limbo dance … a question of where you get down not how low you can get." The point, as Guggemos observes: because they are located in white-ness, their free-fall will always look like success, or at least a rollicking adventure, and they'll face no bottom end.[81] Enlarging on this theme, the second bit of graffiti reads "it's not the fall that kills you – it's the sudden stop." Thus, the perennial question for young white men of how to live finds an answer in the imperative to keep falling, the film's title – *Down by Law* – being Black slang of that period for the ultimate bond, the kind that comes from having fallen in love. What the Italian-as-magical-negro has taught them is simply to keep falling this way, for this is how one escapes; and as young white men, they have no reason to worry that such a long, long fall might reach a sudden stop.

The politics of race and trauma are not so easily finessed in the rest of the major writing that has sprung up around this part of town in recent years. Hurricane Katrina, in particular, has led many to write as a means to recover from extraordinary psychological pain and to preserve cultures and community histories threatened with permanent diaspora, if not complete erasure, by that event and the bungled government response. The 7th Ward native Fatima Shaik did extraordinary work as a journalist profiling the victims and telling their stories, beginning in the immediate aftermath of the event and continuing for the full decade that followed. She first emerged on the national scene as a fiction writer with the publication, around the same time *Down by Law* premiered, of her comic masterpiece, "The Mayor of New Orleans: Just Talking Jazz." A kind of fictional memoir mixed with apocryphal local history, this novella is comprised of rivers of uproarious blather that flow far into the night from a trumpet player who claims to have held, for a time, the city's highest office, until he was ignominiously ousted for some minor, well-intentioned malfeasance. A second novella that appears in the same volume as the latter, "Climbing Monkey Hill," is set in the 7th Ward in the aftermath of Hurricane Betsy in the mid 1960s; a work of straightforward historical fiction, it follows a girl in her early teens as she eyes the emerging presence of the Black Panthers in her community and the dream of a separatist movement. Sheik's long relationship with the area positioned her well to do invaluable work as a journalist in the years that followed Katrina.

Shortly after Hurricane Katrina, Amanda Boyden, who has lived near Bayou St. John just off Esplanade for decades, published her second novel, *Babylon Rolling.* Set in the years just before that storm, in a New Orleans neighborhood where people of very different backgrounds and identities jostle against each other through considerable chaos, a main character is left alone, after most of the others have evacuated for a looming hurricane. In the surreal emptiness of the city, she chooses to step outside her marriage in a dalliance with a younger man. The same year as Boyden's hurricane novel, Tom Piazza, who has lived for many years not far from the end of Bayou St. John, published *City of Refuge*, a novel about the immediate aftermath of Katrina that follows two very different New Orleans families into exile in Chicago, Albany, Houston, and a small town in Missouri. Piazza's follow-up to *City of Refuge*, though not a hurricane novel or even a New Orleans novel, contemplates the related theme of flight: called *A Free State*, the novel follows the fortunes of a runaway slave at the height of the mid nineteenth-century vogue of blackface minstrelsy, in which the runaway – light-skinned, with keen musical talent – realizes that his best chance of remaining free is to hide in plain sight by darkening his face with cork the way the blackface minstrels of the era did and join one of their bands. Beyond the excellent historical understanding of this moment in American music (Piazza's brilliance as a non-fiction writer about music has landed him a Grammy), the novel is a profound meditation on the ways that artists use masks as portals for escaping into the imaginative freedom they need in order to survive and create.

The struggle for freedom defines as well the work of another major contemporary novelist who lives just off Bayou St. John, Ladee Hubbard, whose first novel, a magical realist work called *The Talented Ribkins*, is populated by a group of Black people who have superpowers that call to mind the heroes of Marvel comics and the supernatural capacities of Bras Coupé. They had used their powers during the Civil Rights Era to advance that cause and protect its leaders, but, in the novel's present, they are aging in Florida. One of them in particular, with an uncanny capacity to make maps of places he hasn't seen, drives around the state with a niece, encountering relatives with their own unique superpowers, contemplating the dynamics of this family, the aftermath of the 1960s, and implicitly the possibilities of W. E. B. Du Bois's theory of "the talented tenth."

In her second novel, *The Rib King*, Hubbard uses a different historical moment as backdrop, one more distant from but more directly echoing the racial politics of the post-Katrina exodus of Black people from New Orleans. Set during the Great Migration, in which many millions of Black people fled the white supremacist terror of the South for the hope of different possibilities in northern cities, this novel explores the way African Americans began to navigate the transition from the loyal-servant role to that of independent entrepreneurs, bravely testing the depth of capitalism's relation to racism and violence, as well as the role of vengeance in the larger dream of escape.

Systemic inequality is central to the best contemporary novel about life in the 7th Ward, Margaret Wilkerson Sexton's *A Kind of Freedom*, which tells the stories of three generations of a Black family from this neighborhood: it rotates from vignettes about Evelyn in the 1940s, to Evelyn's daughter Jackie in the 1980s, to Jackie's son TC in contemporary New Orleans, tracking the way the proud Afro-Creoles of the 1940s (Evelyn's father is a respected doctor, and she grows up on a prosperous block) face harder times a generation later as the family has drifted to the new suburbs to the east of the old city in the 1980s, and, in contemporary, post-Katrina times, are mired in the machinery of mass incarceration. The novel's title is ironic, as the descendants of the enslaved are still battling the broader force of a white supremacist society that, no matter how proud or resilient they try to be, is plenty vast enough to overmatch them at every turn.

Concern about racial injustice in the literature of this part of the city reached a climax in the aftermath of Hurricane Katrina. When the storm hit in 2005, the poet Mona Lisa Saloy, who was born and raised in the neighborhood, was already deeply committed to preserving the proud Afro-Creole folkways of the area. In her first book of poems, *Red Beans and Ricely Yours* – the title taken from the way Louis Armstrong signed the many hundreds of letters he wrote – Saloy writes about her ancestors, especially her father, and the landscape and cityscape of the 7th Ward, particularly shotgun houses, and what her Afro-Creole identity means. Her next poetry collection, *Second Line Home*, reckons with the horror of all of this being washed away by Katrina and by the incompetent (and racist) bureaucracies of that era. The volume's first long poem is called "Evacuation Blues," and there then follows a sixteen-poem section called "Requiem for New Orleans"; several more meditations on hurricanes follow, but the remainder of the book then shifts to hopeful tones, with verse on the election of Barack Obama and a new self-consciousness in New Orleans about the city's importance to world culture, particularly for its music. Another writer consumed with her Creole heritage – Sybil Kein, a sibling of the R & B star, Deacon John – writes not in English but in Louisiana Creole, accepting the rather small audience capable of reading such work as worth the place in the historical record for keeping that legacy alive in such a remarkable way. Kein grew up near Saloy, but spent most of her adult life in Michigan, retiring to New Orleans shortly before Hurricane Katrina, which displaced her permanently. Katrina also figured in a crucial way in the development of Barb Johnson's life as a fiction writer. After growing up in southwest Louisiana and living for a time in New York, she worked for nearly thirty years as a carpenter in New Orleans. Her work, *More of This World or Maybe Another*, is set in the neighborhood where she lives along Bayou St. John, and explores questions of class and religion and the queer experience of the South. After Katrina, she notes that writing became an essential tool for coping with the disaster, so much so that she let go of her carpentry business to devote herself to creative writing classes at the University of New Orleans, where she now teaches. Katrina has also been a major subject for writer, editor, and performance-artist Kristina Kay Robinson, who grew up in this part of town and publishes in *The Baffler* and *The Nation*, among other places, and has shown her visual art in a range of prestigious settings. In addition to important work on Katrina, she has also written on Blackness in a global context.

No one in the 7th Ward has hovered closer to the immediate, daily miseries of the months that followed the storm than Jerry Ward, as documented in his 2009 book, *The Katrina Papers: A Journal of Trauma and Recovery*. A diary that begins in the days after the storm and continues for one year, this record of the moment-to-moment experience of that year makes the book of keen interest to future historians. The prose is elegant and incisive, and stands in counterpoint to the overwhelming pain, chaos, and horror of its subject, the uprootedness and vertiginous sense of placelessness that follow the loss of a home and a cultural world. In a different register but with the same ultimate subject of Armageddon, the poet John R. O. Gery, who, like Ward, lives near Bayou St. John, published a book-length poem called "The Burning of New Orleans," as well as a book about the way poets have reckoned the prospect of nuclear annihilation.

Ward was a colleague of Mona Lisa Saloy at Dillard University, an historically Black institution in the northeast corner of the 7th Ward that suffered a greater blow from Katrina than any other university in the area. The themes of trauma and recovery, however, were hardly new to Dillard. The campus opened at 1631 Esplanade Avenue as Straight University some five years after the Civil War ended, but less than a decade later, some arsonists set the main building on fire by way of celebrating the withdrawal of Union troops from the city. The school was forced to move to Canal Street, where it flourished until the Great Depression, at which point it merged with another Black institution, New Orleans University, on St. Charles Avenue, to become Dillard and settle in its present location. Like the Couvent School discussed earlier in this chapter, much of the greatest Black literary talent associated with the city has been affiliated with the school. Most recently, the Dillard alumnus Jericho Brown won the Pulitzer Prize for his book of poetry called *The Tradition*. As Maya Phillips notes, this book "is a catalogue of injuries, past and present, personal and national, in a country where blackness, particularly male blackness, is akin to an illness." The poems, however, delineate a pathway – and are themselves that pathway – by which survival, if not escape, can be imagined.[82]

The process of escaping from a traumatic past is also at the core of the astonishing career of the 7th Ward native whose reach has surpassed all the others – Tyler Perry. His twenty-two films, twenty-four stage plays, and twelve-hundred television episodes have enabled his personal net worth to climb to well over a billion dollars.[83] Perry grew up in the 7th Ward in an abusive home, once attempting suicide to escape his father's beatings; he was also sexually molested. After dropping out of high school, he began to write letters to himself, for he had heard on the Oprah Winfrey Show that writing could be therapeutic. Just out of his teens, he moved to Atlanta with his life-savings of 12,000 dollars and spent the money staging his first play, based on the letters he had been writing himself. The play flopped, and for a few months Perry lived in his car.[84] But he retooled the play over the next several years and, in the late 1990s, presented it again, building the sets and hanging the lights himself, even selling the snacks during the intermission. The play drew more attention, particularly among older Black women.[85] He began to develop a larger and larger following, almost exclusively African American, through a steady stream of stage plays that toured a loose circuit of theaters in Black communities around the country. The Perry phenomenon continued to gain momentum through the first decade of the twenty-first century, as he entered into a partnership with Oprah Winfrey and made a 100-episode sitcom; his drag persona, Medea, became the basis of a film franchise that, alone, has led to nearly a dozen separate works.

His entertainment brand, as Rashida Z. Shaw McMahon notes, has drawn criticism from Black intellectuals for its reliance on unflattering stereotypes that offer what is in effect simply a "new minstrelsy." But Shaw argues that Perry's overwhelmingly Black audience finds new meanings in these figures, winnowing from them not just a comforting sense of familiarity and communal solidarity, but an explicitly church-based affirmation of what is best in themselves. In essence, if Perry offers minstrelsy, he does so knowing that his audience will enjoy what is for them, by now, a long-standing, communal ritual of recognizing it as such, and striving to invert and escape it.[86]

Coda: Armstrong at the Colored Waifs Home
At the far end of the ridge that became Esplanade, beyond where it winds its way across Bayou St. John to become City Park Avenue, beyond Duelling Oaks and the front edge of the cypress swamp where Bras Coupé hid and Marie Laveau conjured High John the Conqueror, and just beyond the old potter's field where the remains of tens of thousands of New Orleanians were laid to rest over the centuries, there stands a pair of small barracks. One of them is now a popular restaurant named Rosedale; for several decades, it was a neighborhood police headquarters; but at the dawn of the twentieth century, these two buildings were part of a larger set that, collectively, were known as the Colored Waifs Home.

It is here that a young Louis Armstrong first lifted a horn to his lips.

He was incarcerated for having fired a pistol into the air on New Year's Eve, and sent there for an indefinite duration. He ended up living there for eighteen months. Until then, Armstrong had been mostly raised by his grandmother, who, in her girlhood, had been enslaved, her physical movements circumscribed within a narrow range of chores. Armstrong's transition into the Colored Waifs Home probably felt like a return to an earlier order, particularly when Armstrong notes, rather cryptically, that before the barracks had been used as a sort of juvenile jail, they had apparently "been used for some other purpose."[87]

Armstrong was initially afraid of the institution's band director, who, he assumed, hated him. The man, as Armstrong explains in *Satchmo: My Life in New Orleans*, would terrorize all the boys there with whippings. However, when the boy who had the job of blowing the bugle each day to announce mealtimes was released, Armstrong took his place, and felt great pride in regulating the day's activities with the horn. Soon, he was asked to join the brass band. He was ecstatic.

After Mr. Davis made him the leader of the band, Armstrong writes,

> I jumped straight in the air, with Mr. Davis watching me, and ran to the mess hall to tell the boys the good news. They ... all rejoiced with me. Now at last I was not only a musician but a bandleader! Now I would get a chance to go out in the streets and see Mayann [his mother] and the gang that hung around Liberty and Perdido Streets. The band often got a chance to play at a private picnic or join one of the frequent parades through the streets of New Orleans covering all parts of the city, Uptown, Back o'Town, Front o'Town, Downtown. The band was even sent to play in the West End and Spanish Fort, our popular summer resorts ... in those days some of the social clubs paraded all day long ... we were so glad to get a chance to walk in the street we didn't care how long we paraded or how far ... playing like mad, we loved every foot of the trip.[88]

1. Charity Hospital – 1532 Tulane Avenue
2. Lulu White's Mahogany Hall 235 N. Basin
3. Josie Arlington's brothel – 225 N. Basin
4. Tom Anderson's restaurant – 115 N. Rampart
5. Countess Willie Piazza's brothel 317 N. Basin
6. Carver Theater – 2101 Orleans Avenue-
7. Dorothy's Medallion Lounge – 3232 Orleans Avenue
8. Economy Hall – 1422 Ursulines St

9. Albert Woodfox's boyhood home – 918 N. Villere
10. St. Augustine Church – 1210 Governor Nichols St.
11. Tom Dent's last home – 1114 Treme St.
12. Earl Palmer's boyhood home 918 N. Clairborne
13. George Herriman's birthplace – 348 N. Villere
14. Jose Marti statue – corner of Banks St and
    Norman C. Francis Parkway
15 Orleans Parish prison, 1837–1895

Map of Basin
Street to
Orleans Avenue
Congo Square,
Storyville, Tremé

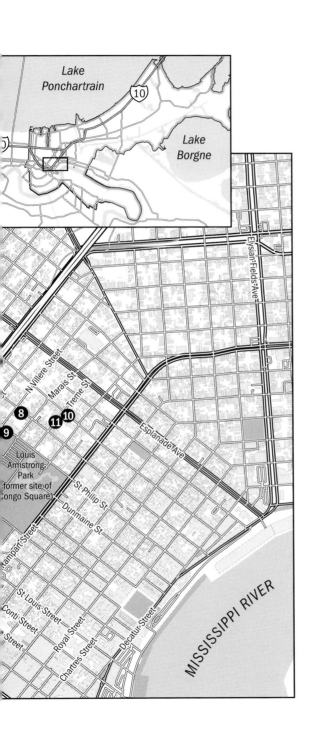

Lake Ponchartrain

10

Lake Borgne

Elysian Fields Ave

N Villere Street

Marais St

Treme St

8

11 10

9

Esplanade Ave

Louis Armstrong Park (former site of Congo Square)

St Philip St

Dunmaine St

Rampart Street

St Louis Street

Conti Street

Street

Royal Street

Chartres Street

Decatur Street

MISSISSIPPI RIVER

Basin Street – Memory and Music

Congo Square – Storyville – Tremé

4

The manuscript for Toni Morrison's *New Orleans: The Storyville Musical*, at some point, caught fire: the edges of its pages in the Morrison archive at Princeton are dark and singed with irregular absences that only flames could have scooped out, and, on some pages, the fire nearly reached the center of the paper. Roughly a hundred continuous pages of typescript remain readable. But, because no serious biography of Morrison has been written, little is otherwise known about this project. Perhaps it was salvaged along with many of her other papers from the basement of her home after a Christmas Day fire consumed everything else in 1993. She seems to have begun working on it in early 1981, presumably soon after she finished *Tar Baby*. In late summer of 1982, she allowed the manuscript a six-week workshop in New York, a "no-frills test run," according to *The New York Times*, "before going into rehearsal for an opening in the fall."[1] Morrison had never worked as a lyricist, but was jotting down verses, she said, until the company could hire one. Ultimately, she created twenty-six songs for the musical.

Noting the generally solitary work of the writer, the *Times* article quotes Morrison as saying, "I thought that working with other people would be difficult for me, but something magical has happened." While the flame-gnawed front page of the manuscript notes that she was revising it as late as June of 1984, the musical was never performed: the project was scrapped. But something magical indeed must have occurred within Morrison, for, as she set the manuscript aside, she began to work on a new project that she would call *Beloved*. It appeared in 1987, and, five years later, as the world came to know that novel as a masterpiece of the highest order, she was awarded the Nobel Prize for literature. What happened within Morrison as she shifted from *New Orleans: The Storyville Musical* to *Beloved* is impossible to say, but a close look at that manuscript points to themes that define much of the major writing associated with the neighborhoods just north of the French Quarter. Perhaps her work on *New Orleans* brought her to a new relationship with the collective memory of African America, for that is what the manuscript is about – as is much of the writing that is set in or inspired by this particular part of town.

The primary artery of Storyville is Basin Street, a thoroughfare that bends to the north, away from the river, a few blocks downriver from Canal Street, to become Orleans Avenue, a primary artery, in turn, of the neighborhood known as Tremé. However, the story of this part of town – and, arguably, of African-American culture in general – begins, as does Morrison's musical, in a place a few minutes' walk downriver from Basin Street called Congo Square.

This territory is invoked in the opening set directions of Morrison's musical – specifically, what Morrison wanted the audience to see first is Congo Square in the nineteenth century morphing into the nearby Storyville of 1917. Morrison's directions require that a tall, masked figure descend, dancing, and, as it makes its way down to the street, to shape-shift from "a god to a tribesman to a slave to ragged and indistinct mendicant." The street toward which the dancing shape-shifter descends is filled with dancing workers who chant the names of streets in New Orleans and call out "Don't break" and "Don't break on me." As these dancing workers set up stalls for marketing their goods, the ragged mendicant moves among them, trying to sell blessings in the form of brightly colored scraps of cloth, but he is ignored. His name is Omar, and he sings, "Every hello ain't a welcome / Every goodbye ain't gone." Those last four words – suggesting that what leaves can come back – suggest further that the ragged mendicant can shape-shift back into his earlier form as a god and that perhaps in turn the keys to the future are hidden in the remote past.

Omar approaches a young couple named Johnny and Cally, who will be at the center of the musical's plot, along with their son Beau, and asks if they would like to buy a blessing. They tell him they don't need one. A mistake. After this prelude, the action of the plot begins. We learn that Johnny and Cally live in a "quiet, colored neighborhood" named Algiers, across the river from the heart of the big city, but Johnny has been gone for two weeks, and Cally is "listless, almost dotty with grief." Her household is in disarray, and her son Beau complains that there's nothing to eat. Her friend and neighbor, Geneva, introduces Cally to a conjure-woman, a hoodoo queen, named Madame Jessica Five, who will cast a spell for Cally, guaranteeing that "he'll be back in your bed in five days." First, however, Cally must deliver several small items belonging to Johnny to Jessica Five, through which she'll work her hoodoo.

One of them is Johnny's hat, which Beau, the son of Johnny and Cally, must snatch off Johnny's head; this will require Beau to cross the river and brave the perils of Basin Street – the red-light district, known in its day simply as the District or Storyville, where the fleshpots hiss, sizzle, and boil – and where Johnny presumably has been trapped and held captive, ensorcelled and enslaved by one siren or another. Beau accomplishes his mission, brings the hat to Madame Jessica Five, and

Johnny is thus liberated to reunite with Cally at the musical's end. The hoodoo spell succeeded.

But this short, incomplete, and abandoned manuscript is more than a simple tale of love lost and regained. To walk onto Basin Street, is, in the world of this manuscript, to step outside of ordinary time and to risk becoming trapped in something like a dimension of timelessness. The District is like a black hole in space or the collective unconscious, where the remote past and the distant future are pressed together in the impossible intensity of an eternal present. Specifically, the past is here in the form of sex workers who, as bodies with price tags, call to mind the antebellum slave market; and the future is here in the African-American music that would soon be at the center of both the popular and high culture of the twentieth century, where it still reigns.

As Beau prepares to risk the journey into the District to snatch his father's hat, his friends warn him that the only thing that will get snatched is him: "You go in the District – you never coming out. Crib women eat you alive." Beau insists he'll only be in there an hour, but his friends warn that it will swallow him up for decades, that he won't re-emerge till he's an old man, that he's dooming himself to the same fate that apparently befell his father, that he's essentially just reducing himself to an echo of the latter. They present Beau with a vision reminiscent of the climactic episode of Joyce's *Ulysses*, when the main characters in that novel enact an hallucinatory theater or psycho-drama in Dublin's red-light district, as the several voices of Beau's friends alternate in quick staccato, warning him that, in Storyville, "You'll be crawling on all fours, howling like a dog, slobbering at the mouth, grunting like a hog," for the women in there "got crazy juice and funny cigarettes, and they give you dream powder," adding "They'll melt you like butter in a hot skillet, truss you like a chicken, split you so wide open you think you a twin."

In the next instant, a group of sex workers replaces Beau's friends, emerging out of a large blue book of the sort that, historically, listed all of the women working in Storyville, a directory with descriptions of the particular talents and charms of each. Each woman sings for Beau, each one a different song derived from the language that advertised her services in the blue book, and then they all sing together by way of folding Beau up in its pages, apparently sealing his fate. But Beau has not simply been swallowed up in the advertising of Storyville but rather, given what comes next in the musical, he – and the audience – are delivered into a vision of the remote past.

MISS LULA WHITE.

This famous West Indian octoroon first saw the light of day thirty-one years ago. Arriving in this country at a rather tender age, and having been fortunately gifted with a good education it did not take long for her to find out what the other sex were in search of.

In describing Miss Lulu, as she is most familiarly called, it would not be amiss to say that besides possessing an elegant form she has beautiful black hair and blue eyes, which have justly gained for her the title of the "Queen of the Demi-monde."

Her establishment, which is situated in the central part of the city, is unquestionably the most elaborately furnished house in the city of New Orleans, and without a doubt one of the most elegant places in this or any other country.

She has made a feature of boarding none but the fairest of girls—those gifted with nature's best charms, and would, under no circumstances have any but that class in her house.

As an entertainer Miss Lulu stands foremost, having made a life-long study of music and literature. She is well read and one that can interest anybody and make a visit to her place a continued round of pleasure.

And when adding that she would be pleased to see all her old friends and make new ones. What more could be added ?

A typical page from a Storyville Blue Book. Courtesy of the Historic New Orleans Collection.

Clara Miller.

Demure everybody's friend, can sit up all night if necessary, and handicap to put a friend on to a good thing. Why? Because it is her disposition, and who don't want to meet such a young lady? Not one with real blood in his veins. She has been in the principal cities of Europe and the Continent, and can certainly interest you as she has a host of others. When we add that the famous octoroon was born near Baton Rouge we trust you will call on her.

The next scene opens in the brothel owned by Ana La Premiere, where a group of sex workers with names like Knockout, Sweet Justice, and Cobalt Blue is chatting. Cobalt Blue embarks upon a long reminiscence of what the surrounding area used to be, saying,

> Africans would walk all over this town in their own clothes – from Africa. They was slaves from Santo Domingo and Africa, but they didn't wear those old missionary dresses and pants. And they didn't wear no tied up shoes. Oh no. They had robes in sapphire blue and green and yellow the color of butter. And not only did they wear their own clothes, they spoke their own language and used their own true names. You know there were places in the city and right outside of it where no white man could set foot and expect to come out alive. African places. And sometimes at night or on Sunday – that was the free day for slaves – they would go into the very middle of town, to a big square, and they'd have drums and flutes and rattling things. And right there under a sky full of stars they'd dance and dance and dance.

Cobalt Blue is talking about Congo Square.

Immediately after this vision of Congo Square, as if by magic, Beau reconnects with his father, Johnny. The latter explains that he's been gambling, that he started winning and kept winning, and thus couldn't leave; he implies too that he eventually started losing, and is waiting for his luck to return so he can go home with the winnings of earlier in his spree. When Beau turns to leave, he seems poised to succumb to a version of the same siren song as his father, for, as a budding musician, he becomes enthralled with the sound of a piano emanating from nearby and can't help but linger. Beau does manage to tear himself away and deliver the hat, but he returns right away to find the pianist, this time bringing his horn – and asks for lessons. Beau is warned by the pianist that his father might not want him to learn this music, for some people hate its power to make them think and feel things that they would rather repress and forget. Beau is also told that, while some people think this music is mere entertainment, it is, in truth, a "secret weapon," and what's more, "They can't kill a man's music, and they can't kill a man who knows that."

The pianist then sings Beau a song called "In My Sound":

Here, in my sound,
Is a letter for you.
Read it by the light inside me

What you feel is not complex
The closer you get
To my sound: Lost is found;

Suffering will die
My O my

My sound is a room with a view
Waiting just for you.

In the pianist's sound, "lost is found," echoing Omar's assertion at the beginning of the play that "Every goodbye ain't gone." The idea that music can serve as a cue to memory, virtually reconstituting what, in actuality, has passed away, is at the heart of Morrison's project, for it is itself a musical that seeks to conjure the social terrain within which

Jazz music first came to be known and, within that terrain, to gesture in turn to the situation many decades earlier and a short walk downriver, in Congo Square, where, most generally, African-American music is widely understood to have begun and where the memory of Africa itself – and of freedom – was kept alive in the eighteenth and nineteenth centuries.

Morrison may have first taken up this dynamic of music and memory from Sidney Bechet's memoir, *Treat it Gentle*. Though Bechet was born and raised in the nearby 7th Ward, just below Esplanade from Congo Square and Storyville, his prodigious capacities for music-making led him into Storyville constantly in his youth as the new music was exploding there during the first two decades of the twentieth century. As he reflects on the origins of this music in Congo Square, where the enslaved would gather on Sundays to entertain each other and sell goods to each other, Bechet writes, "That's why there was this music in them; music was all they had to forget with. Or they could use it for a way of remembering that was as good as forgetting."[2] He continues, "The only thing they had that couldn't be taken from them was their music."[3] At the end of the book, he circles back to the legend that he recounted at its opening, the story of his grandfather, whom he understood to have been the greatest dancer in Congo Square and the inventor of Jazz – and also a version of the one-armed cop-killer named Bras Coupé discussed in the last chapter. In Bechet's telling, his grandfather was ultimately hunted down by a lynch mob and killed by a friend. The grandfather's name was Omar – the same name as the shape-shifting entity in Morrison's musical – and Bechet explains the origins of jazz in terms of the memory of him:

> It was Omar started the song … and all the good musicianers have been singing that song ever since, changing it some, adding parts, finding the way it has to go. But if you're a musicianer, if you're any good musicianer, it's Omar's song you're singing. I met many a musicianer in many a place after I struck out from New Orleans, but it was always the same: if they was any good, it was Omar's song they were singing. It was the long song, and the good musicianers, they all heard it behind them. They all had an Omar, somebody like an Omar, somebody that was *their* Omar. It didn't need just recollecting a somebody like that: it was the feeling of someone back there, hearing the song like it was coming from somewhere … It's the remembering song.[4]

When Bechet describes "hearing the music like it was coming from somewhere," he frames it the same way that the pianist in the Morrison musical does when he says, "My sound is a room with a view." The sound anchors and emanates from a particular location – one is no longer lost; a "room with a view" creates an experience of perspective, a sense of what is behind and what lies ahead, a narrative, and as such the stuff of memory. Echoing both Bechet and Morrison, when Joseph Roach writes about the cultural phenomena of Storyville and Congo Square, he ultimately suggests that all performance is an act of recovering, reconstituting, and re-membering that which has been lost, a kind of ghost-dance that seeks to substitute a new entity (a memory) as partial effigy for the missing, earlier actuality, replacing it within a larger structure where some spot has been vacated, a kind of haunting. This, in turn, is how diasporic communities constitute themselves and manifest, over time, a culture. Roach would likely argue, based on his studies of Congo Square and Storyville, that all culture can be defined in Bechet's terms as "the remembering song."

All of the major writers associated with this part of New Orleans would surely concur. Between Rampart Street, the northern border of the French Quarter, and Broad Street, the northern border of Tremé, and between Canal and Esplanade – this particular area, combining the 4th, 5th, and 6th Wards, includes the sites of Congo Square, Storyville, and Tremé, places that collectively constitute the original "Back o' town," or "Backatown."[5] The major writing of this area often defines itself – like Bechet's concept of music – as the servant of memory, casting the area itself as a living repository of the most extraordinary history. As Michael E. Crutcher puts it, if the French Quarter has long been the city's showpiece, the public face it presents to visitors, then Backatown, running along Basin and out Orleans Avenue, spreading to Esplanade and Canal, is its soul.

Backatown I: Black Memory and Congo Square
The definitive study of the particular expanse of ground that, for many, is a holy site, is Freddi Evans's *Congo Square: African Roots in New Orleans* (2011). Evans notes that, according to the history of Louisiana that Le Page du Pratz published in the 1750s, the enslaved would gather on this location every Sunday as early as 1726, less than a decade after the founding of the city, to sing and play music, to dance and do business, to masquerade and have fun together. Le Page du Pratz reported that he regularly saw as many as 400 people of African descent gathering there in an era when the entire population of the city was roughly 2,000.[6]

And, while parallel phenomena are well documented in other parts of the African diaspora, most notably in Cuba, Haiti, and the West Indies, as well as in the US, what transpired on this ground persisted for far longer and on a greater scale and with greater reach than in any other US location,[7] traces of it boldly on display even today in the Sunday street theater of Mardi Gras Indians.[8]

The place, not surprisingly, has been a scene of conflict with the official powers of the city, its complicated history reflected in the various names by which it has been identified over the decades: Place Publique, Place des Nègres, Place du Cirque, Circus Park, Circus Place, Congo Park, Place Congo, Place d'Armes, even Beauregard Park.[9] The name, however, most often used to refer to this place, historically, is Congo Square.

The first use of the word Congo to refer to this area, according to Evans, came in 1786 when Bishop Cyrillo of Tricali, with authority over the Gulf Coast region and as far to the northwest as the Mississippi River, denounced, in writing, the habit of people of color gathering there on Sunday afternoons to dance the various dances "imported from Africa."[10] The term "Congo," at this time, most often referred to a particular dance, though it was also used to refer to any dance imported from Africa. A further distinction: when spelled with a "K," Kongo refers to a particular ethnicity based in southeast Africa.[11] By 1820, at least half of the enslaved in New Orleans had roots in Kongo, but those who were gathering in Congo Square in the preceding century constituted a veritable melting pot of the African diaspora, drawing people from the Bambara, the Mandinga, the Wolof, the Fulbe, the Nard, the Mina, the Fon, the Yoruba, the Chamba, the Ado, the Caraba, the Ibo, and the Moko.[12] In short, Congo Square on Sunday afternoons in the eighteenth century was a radically cosmopolitan phenomenon whereby traditions from various parts of Africa and the Caribbean and the southern US came together to create new forms for a newly cohering, diasporic, African-American identity, all of it serving as a remembrance of their shared, if diverse, heritage as Africans.[13]

Of cardinal, long-term importance to this collective memory-project was music. Evans describes the perpetuation of African rhythmic cells among the drummers, from which much modern music derives: a prime example is the tango, a word, as Evans notes, of Kongo origin.[14] These same rhythmic cells would still be heard at the end of the nineteenth century in early Jazz and can be heard even today in the popular street songs of Mardi Gras, such as "Hey Pocky Way."[15] Evans describes at length the varieties of drum that were fashioned out of logs and animal skin for use in Congo Square, the wind instruments also carved from wood, and the songs and dances that were performed there in a tour-de-force of interdisciplinary scholarship that will serve well all those interested in the topic for generations.

But, as Evans explains, Congo Square was not simply a music scene, for a great deal of commerce was conducted there, particularly by women. Because the enslaved could keep small gardens of their own, they sometimes had a little surplus to sell, and because they could hire themselves out for additional work when not serving their masters, they sometimes had some extra money to spend. The commerce here, however, was hardly small-scale. As Lawrence Powell notes, during the middle decades of the eighteenth century, as the European colonial projects flailed and floundered in south Louisiana, what arose instead was essentially an African market town, a commercial crossroads of considerable reach.[16]

What was happening in and around Congo Square was substantial enough to draw the attention of many writers who passed through the city in the early decades of the nineteenth century. In fact, the first play ever written in Louisiana – a five-act tragedy that Paul Louis Le Blanc de Villeneuve wrote in 1809 and called *The Festival of Young Corn or the Heroism of Poucha Humma* – engaged the meaning of this territory before Africans and Europeans arrived by commemorating the

"Dancing in Congo Square" by Edward Winsor Kemble, 1886. Wikimedia Commons – Public Domain.

ceremonial feasts indigenous groups had held there for centuries. But the phenomenon of Congo Square itself is what most compelled the attention of travellers, who wrote about it in their diaries and the letters they posted from the city: Henry C. Knight and Timothy Flint, to name just two, recorded observations of Congo Square, and Johan Gottfried Flugal referred in his *Journal of a Voyage down the Mississippi to New Orleans* in 1817 to having seen "richly ornamented" Africans in Congo Square, noting that they had to have been royalty back in Africa and were extraordinary dancers.[17] And Benjamin Latrobe's observations (noted in Chapter 2) are crucial to the historical record of this phenomenon: in 1819, he witnessed some 500 people gathered there dancing and drumming, even though it was a cold Sunday in February; another account, by a man from Buffalo named John Lay, mentions 5–6,000 people gathered there one day in 1822.

Perhaps these writings were part of why the scene increasingly drew white gawkers,[18] for writers described a considerable spectacle there: many of the revelers, they said, wore bells on their pants, and fashioned regalia that included a profusion of tassels and streamers. In fact, a story called "The Singing Girl of New Orleans" by Mordecai Manual Noah that *The Sunday Times* published in 1849 includes a description of a dancer in Congo Square who was wearing so many feathers he resembled a giant rooster, an account that unmistakably calls to mind what would become the Mardi Gras Indian tradition that reaches down to the present day.[19] What that elaborately feathered dancer might have been doing, theorizes Jeroen Dewulf, aside from making an extraordinary impression on the larger and larger white crowds who gathered to witness him, was remembering, reviving, and preserving the mock-war dances that were an important part of Kongo culture.

One particular observer of Congo Square who spread news of it most widely across the US and even Europe was the blackface minstrel performer E. P. Christy. When he was a child in 1825, his family moved to New Orleans, and he began to visit Congo Square for the Sunday gatherings quite frequently. He eventually joined one of the travelling circuses that passed through the area as a supervisor to a group of enslaved Africans. He later said in his memoir that, between his time in Congo Square and in the circus, he learned to mimic what he thought he was seeing and thereby developed the repertoire through which he became a minstrelsy star. Though Christy was not the first blackface minstrel, he was probably the most influential and grew very rich from his performances,[20] as he carried the African and African-derived songs,

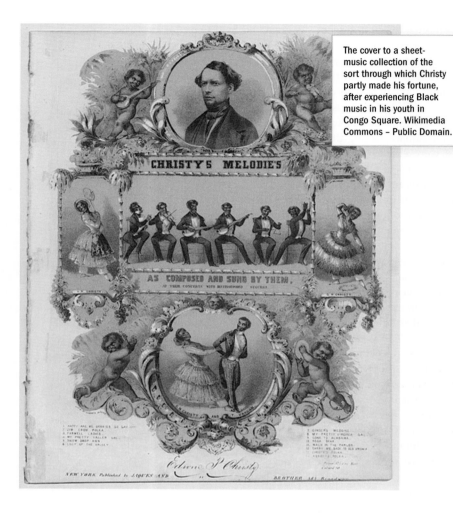

The cover to a sheet-music collection of the sort through which Christy partly made his fortune, after experiencing Black music in his youth in Congo Square. Wikimedia Commons – Public Domain.

dances, and even the instruments from Congo Square all over the US and Europe.[21] Despite his wealth and fame, he committed suicide in 1862.

Major literary figures in the latter decades of the nineteenth century recognized the significance of those Sunday gatherings. William Wells Brown, for example, was compelled to include an excerpt from a local newspaper article about the phenomenon in his book *My Southern Journey or the South and Its People* in 1880. A few years later, Lafcadio Hearn reported hearing a purely African song there, and George

Cable's *Creole Slave Songs* includes several examples of songs sung in Congo Square – songs that Cable himself would sing from the stage before large audiences when he toured the country with Mark Twain. In 1902, Clara Gottschalk Peterson, the sister of the famous composer born at the corner of Royal and Esplanade (as discussed in Chapter 3), published a collection of songs associated with Congo Square that, she said, influenced her brother's music.[22] And during the Great Depression, the Federal Writers Project captured stories from people who had seen, as children in the nineteenth century, what transpired in Congo Square. Most recently, Ruth Salvaggio has written about the old songs of the enslaved in Congo Square in her post-Katrina meditation on the city, *Hearing Sappho in New Orleans.* Aside from this literary interest, countless musicians, from Duke Ellington to Teena Marie to the Neville Brothers, have referred to Congo Square in their recordings.[23]

> **Lafcadio Hearn** The tradition of visitors writing home to share their experience of Congo Square blossomed into a major literary achievement in the career of this newspaper- and magazine-writer, who lived in the city for a little less than a decade in the 1870s. No single writer, as S. Frederick Starr explains, did more to conjure New Orleans in the public imagination of the US than he did. Most of the primary tropes of the tourist industry – ghosts, romantic decay, duels, voodoo, humidity, cemeteries, cuisine, Creolism, and so on – got some of their first, best, and most widely disseminated coverage through this master prose stylist.

What would ultimately emerge from Congo Square – Jazz – owes a great deal to a particular infrastructural development of the 1790s: the Carondelet Canal. This canal, named for the man who was then the governor of Spain's colony in Louisiana, was intended to serve as drainage during heavy storms and also to create a waterway that would connect Bayou St. John to what was then the rear of the city. The Carondelet Canal would be a much more efficient alternative to the muddy portage that would become Esplanade Avenue.[24] The mile-and-a-half channel, dug by convicts and slaves over a two-year period, was completed in 1796. It soon fell into disrepair, but James Pitot, who understood the importance of keeping the city connected to the lake as it began to boom with newly arriving Americans and those fleeing Haiti in the early nineteenth century, restored it and dug a massive basin at the end closest to the city where the boats could turn around. This inland harbor is what gave Basin Street its name, for right where that thoroughfare bends to the north to become Orleans Avenue, that bend originally wrapped around the canal's turning basin.

Business boomed around this inner harbor: the Tremé market developed nearby, as did the Globe Theater, and the Orleans Parish Prison. Most important, however, for the cultural legacy of the area were the

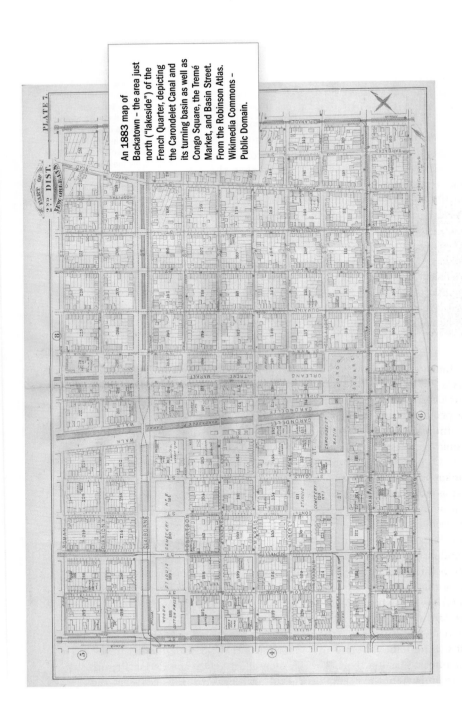

An 1883 map of Backatown – the area just north ("lakeside") of the French Quarter, depicting the Carondelet Canal and its turning basin as well as Congo Square, the Tremé Market, and Basin Street. From the Robinson Atlas. Wikimedia Commons – Public Domain.

An oyster lugger, moored in the turning basin of the Carondelet Canal, circa 1910, near Congo Square and Basin Street. Wikimedia Commons – Public Domain.

brothels that flourished along the basin, courting the business of travellers and sailors, who would disembark there at the end of what might have been a long journey. For what was in those brothels was not only the promise of sex, but, eventually, the sound of a new music that would constitute the fullest flowering of the musical interactions that had first begun in the 1720s in Congo Square.

Backatown II: White Nostalgia and Storyville
Just as Storyville played a key role in the development and dissemination of Jazz, what played a key role in the development of Storyville was the idealized, semi-mythic figure of the mixed-race woman, known either as a quadroon or an octoroon, depending on whether she had one grandparent of African descent or one great-grandparent. Emily Clark, who published the definitive study of this figure in 2013, locates the origin of this archetype in the 1790s, around the same time the Carondelet Canal was dug. In that moment, the white establishment's horror in the face of the Haitian Revolution gave rise to the fantasy of the quadroon and octoroon woman as a bewitchingly gorgeous lover who would submit willingly to white male ownership. This fantasy transmuted white fear into desire – a desire, in particular, to regain a most intimate and complete control over manageable traces of Blackness, a control that

had been upended by the hordes of machete-swinging revolutionaries in Haiti.[25] The mixed-race lover's body, in short, was a way for white men to remember what had been, for them, a much more comfortable time, a souvenir.

In 1809, as we saw in Chapter 1, nearly 10,000 refugees from the Haitian Revolution, who had settled first in Cuba, began to make their way to New Orleans. That first cohort, as Clark reports, numbered a little over 1,300 people, half of them free people of color – of these free people of color, only 178 were men; 608 were women, a ratio of 1:3.[26] Ned Sublette hypothesizes about this disparity in blunt terms: the white men were bringing their mistresses.[27] A few decades earlier, people of European descent had already begun to entertain certain ideas, says Clark, about women of African descent: Justin Girod de Chantrans published on the sexual dangers posed by free women of color in 1785, claiming that women with African blood are much more lascivious than women who are of purely European descent, and, as Clark observes, this document was the key precedent for similar writings by Baron de Wimpffen and Moreau de Saint-Méry that both appeared in 1796.[28] These latter two supposed that the great uprising of the enslaved in Haiti could be blamed on the weakening of French resolve there, a weakening accomplished by the capacities of women of color to overwhelm, sexually, the European men in their midst. Just a year before these two publications, John Murdock's *Triumph of Love* cast a free woman of color as sexually precocious, but the key text in codifying this myth appeared in 1808, immediately prior to that massive influx of those fleeing Haiti into New Orleans, when Leonora Sansay, a Philadelphia native married to a refugee of the Haitian Revolution, published *Secret History or the Horror of St. Domingo*. She describes these mistresses of color as exerting extraordinary sway over their infatuated white lovers.

The first iteration of the New Orleans version of this type appears in an 1806 memoir written by another Haitian refugee named Pierre-Louis Berquin-Duvallon.[29] His memoir portrayed free women of color in New Orleans as being much the same as they had been in Haiti: "Money will always buy their caresses ... [and they are motivated in their relationships with white men] more by money than any [heartfelt] attachment."[30] Thomas Ashe published in 1806 his *Travels in America*, which included a vision of the free women of color in New Orleans that was based closely on the descriptions in Wimpffen and Moreau de Saint-Méry.[31] After Ashe's publication, says Clark, all who visited the city had certain expectations of titillation or outrage that put the hyper-sexualized free woman of color at the center of their fantasy of the city.[32] The larger meaning of this figure, however, was crystallized in Sansay's 1808 *Secret History*: they lured white men away from their proper role as husbands and fathers, spurred them to debauch themselves in riots of lust, and thereby undermined the civilization that these men, otherwise, were expected to embody and uphold. In short, the quadroon or octoroon was a softer and lighter – feminine and highly sexualized – version of the dark, male, machete-wielding menace that had toppled French rule in Haiti.[33]

A version, that is, that white men imagined they could own, and, on the most intimate terms, control. This, in essence, was the template that shaped how New Orleanians greeted the massive influx from Haiti in 1809,[34] dominated as it was by women, and moreover how the city's decadent, elite white men began to imagine the market value of the daughters they had long been siring on the women they enslaved. These daughters were versions of the enchanting free women of color in Haiti, but born as their father's literal property, to be traded or sold to other men of similar status. Thus arose the notion of *plaçage*, as discussed in the last chapter, whereby rich white men "placed" lovers and the children born of these relationships a short walk from the mansions of the French Quarter they inhabited with their purely white wives and children – and where these mistresses of color were incentivized to cultivate as much love in their owners as they could, given the possibility of being named in their owner's will, as a recipient rather than merely a marker of his wealth.

Within just a few decades, says Clark, the mythical archetype of the "irresistible, mixed-race seductress" was turning up with considerable frequency in literature – but with an additional meaning. Joseph Holt Ingraham's 1841 novel *The Quadroon, or, St. Michael's Day* marks this shift, for instead of undermining the white man's devotion to civilization, the mixed-race lover becomes the paragon of the tragic feminine, subject to the depraved lusts of her owner in a relationship that could only be understood as a protracted experience of rape. Earlier in this same decade, as already noted in Chapter 1, the group of poets known as Les Cenelles were cautioning women away from *plaçage* as a highly unreliable pathway to wealth. As the writing about this arrangement accumulated, in the middle decades of the nineteenth century, it increasingly served anti-slavery activists as a vision of the supreme damsel-in-distress, held captive by forces that were, as Clark notes, foreign to the wholesome values of mainstream, normal Americans.[35] Perhaps the most famous of all of these nineteenth-century literary representations is Dion Boucicault's *The Octoroon*; it opened in New York in 1859, an instant hit, and has been performed many times since.[36]

Clark counts more than three dozen novels, poems, and plays written between 1834 and 1865 that focus on this theme by authors as different as Henry Wadsworth Longfellow, Hans Christian Andersen, and Harriet Beecher Stowe. And in the decades that followed the Civil War, the mythic figure became codified as a primary archetype in the American imagination, showing up in work by William Faulkner, as we've already seen, and also in Langston Hughes, and, most recently, Isabelle Allende. So widespread was this stock figure that, as the Harlem Renaissance arrived, the poet Sterling Brown would list the "tragic mulatto" as one of the seven types of African Americans to appear in US literature.[37]

Perhaps spurred by fantasies that orbited around this stock figure, many male visitors to the city began to spend money in the brothels around the turning basin at the end of the Carondelet Canal. By the end of the nineteenth century, what we today call sex tourism had become a major industry in New Orleans, and though business was especially prevalent around the old turning basin, it was a general phenomenon through-out the city, particularly in the city's public ballrooms, where visitors could find traces of the *plaçage* culture of early decades. In particular, in the tradition of quadroon balls in the Quarter in the early decades of the nineteenth century, women of color (either mothers or agents mas-querading as mothers) would debut their daughters as potential concu-bines for rich white men. However, over the course of the century, these relatively elite events had given way to cheap, rowdy affairs, as Clark notes,[38] and migrated increasingly to the rear of the city near the big basin at the end of the old canal. There were a number of large dance halls there in the middle part of the nineteenth century, frequented by male transients, often sailors and soldiers. The Globe Ballroom was the most famous such place, directly on the banks of the old basin, and the women who danced there were almost certainly professionals, highly skilled in the arts of flirting with and fleecing tourists.[39]

This was a primary seed for what became "The District."[40] In 1896, amidst concerns about the need to make the city more "respectable," a bold new plan was hatched to quarantine vice. The idea was proposed by a city alderman named Sidney Story, who had seen several similar such schemes work in European cities he had visited; Dublin's "Monto" was a key precedent for what Story had in mind. As he had led the discussion of the idea, the new area in New Orleans was unofficially named after him – Storyville – and began its tenure as the official red-light district on January 1, 1898. The social experiment was, for just less than two decades, a success beyond anyone's wildest dreams.[41] By 1901, there were estimated to be 2,000 sex workers plying their trade in the district daily during the high season, supporting, in turn, an elaborate economy around the district, in bars, restaurants, and laundries.[42] Among the legendary denizens of this underworld were figures who, though lost to history, were known by names that suggest something of their stories: Coke Eyed Laura, Mary Meathouse, Titanic, Stack O'Dollars, Gold Tooth Gussie, Charlie Bow Wow.[43]

Basin Street was for the elite. One block north of Basin, running in the same direction, was Franklin, where rather less ritzy businesses flourished amidst the cheap taverns that were crucial to the development of the new music. Each successive street parallel to Basin and Franklin became more outwardly raunchy, seedy, less expensive, and more chaotic: first, Liberty, then Marais, then Villere, and finally Robertson. The streets that intersected these four – St. Louis, Conti, Customhouse (now Iberville), and Bienville – were lined with one-room shanties called "cribs," rented on a day-to-day basis by street-level sex workers.[44]

Several of the wealthiest and best-known madams on Basin Street capitalized on the quadroon and octoroon lore, their large, upscale brothels being memorials of sorts to the old traditions of *plaçage*. For example, at 225 Basin, Lulu White's Mahogany Hall explicitly specialized in interracial sex, advertising a roster of octoroon women. White herself claimed to be an octoroon.[45] She became the model upon which Mae West crafted her public persona and made a fortune.[46] Another major figure on Basin Street was the Countess Willie Piazza, who also identified as an octoroon; she was most likely the daughter of a first-generation Italian shopkeeper in rural Mississippi and an illiterate woman of color who had probably been enslaved. Nonetheless, she kept a large library in her brothel.[47] She was the first to hire a band that would play the new music and help her compete against the entertainment offered at the lakefront resorts.[48] The famous jazz standard, "Basin Street Blues," memorializes the business model of these two madams in the line, "where the black and the white folks meet."

That music, the earliest traces of which were first heard in nearby Congo Square as a way of remembering Africa, would now flourish in a place where many travellers visited, including major celebrities like

Babe Ruth and Teddy Roosevelt, thereby becoming poised to sweep the country within a few decades via the new technologies of radios and record players, giving rise to what would be called the Jazz Age.

Aside from adapting and extending an African musical aesthetic, a different kind of memory-work was also afoot in those brothels – a particularly sinister brand of white nostalgia. As Joseph Roach suggests, these brothels also functioned as half-conscious memorials to the city's vast antebellum network of slave markets. Just as slave auctions were often staged as grand spectacles with live music and considerable nudity, so too were the auctioning off of young octoroon and quadroon virgins in the Basin Street brothels.[49] As Roach notes, when Jelly Roll Morton recounted his glimpses of these auctions where he worked as a young pianist, the word he used to describe them was "cruel."[50] Roach notes further that when Al Rose interviewed in the 1960s women who worked in Storyville in their youth, their life-stories read like slave-narratives,[51] particularly as one woman tells the story of being sold on the auction block at Emma Johnson's brothel when she was 12 years old.[52] This idea has been explored at book length in Emily Epstein Landau's *Spectacular Wickedness: Sex, Race, and Memory in Storyville, New Orleans*, in which she notes for example that the near simultaneity of the founding of Storyville and the Supreme Court decision in *Plessy v Ferguson* that instituted the Jim Crow system of separate-but-equal was no mere coincidence: both were attempts to re-inscribe white supremacism in boldest terms after the shocks delivered to that system by the Emancipation Proclamation and the early, progressive years of Reconstruction.[53] Storyville advertised mixed-race women as an opportunity for white men to lease – rather than, as in decades prior, to own – people of partial African descent, a kind of sexual nostalgia for the bygone era of octaroon balls and *plaçage* that had figured so prominently in the nation's literary imaginings of New Orleans. In other words, the mixed-race siren functioned in early twentieth-century Storyville exactly the same way she had, in superficially different circumstances, exactly a hundred years earlier, when, in the aftermath of the Haitian Revolution, white men constructed her as a platform for enacting their fantasies of the most complete, most intimate domination of Blackness.

House of the Rising Sun Ted Anthony lists about 150 different recordings of the song, but notes that the list is by no means exhaustive and that new versions are being recorded all the time. The title has been borrowed for pulp detective novels and porn films, the melody turning up as a popular cell-phone ringtone and a sports-drink TV commercial. An American soldier reported playing it on a guitar on Christmas Eve, 1968, in the Cambodian jungle, and thought he heard an echo; he then realized that enemy soldiers, camped not far away, were singing along in the darkness.

Ironically, what is surely the most widely promulgated piece of writing about sex work in New Orleans – the song "House of the Rising Sun" as performed by The Animals – casts the customer as victim, much like the French were thought to be when they fell in love with their mixed-race mistresses in what became Haiti: this brothel "has been the ruin of many a poor boy, and god I know I'm one." (In earlier versions, the narrator is a girl, but Leadbelly changed it to a boy, and the baby-boomer anthem that swept the world retained that change.) The irony is compounded by the fact that the song, which has been recorded by countless artists over the last several decades, probably has little connection to Storyville, for an 1820 newspaper advertisement for the Rising Sun Hotel was recently discovered, the address being in the 500 block of Conti, in the Quarter; some archaeological evidence – a significant deposit of discarded bottles of rouge and perfume – suggests the hotel functioned as a brothel, but the evidence is by no means conclusive. Several other possible New Orleans locations for the House of the Rising Sun have been proposed, none of them in Storyville. And, in fact, the House of the Rising Sun might well have been in England, for, in 1953, Alan Lomax encountered a version of the song in Norfolk in eastern England, sung by an elderly man who learned his repertoire from his father who, in turn, had performed in rural taverns in the area in the late nineteenth century, where even then it was understood as a melody that had been around for a long time.[54] And, in Lowestoft, on the eastern seaboard of England, there was once a pub called the Rising Sun, Lowestoft itself sometimes being called the Town of the Rising Sun, given that it was so far east on the island.[55] Thus, the original melody and lyrics could predate the founding of New Orleans, to say nothing of Storyville, by centuries. And the song might not even be about a brothel, as some have suggested that it could refer to a casino or been the nickname of the local women's jail.

Nonetheless, the power of Storyville, in particular, to "ruin a poor boy" was not only unambiguous but rose to the level of a national security issue when the US military cited in 1917 the high rates of venereal infection among the troops stationed nearby, and closed it down. And, seven years later, the Carondelet Canal and its turning basin adjacent to Congo Square were filled in and closed. Today, what had been the canal is a long public green space for bicycling and jogging; Basin Street itself is home to a gas station, some parking lots, and a block of featureless condominiums; and where the waters of the old turning basin glittered shiftily in the moonlight, there now sit some offices of the tourist bureau and an RV parking lot. Foot traffic is nearly non-existent.

A newspaper clipping from *The Louisiana Gazette*, January 27, 1821, discovered by Ted Anthony after Shannon Dawdy found an abundance of perfume bottles during an archaeological dig at this address. The presence of such bottles is often interpreted as a sign that a brothel had operated on the site.

RISING SUN HOTEL,

LO.TI STREET,
Nearly opposite the State Bank.

THE undersigned inform their friends and the public that they have bought out the interest of JOHN HILL & Co. in the above establishment. No pains or expence will be spared by the new proprietors to give general satisfaction, and maintain the character of giving the best entertainment, which this house has enjoyed for twenty years past.

Gentlemen may here rely upon finding attentive Servants. The bar will be supplied with genuine good Liquors; and at the Table, the fare will be of the best the market or the season will afford.

The business will be carried on under the firm of

L. S. HOTCHKISS & CO.

Jan. 27

Nonetheless, the place still looms large in the literary imagination of the US. The word "Storyville," when typed into the Amazon search-window, generates well over 10,000 items; to narrow the search only to books still yields over 300. It is surely the best-known vice-district in all of American history – perhaps in the history of the world.

Much of the writing about Storyville takes the form of popular histories or historical novels, either romances or detective fiction. In the former category, Lois Battle's *Storyville* stands out as particularly well-researched, as does, in the latter, David Fulmer's seven-volume detective series centered around the Creole-Sicilian sleuth, Valentin St. Cyr.

Aside from genre fiction, a few self-consciously literary works have situated themselves in Storyville, among them Patrick Neate's Whitbread Award-winning *Twelve Bar Blues*, a rollicking, wide-ranging novel that is derived in fairly direct ways from Tom Robbins's *Jitterbug Perfume*, which is inspired in turn by Ishmael Reed's partly New Orleans-based counter-narrative about the Jazz Age, *Mumbo Jumbo*. Neate's novel begins in the 1790s in Africa, where two men compete for the charms of a woman, one casting a spell on the other that sends his rival to New Orleans on a slave-ship, where, a century later, one of his descendants is an emerging star on the cornet with a quadroon stepsister whom he adores. The novel then bounces back to Africa and yet another century forward in time to start another storyline, this one about local reactions to an archaeologist from Northwestern University, who has unearthed a magnificent, ancient head-dress; meanwhile, back in the early twentieth century, the young cornetist has arrived in Storyville, but doesn't stay long, as his beloved quadroon stepsister is rumored to no longer be there. There are other sub-plots, but the upshot is that these stories are, in large part, about the process of assembling an understanding of one's lineage, reconstructing it against the riptide of diasporic entropy, a coherent, collective memory of a family. The music scene in early twentieth-century New Orleans is only a small part of what the novel engages. In a similar key, Alex Jennings recently published the novel, *The Ballad of Perilous Graves*, a tale about nine New Orleans songs that have kept the city alive, which have escaped from a magical piano where they live, leaving the city poised for an apocalypse.

A more nuanced engagement with related territory is Michael Ondaatje's *Coming through Slaughter* (1976). Ondaatje had been publishing poetry for a little over a decade when he spent three weeks in the Hogan Jazz Archive at Tulane University, and, from his notes, assembled this collage-like detective narrative, much fictionalized, about how Buddy Bolden – the first star of the new street music at the dawn of the twentieth century – vanished from the District.

Though Bolden's career ended before recording technology could have captured his playing, the memory of his career is central to every origin-story of jazz. The bare facts known about the actual, historical person, as Gary Krist notes, are few: the grandson of slaves, he was born uptown on Howard Street, then spent his boyhood at 385 First Street, near the corner of Liberty.[56] As his musical career took off, he was adored by women, even followed around by groups of them. His popularity peaked around 1905, and by 1906 he began to unravel: severe headaches set in, plus some erratic and delusional behavior, even eccentric paranoias in which he seemed to fear his own horn. Some have suggested that he had an untreated ear infection, others that he was going mad from playing too loud.[57] Ned Sublette, in particular, makes a compelling argument that Bolden's demise owed to cocaine addiction.[58] Whatever the cause, after a few episodes of deranged violence at home, his mother and his mother-in-law had him arrested, and neighbors told their children to stay away from him. His mother then had him arrested yet a few more times on charges of insanity, and, on the forms she filled out, under "cause for insanity," she wrote "alcohol."[59] He spent the next two-dozen years in an asylum in Jackson, Louisiana, where he would eventually pass away. Beyond these bare facts, though, are the stories told by the second generation of Jazz horn players who picked up where he left off and who cite him as the spark that they fanned into a nationwide fire in the years that followed his departure: Louis Armstrong, Sidney Bechet, Freddie Keppard, Bunk Johnson, King Oliver, Kid Ory, and others.

In Ondaatje's fictional account, Bolden runs a barber shop and edits a local scandal sheet. He has even struck up a rather far-fetched

friendship with the historic photographer, E. J. Bellocq, whose portraits of Storyville sex workers were discovered in the early 1970s in
a watershed moment for those interested in that history and in documentary photography in general. Another Ondaatje invention: a friend
of Bolden's youth named Webb, who now works as a detective, investi-
gates Bolden's disappearance as though it were a missing person's case.
None of this is true, but it allows Ondaatje to sift through various fragments of found text by way of reconstructing the world of Storyville
at the turn of the twentieth century. And this, rather than the detective
plot pasted onto that material or the unlikely interactions of Bellocq
and Bolden, is the book's great value, making it read, at its best, like an
unearthed time-capsule.

In Ondaatje's vision of Bolden, what drove Bolden mad was the
domain of memory, for memory, in the context of this book, stands
in opposition to freedom. This antagonism – specifically, the memory of slavery as the fatal counterweight to the all-important sense
of imaginative freedom and spontaneous playfulness that enables, in
Bolden, the making of his music – is the essential conflict and tension
that drives the book. Bolden is obsessed with the experience of freedom, especially as cultivated in his musical performances. He imagines

One of E. J. Bellocq's portraits of a
Storyville sex worker, circa 1915. Wikimedia
Commons – Public Domain

playing with his band as "sending forth musical notes, sending them forward and forth and forth till, as he could see them, their bursts of air were wild animals fighting in a room," as if trying to break free in their legendary loudness back into the great outdoors and the infinity of space. This imaginative freedom is what he seems to prize above all else in his wife, Nora, "who believes in the sandman when putting the children to bed, when even the children don't."[60] Ondaatje ultimately describes Bolden's absorption in open-ended playfulness as "fears of certainty."[61]

As Webb begins to look for him, he supposes as a starting point that Bolden may have wanted to get free of the stardom, the grand public life he had spun up about himself in Storyville. In vanishing, perhaps Bolden was turning all of that into memory, and then expelling the memory, "wiping out his past ... in a casual gesture, contemptuous."[62] For he has learned that "reputation" makes the available space for creativity "narrower and narrower, til you were crawling on your own back, full of your own echoes, til you were drinking in only your own recycled air."[63] Later, Bolden reveals that he has been hiding out at some friends' house in Shell Beach, some 30 miles downriver from New Orleans, because, in that situation, he felt he could regain his all-important creative freedom: "anonymous ... alone ... with no history and no parading," free to "make something unknown" and re-locate that "fear of certainties" that drives his spontaneous improvisations on the bandstand.[64]

Given this fear of certainties, Bolden had to have been hit hard by Bellocq's photos, for Bellocq seems to capture the souls of the women he photographs, locking them for all time onto a flat surface. Here is how Ondaatje describes what Bellocq does:

> One snap to quickly catch her scorning him and then waiting, waiting for minutes so she would become self-conscious towards him and the camera and her status, embarrassed at just her naked arms and neck and remembers for the first time in a long while the road she imagined she could take as a child. And he photographed that. Then he paid her, packed, and she had lost her grace.[65]

After he gets his wife, Nora, to pose for Bellocq, she argues with him, saying "Look at you. Look at what he did to you. Look at you. Goddamn it. Look at you."[66] The photographs, for Bolden, have become mirrors, which Bolden then attacks in a furious act of "Defiling people he did not wish to be."[67] Bolden experiences Bellocq's photography as a freezing of time, as the instantiation of memory. And, particularly in those sex workers – bodies with price tags – Bolden must confront a brutal, even devastating reminder of that all-too-fresh wound that is slavery, a memory which, for him, is antithetical to the part of his mind that makes his music.

Curiously, Ondaatje's text begins with a short excerpt about the way dolphins use echolocation, making sounds and following echoes to remember where they are and to keep track of where they are going. Sound, for dolphins, is a way of mapping and remembering, of creating, in the terms of the pianist in Morrison's musical, a "room with a view," such that "lost is found." For the dolphins, sounds also function as a signature, a way of locating the self amidst free movement. This presumably is what Bolden was building with his horn, a legendary persona, a recovery of humanity in the aftermath of having come through slaughter, through the supreme dehumanization of slavery. Thus, the recovery of freedom and humanity was as yet still too tentative and fragile, for all Bolden's loud swagger, to survive the presence of machines, whether cameras, record players, or radios, that would capture and commodify it.

A quarter-century after Ondaatje's *Coming through Slaughter*, another major achievement appeared that uses Storyville as its primary context for exploring themes of memory. This more recent book – *Bellocq's Ophelia* by Natasha Trethewey – does so in more complex and profound ways than Ondaatje did, linking the theme of memory to questions about the power that inheres in the act of naming and of image-making, processes always suffused, in turn, with the power of desire and the dynamics of gender. This work chronicles the growth of a young woman, who, early in the book, arrives in Storyville, a desperate refugee from the cotton fields of the rural South, and learns to become a sort of living statue in a Storyville brothel, devoid of agency, a projection and a target of the male gaze. Within a few days, she is auctioned off. In a little over a year, however, she evolves when she discovers, first, through reading and writing, her own subjectivity and agency, and then becomes interested in using a camera to document and preserve moments of change. In the larger context of the book, this means taking control of the domain of memory, and, in turn, of the power of naming.

The first half of the book is presented as letters that the young woman, new to the work of prostitution in Storyville, writes home to her former schoolteacher back in Oakvale, Mississippi. In the second half of the book, the letters have stopped and what follows takes the form of diary entries. All but the final poem of the book come from her point of view and her voice, and this simple fact constitutes an historic intervention in the discourse of Storyville, an inversion of the dominant order that has positioned those women as silent objects. Among the first poems in the book is one that crystallizes this dominant order by invoking the conduct manuals for young ladies of that era:

"Countess P–'s Advice for New Girls"

Look, this is a high-class place – polished
mahogany, potted ferns, rugs two inches thick,
The mirrored parlor multiplies everything –

One glass of champagne is twenty. You'll see
yourself a hundred times. For our customers
you must learn to be watched. Empty

your thoughts – think, if you do, only
of your swelling purse. Hold still as if
you sit for a painting. Catch light

in the hollow of your throat; let shadow dwell
in your navel and beneath the curve
of your breasts. See yourself through his eyes –

your neck stretched long and slender, your back
arched – the awkward poses he might capture
in stone. Let his gaze animate you, then move

as it flatters you most. Wait to be
asked to speak. Think of yourself as molten glass –
expand and quiver beneath the weight of his breath.

Don't pretend you don't know what I mean.
Become what you must. Let him see whatever
he needs. Train yourself not to look back.

The meaning of those last words – "train yourself not to look back" – multiplies upon reflection like that champagne glass in the opening stanza. At first, of course, it means simply that the new girl should not meet, much less challenge, the male gaze, with her own; it means thus essentially the same thing as that first precipitous command that falls from the first stanza to the second: "Empty / Your thoughts." But it carries another meaning as well: don't think about the past, don't try to retrace the path that led you here; rather, you must learn to forget, for forgetting is the ultimate step in dissolving your personhood. The implication is clear: it is through our sense of history that we cultivate our humanity, and thus the most essential key to "success" for a young woman arriving in Storyville is to learn to do the opposite – become an object that pleases those who would look upon it and use it. But the very first word of the poem – "Look" – sounds the opposite note and indicates how she'll save herself.

The broader question of what the protagonist saves herself from in the latter half of the book gets a partial answer as we learn more about her background a few poems after "Countess P–'s Advice for New Girls." She has been raped: "I am back at the farm store / the man leaning over me ... as I stare at the lines on the floor / and they blur into one smooth path / leading me out of this place."[68] What she then desires, she says, is "freedom from memory."[69] Thus her flight away from that scene becomes a flight into the still broader sort of self-erasure or amnesia that working for Countess P– requires, the rape's shockwaves or echoes taking shape as her life in the brothel. In the very next poem, still more backstory emerges, as her mother taught her "to curtsy and be still / so that I might please a white man, my father."[70] In the same poem, she defines herself as an odalisque, a concubine of color, and says that she began to take arsenic tablets to whiten her skin, implicitly as a means to enter "the white space of forgetting."[71] The opposite of that arsenic regimen is her letter- and diary-writing, for there the white space of forgetting is the blankness of the empty page – against which her writings, the ink marks themselves, literally instantiate her Black memory, and in turn her living humanity.

Toward the end of this first section, she begins to discover the brothel's library, where there is a globe she can spin with her hand. This poem recalls the pride she takes in her literacy earlier in the book in the first of her letters home. The next poem marks a kind of rebirth, and what follows that one is a vision of human desire, how it always recurs and is thus outside of the flow of time and is itself, in its urge to realize itself, seeking to stop time, to capture and eternalize its own moment of flowering. This ultimate act of remembering is carried out through writing and reading, and, in the second half of the book, through her discovery of photography – not in having her picture taken, but in taking pictures herself, and thus reclaiming the entirety of her life as her own. She has turned on its head Countess P–'s injunction "Don't look back," when she says,

> *I know now that if we choose*
> *to keep any part of what is behind us*
> *we must take all of it, hold each moment*
> *up to the light like a photograph*[72]

This work of collecting, preserving, and holding fragments of the past – even the entirety of the past itself – "up to the light like a photograph" defines the primary purpose of the most important writing situated in the neighborhood directly adjacent to Storyville, the one known as Tremé.

Backatown III: Black Memory Again and Tremé

Soon after the Carondelet Canal was dug in the 1790s, the owner of a nearby plantation named Claude Tremé must have realized that the value of his land would soon rise considerably, especially as Americans began to pour into the city in large numbers in the years that immediately followed the 1803 Louisiana Purchase. He had come into possession of the property when he married Julie Moreau, a manumitted slave who had inherited the plantation. He ultimately must have been prompted to start selling it off in small parcels by the 1809 influx of refugees from what had just become Haiti, for by 1812 the word "Tremé" starts showing up on maps of the area.[73]

Street Photography The joyful spectacle of second-line parades and Mardi Gras Indians has been captured by a number of brilliant photographers whose work is easy to find online: Abdul Aziz, Malik Bartholomew, Jeffrey Ehrenreich, Bernard Hermann, L. Kasimu Harris, Freddye Hill, Pableaux Johnson, Kevin Kline, Fernándo López, Jafar M. Pierrre, Kevin Rabalais, Akasha Rabut, Vincent Simmons, Michael P. Smith, Zach Smith, Tyrone Turner, Eric Waters, and Christopher Porche West. In a different key, the built environment of the city, as well as its swampy surroundings, are the subjects of Frank Relle's astonishing pictures.

Today, Tremé is commonly understood to be the oldest African-American neighborhood in the US,[74] densely built with varieties of shotgun house – single, double, and camelback – as well as plenty of Creole cottages.[75] The area is also thick with cultural institutions and traditions that exude a broad and subtle sort of resistance to the cultural patterns of the larger US, ways of building and sustaining cultural memory through the ritual of parades, meetings, and dances, to say nothing of funerals. These sorts of organizations recall those of Kongo, where fraternal orders and secret societies of various kinds

Old Parish Prison, opened in 1834 in the area bounded by Marais Street, Tremé Street, Orleans Avenue, and St. Ann Street, directly adjacent to Congo Square. It was demolished in 1939.

PARISH PRISONS.

have enjoyed utmost importance for centuries.[76] In the decades after the Civil War, some 80 percent of the New Orleans population belonged to some kind of benevolent association, and, between 1862 and 1880, the city had more than 220 such organizations.[77] And nowhere in New Orleans has this quasi-Kongolese devotion to clubs and societies been deeper and more widespread than in Tremé.

These organizations have also been great repositories of memory in written form, as delineated in Fatima Shaik's magnificent new history of one of the most vibrant and powerful such orders, La Société d'Économie et d'Assistance Mutuelle, an organization whose headquarters – Economy Hall – stood at 1422 Ursuline Street for much of the nineteenth century and well into the twentieth. This group was devoted to the cause of protecting the poorest and most vulnerable people of color in the city, particularly through education. Similarly, in the 1830s, a group of women organized themselves at what was then the brand-new St. Augustine Church, one block north of the French Quarter, to devote themselves to the education of children of color. They called themselves the Sisters of the Presentation, but a few years later they were officially

Revelers from the Sudan Social Aid and Pleasure Club enjoying their annual November parade. Courtesy of the photographer, Kevin Rabalais.

recognized, under the leadership of Henriette Delille, as the Sisters of the Holy Family, the first female religious order in Christendom that would admit women of African descent. Delille had been born in the French Quarter and lived, in her teens, within the *plaçage* system, but after two of her children died, she devoted her life to helping the poor and educating the enslaved. In 2010, she was declared by Pope Benedict XVI to have attained the status of "venerable," just two rungs shy of full sainthood. She may soon attain that status, the first African American to do so, as two miracles – the key criteria for canonization – that are attributed to her are currently being studied for verification.[78]

Whether or not Delille is ultimately memorialized with this highest honor, the work of remembering Tremé has grown especially urgent in recent times. Because there are, even today, pockets of dire poverty in Tremé, the area has been vulnerable to a series of

Henriette Delille A block away from St. Augustine Church, Henriette Delille purchased a house in 1850 that she would soon use as a convent and call the House of the Holy Family. Women of color were welcome. Her mission: to feed and educate the most downtrodden and vulnerable around her. When she died ten years after creating this religious order, her obituary, as Virginia Gould notes, praised her as a "servant of slaves." A hundred years later, the Sisters of the Holy Family had come to include hundreds of women of African descent who would operate orphanages, nursing homes, and schools as far away as Belize and Nigeria.

disastrous "urban renewal" programs. The first came in 1930, when the Municipal Auditorium was built on some of the grounds known as Congo Square. This required the demolition of the Globe, an historic dance hall and theater discussed earlier in this chapter, as well as eight square blocks of houses, many of them a hundred years old at the time, if not older. In the 1940s, a city ordinance removed Rampart Street, the border between the Quarter and Tremé, from the protections instated by preservationists in the Quarter. And so there are now mid twentieth-century structures there – gas stations, parking lots and garages, motor courts – that directly abut 200-year-old Creole cottages and townhouses. But the most devastating blow came in the mid 1960s, when city officials created a raised expressway on pilings that held it one story above Claiborne Avenue. That street had been the primary commercial and cultural artery of Tremé, the epicenter of the vibrant social life of downtown New Orleans, where benevolent societies and social aid and pleasure clubs held their annual marches, a different weekend for each group. But the new construction meant ripping out a vast stretch of old oaks and fitting a long expanse of concrete, like a sarcophagus, over these once proud blocks of the old parading ground, turning them into a dank and dark stretch of parking spaces that, today, is marked, at one end, by the sprawling squalor of a homeless encampment. When the Claiborne Overpass was built, as Holly Devon notes, residents in the immediate area referred to it as "the monster."[79] For "everything in our lives was on Claiborne," said one resident, adding that the building of that overpass "devastated our community." There is now a significant movement to remove the Claiborne Overpass as poorly designed. Some worry, however, that such a move would only further accelerate the gentrification that has transformed at warp speed, and on an American scale, much of the historic downtown neighborhoods: in the years before Hurricane Katrina, Tremé was 92 percent African American; today, 56 percent.[80] If and when that expanse of concrete is no longer squatting over the parading ground, property values will skyrocket like never before, which will likely mean a white majority in Tremé, an eventuality entirely unthinkable less than two decades ago.

Thus, the work of memory has never been more necessary than it is now, and this has long been the task of the major writers of this area. In fact, as if making a supreme memorial to the ultimate meaning of the cultural activity of Tremé, St. Augustine Church created in 2004 a monument in which large, grim, rusting chain shackles are fashioned into a crucifix that leans on its side, with a few other small metal crosses

TOMB OF THE
UNKNOWN SLAVE

TOMB OF THE
UNKNOWN SLAVE

Tomb of the Unknown Slave,
along the downriver side of St.
Augustine Church. Photo by the
author.

nearby. At first glance, it appears to be the anchor of a massive ship. It
is called the Tomb of the Unknown Slave. Because construction in the
area still turns up fragments of skeletal remains, this part of town, just
north of Rampart Street and thus beyond the old city, could well have
been the scene of slave burials. The most important books situated in
Storyville and Tremé constitute, in effect, more or less explicit memorials to honor the otherwise unmarked graves of the enslaved, a kind of
counter-gesture to the urban renewal projects and gentrification that
have robbed the community of so much in recent decades.

The most recent musical activity of historic significance along the Basin Street corridor offers in microcosm some of the same dynamics. At the thoroughfare's opposite end from Storyville, at 3232 Orleans Avenue, just before the street crosses Bayou St. John, the singer Johnny Adams held court on Saturday nights through the 1970s and into the first half of the 1980s at Dorothy's Medallion Lounge. Adams was nearly signed to Motown a few different times in the early 1960s, but, according to Adams's wife and biographer, Judy Adams, Joe Ruffino kept him "shackled" to a bad contract, even threatening and intimidating Adams to the point that he feared for his and his family's safety if he recorded for anyone else.[81]

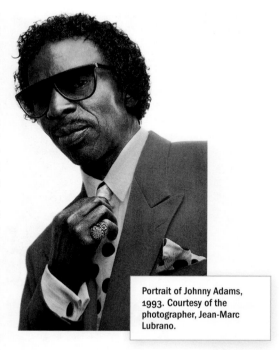

Portrait of Johnny Adams, 1993. Courtesy of the photographer, Jean-Marc Lubrano.

Dorothy's Medallion Lounge always hit its stride after midnight, when, as one observer put it, "Rubenesque" women in bikinis would shoulder live boa constrictors to do the bump and grind in cages along the sides of the bandstand. But they were merely the sideshow. The singer – always dressed in an immaculate Italian suit and an expensive-looking pair of sunglasses, even though he lived in the nearby Lafitte Public Housing Project – sang with such power, skill, range, and charm that even today those who saw those performances can usually only stammer about their memory of them. The dozen albums he made for Rounder Records, beginning in the early 1980s when Dorothy's was heading into its twilight, up until the late 1990s when he himself passed away, are timeless, especially *One Foot in the Blues, Man of My Word*, and *A Room with a View of the Blues*. Outside of New Orleans, he is known only to a tiny cult of rare soul-music obsessives.

Around the time Adams began to record for Rounder, somewhere along Orleans Avenue, between Adams's home in the Lafitte Projects and his

Dorothy's Medallion Lounge at 3232 Orleans Avenue, some forty years after Johnny Adams stopped performing there. Photo by the author.

kingdom at Dorothy's Medallion Lounge, is the house where, at a party in 1983, James Booker – perhaps the most extraordinary pianist in the history of the city – began to complain of ominous pains, and within hours passed away at the nearby Charity Hospital. The colorful, but tragic story of Booker's career – enslaved to alcohol and heroin, he lost an eye, probably during a beating when he was in the Angola Penitentiary, though there are any number of other legends about how that eye went missing – is told exceptionally well in Lily Keber's documentary *Bayou Maharajah.*

The experience of growing up in the musical cultures of Backatown is at the heart of *Backbeat: The Earl Palmer Story* by Tony Scherman. Palmer lived at 918 N. Clairborne and transformed the drumbeat of R & B to create rock'n'roll in Cosimo Matassa's studio on Rampart Street in sessions with Fats Domino and Little Richard; and then, through his session work in Los Angeles from the 1960s through the 80s, Palmer became the most recorded drummer in music history (in 1967 alone, he was documented on 450 sessions.)[82] His

Chinatown A Chinatown district just across Canal Street from Storyville developed in the 1880s, when Lena Saunders began offering classes on Christianity and the English language from her home at 215 S. Liberty to a small group of Chinese immigrants. The Chinese had come to the area to fill the labor shortage that followed Emancipation. Saunders's small school soon became the Chinese Mission, and by 1915, as Campanella notes, there were fifteen Chinese businesses in the area. By 1940, however, Chinatown was gone, an ominous indicator for the much larger and rapidly gentrifying Tremé of how quickly a vibrant cultural world can vanish.

drumming anchored pop classics of that era numbering in the dozens, though late in his life he lamented that he was never given a gold record, of the many he helped to create, to display on his wall.[83] As extraordinary as Palmer's story is, the most artful storytelling about the Backatown music world can be found in the Danny Barker memoir, *A Life in Jazz*, which conjures his youthful experiences of police raids on neighborhood juke-joints, the racist taunts of white tourists, and the pervasive effects of trauma within the culture of Jazz. The latest musical legend in this tradition is Jon Batiste, a graduate of Tremé's St. Augustine High School, who was nominated for an historic eleven Grammy Awards for his 2022 album, *We Are*.

The essential aesthetic component of Jazz, especially early Jazz – the sense of playfulness that peaks in ecstasies of freedom that Ondaatje equates with Bolden's experience of becoming a local star – resurfaces in a number of other ways in the writing of Tremé. Consider the figure of Krazy Kat, created by Tremé-born cartoonist George Herriman, to whom Ishmael Reed dedicated *Mumbo Jumbo*. Echoing something close to the same tone as in Reed's title, the main title of the Herriman biography by Michael Tisserand is simply *Krazy*. Born in 1880 at 348 Villere Street, Herriman's ancestors were involved in the *plaçage* system, which is why he was born with a "passing" complexion. As a 10-year-old who was fluent in French, Herriman moved away from New Orleans with his family and presented himself as white for the rest of his life. He was a distant relative of Jelly Roll Morton, but no record exists of their having met, as the Herriman family left New Orleans around the same time Morton was born. After spending ten years in Los Angeles, Herriman moved as a 20-year-old to Coney Island and soon thereafter launched his career. He would become one of the most beloved newspaper cartoonists the US ever produced, having drawn, by the end of his life in the mid 1940s, some 10,000 comic strips.[84]

The same spirit of creative freedom and fun appears in much of Arthur Pfister's poetry, a great deal of which is explicitly about or inspired by Jazz, or written in a form that is clearly meant to serve as script for vocal performances structured like Jazz. Pfister grew up in Tremé on N. Roman Street. His poems are often built on repeated syntactic structures, creating a profound rhythmic pulse or echo effect, as in chanting or drumming. For example, in riffing off Marcus B. Christian's famous poem, "I Am New Orleans," Pfister's poem "My Name Is New Orleans" offers nearly 300 lines of verse that begin with the words "I am," followed by a set of cultural associations with where he grew up. But Pfister's exuberant playfulness, sometimes reaching full hilarity, are mixed with very different kinds of work, such as the solemn, spiritual devotion of his ten-page political rhapsody called "Malcolm." A short sample of lines from his poem "To a Black Girl on Her Birthday" offers in microcosm the range of tones and the balance of seriousness with his free-wheeling playfulness.

> *Now, I'm no Michael Jackson*
> *(I'm just here relaxing)*
> *Writing of the truth*
> *Of your beauty and your youth*
> *Your silence and your song*
> *Your spirit, ever-strong,*
> *And so it all will be*
> *Throughout eternity.*[85]

Pfister also writes love poetry, some of it salty but no less successful for that, as in "The Last Time I Saw Janine," his performance of which can be found online. No writing situated in Backatown, however, takes up this terrain with greater whimsy or raunch than Steve Cannon's 1969 cult classic, *Groove, Bang, and Jive Around.* The first half of the book is a pornographic romp with motifs of Jazz and voodoo, the second an Afro-Futurist vision of utopia. A partial inspiration for Ishmael Reed's *Mumbo Jumbo* (1972), the book ends with an editor's note through which it comes to seem a self-deprecating political cartoon:

> This manuscript was found under a coffin in St. Louis Cemetery #2 which was removed to make room for an Urban Development Program. Centuries ago. Unsigned, but said to have belonged to some mysterious nun – a Da Da Hoo Doo Voo Doo Surreal List #2, of the Seventh Order of the Holy Ghost Church, New Orleans, Louisiana. It fell into my hands as a deal for some reefer.[86]

Despite this tone, the political seriousness of Cannon's Afro-Futurist vision was anticipated by his founding – with Ishmael Reed, Archie Shepp, Tom Dent, and others – the Umbra Writer's Workshop on the Lower East Side of Manhattan in 1962, an early trace of what would become the Black Arts Movement that flowered in the aftermath of Malcolm X's murder three years later. Cannon, who was blind for the final thirty years of his life, continued to be a major force in the New York arts and literary scene long after the passing of the Black Arts era. His magazine *A Gathering of Tribes* published the Man Booker Prize–winning satirist Paul Beatty, among others, and the legendary salon that ran for decades out of his Lower East Side home (a home he almost never locked) featured performances by members of the Sun Ra Arkestra. He was nicknamed "The Heckler," and named his son Karl Marx.[87]

Cannon's political seriousness and that of his fellow New Orleanian Tom Dent had no shortage of precedent in the Backatown lore circulating in their youth. Consider that José Martí, the white nineteenth-century Cuban poet and political theorist who helped to spark the independence movement in his home country, used to spend time at the Tremé household of the Afro-Cuban war hero Antonio Maceo.[88] When Cuba's war for independence began in 1895, General Maceo led a guerrilla army of Afro-Cubans on horseback fully 1,000 miles across Cuba over three months, engaging in some 30 separate battles against the army of Spain. Though Maceo was killed near the end of this campaign, his cause prevailed, as Cuba was, the following year, liberated from its colonial masters.

Perhaps Tom Dent was thinking of Martí and Maceo when he joined the group that demonstrated at the United Nations in the winter of 1961 to protest the murder of Congolese anti-colonial leader, Patrice Lumumba, and to honor Fidel Castro's triumph in Cuba. Dent was raised among the Black cultural and financial elite of New Orleans, his father the president of Dillard University, and groomed from an early age to lead. Dent moved to New York City in 1958, when he was in his mid twenties, working as a reporter for a Harlem newspaper and as a press attaché for the NAACP. But after helping to found Umbra the year after the UN demonstrations, he was back in New Orleans by 1965 to embark upon a five-year stint as director of the Free Southern Theater. After his time at the helm of FST, he founded the Congo Square Writers' Union, and, with Jerry Ward (discussed in Chapter 3) and Charles Rowell, the historic journal of African-American literature named *Callaloo*. Though he moved around New Orleans a lot over the ensuing decades, he lived, in the final decade of his life, when he was at the height of his powers as a writer and a cultural activist, at 1114 Tremé Street, just behind St. Augustine Church, around the corner from the Tomb of the Unknown Slave. Many feel that Dent's final project was ultimately his most important: *Southern Journey*. Dent had been serving for a few years as the executive director of the New Orleans Jazz and Heritage Festival (aka "Jazz Fest"), but quit to devote all his energies to creating this work.[89] He had composed two volumes of poetry and some plays, including the widely praised and frequently performed *Ritual Murder*, and co-edited with Richard Schechner and Gilbert Moses *The Free Southern Theater by the Free Southern Theater*,

1 Chris Ferrand, the 2021 King of the Dumaine Street Gang, at their December second-line parade. Photo by author.

2 Unknown reveler, St. Joseph's Night, Central City. Photo by author.

3 A young Mardi Gras Indian, being raised in the tradition. Photo by author.

4 A masked reveler with Uganda Roberts on conga in the background. Photo by author.

5 A home in the 9th Ward. Photo by author.

6 Leo "Bud" Welch, performing on Frenchmen Street. Photo by author.

7 A home in the 7th Ward. Photo by the author.

8 A backyard fence in the 9th Ward. Photo by the author.

9 Kidd Jordan, with James Singleton behind him on bass. Photo by author.

10 Contemporary fishing camp. Photo by the author.

11 The aftermath of Hurricane Katrina. Wikimedia Commons.

12 The aftermath of Hurricane Katrina. Wikimedia Commons.

but this work, *Southern Journey* – a poetic travelogue through and personal meditation upon seven southern cities that were flashpoints of the struggle for Civil Rights, with extensive interviews of those directly involved – creates a treasure-house of memory that Dent renders in ways fully attuned to the dramatic and poetic power of the testimonies he gathered. He published the work in 1997, and, a year later, at the age of 66, he died.

Today, the neighborhood of Tremé is probably most widely known through the thirty-six-episode HBO series named after the neighborhood that writer-producers David Simon and Eric Overmyer debuted in 2010. Though not restricted in its focus to Tremé (the plot and characters range through all parts of the city) it shares in the neighborhood's singularly intense focus on memory – and on music, in turn, as a tool of remembering. The drama unfolds in the years immediately following Hurricane Katrina among the deep anxiety over what aspects of the city's glorious cultural traditions would find a way into the future. The series will perhaps be most treasured in the years ahead for its quality as a time capsule, capturing as it does many of the greatest musical performers who were active at the time but no longer are: Allen Toussaint, Kidd Jordan, Dr. John, Fats Domino, Lloyd Price, Tim Greene, Uganda Roberts, Coco Robichaux, and Lionel Batiste. For these moments alone, the work of Simon and Overmyer in documenting these personalities, particularly at this most crucial and vulnerable moment in the city's history, will be increasingly valued.

There are three masterpieces of memory-work situated in Tremé – one a novel, another a body of poetry, the third a memoir. The novel is Erna Brodber's *Louisiana* (1994). It begins with a fictional editor's note that explains that the manuscript simply appeared on the editor's desk in 1974, some forty years after a certain Ella Townsend had disappeared; Townsend was a young African-American woman who was doing graduate work in sociology in the early 1930s, much as Zora Neale Hurston had been doing in the same period; like Hurston, she was studying the folkways of African Americans in south Louisiana, using a tape recorder to gather oral histories, but an old woman with whom she had been speaking passed away, and her spirit seemed to take possession of the main character. None of this, however, happens in detached, expository prose, for Brodber's tour-de-force uses the notion of spirit-possession to disrupt the category of character, and so the question of whose voice and point of view the reader is following becomes ever more slippery.

Straightforward, traditional points of view return from time to time to guide the reader in a familiar way through key developments of plot. We learn, for example, in the second chapter, that the old woman had been a person of highest importance to her community and that, at her funeral, her spirit came to reside within Ella. We learn, further, that the dead woman's spirit can connect Ella in turn to the spirit of her own deceased grandmother, Sammy, who passed away back in Jamaica. We learn too that Ella's boyfriend, Reuben, has grown interested in the Black music of south Louisiana. When Ella receives a message from one of the elders in the community she had been studying to move to Congo Square, she and Reuben resettle there. In discovering the music in the Jazz clubs along Rampart Street, across from Congo Square, the narrator comes to find in the songs exactly what she had been capturing on her tape recorder while doing fieldwork toward her sociology degree: memories.

One song makes her think of her dead grandfather, and the sense of peace she associates with him; others carry different content, "one sweet sad poignant memory after another,"[90] songs that cause her to begin "seeing things as if on a rolling screen, a movie screen," an absorption in memory so acute as to constitute visionary trance, through which she takes great comfort.[91] Through these songs, she settles into her life in Tremé, and grows confident in her new spiritual vocation, the city allowing her to understand for the first time exactly what is expected of her – and that she can deliver it. Like "salvation" or "getting over," she has begun to experience what she calls an "hegemony of spirit" through which she is "left to the fullness of time."[92] She stops straightening her hair and wears it naturally under a traditional headwrap; she changes her name to Louisiana, and sets aside her tape recorder to begin channeling spirits through a piece of jewelry; she is surrounded by her husband's work in the Jazz scene and immerses herself in her own life's work: "I give people their history. I serve God and the venerable sisters."[93]

Those last lines could have come from the poet Brenda Marie Osbey, who in the decade before Brodber published *Louisiana* embarked upon an extraordinary career when her first book, *Ceremony for Minnieconjoux,* was published in 1983. Osbey is commonly understood to be the greatest poet to have emerged from New Orleans in the last several decades. Most would agree that no poet in the city's entire history has ever written about New Orleans with greater power. She was born and raised in the 7th Ward, but, with the exception of some intervals at Harvard, Brown, and UCLA, and in Kentucky and France, she has spent most of her adult life in Tremé, most recently keeping a place on Ursulines Street near Broad. Her father was a prizefighter;[94] some of her grandparents were devoted to writing and were friends with the otherwise reclusive Marcus B. Christian, and she herself has been immersed in archives, studying history and religion for much of her life.[95] In 2005, she became the first peer-selected poet laureate of Louisiana.

Near the beginning of the first poem in her first book, *Ceremony for Minneconjoux*, she writes "I live inside the city / I am telling only / as much as you can bear." What follows is thus at the outermost limits of the intelligible, the other, but coming from within the city, the realm of the familiar. This theme is elaborated a little later in that first book, when the same first-person narrator describes what happened as she grew into the habit of working in her garden at night, where

> *it was like I could feel this something*
> *pulling me*
> *just pulling at me from down under the ground*
> *and that was how I discovered my throat*
> *and commenced to singing*

She continues, noting that after her "throat opened up,"

> *it was like hearing a language that had never been*
> *it was like having a whole other woman*
> *standing in your middle*
> *singing out your insides*[96]

She refers later in the same poem to her song as a "somniloquy," suggesting something like talking in one's sleep, a dream-song, in the voice of what some call the unconscious and others the soul, that vast, communal repository of desire and memory. In yet another poem in this first book, the narrator declares that she has things moving around inside her,[97] and in yet another these things are more specific: "I carry dead things inside me / songs and photographs and dead flowers." She would seem to comment on this first book as a whole, when, near the end, she writes, "these are only shadows / of endless histories / randomly attached to me."

Five years later, she published a second book of poems, culled mostly from material that her mentor, *Callaloo* co-founder Charles Rowell, urged her to cut from the first one. The second book, *In These Houses*, appears on the surface to anticipate Brodber's novel in its portraits of women who have been driven mad, but, in whose madness, something much more becomes discernible. The poem "Thelma," for example, echoes the interest noted earlier in this chapter in Ondaatje's vision of Buddy Bolden as consumed with the experience of freedom, for "they say that Thelma was so loose / she couldn't even hold onto herself." The woman simply "came unstopped one day / and nothing could hold her after that," and the poem ends:

> *i saw her heading out the front door*
> *naked as she come into the world*
> *and before i could say a word*
> *thelma was out in the middle of the neutral ground*
> *dancing and screaming*
> *eating the black dirt*
> *calling freedom*
> *freedom*[98]

In a related poem called "Elvena," the madwoman stands near the street and asks passersby "what have you lost today?" as if offering to aid them through their grief and to restore what has been lost by helping to build a memory of it. The final stanza of the final poem in this book would seem to refer to the poetry itself contained in these pages, which fuses her literal body with her body of poetic work, what she'll later refer to as one entity, a "bone-sack and house of memories":

> *This is the house*
> *I have carried inside me*
> *This is the house*
> *Made of artifact and gut*
> *This is the house*
> *All my bones have come from*
> *This is the house*
> *Nothing*
> *Nothing*
> *Nothing can tear down*[99]

The theme of memory saturates Osbey's art. Her third book, for example, a single, long, narrative poem set in Tremé called *Desperate Circumstance, Dangerous Woman* (1991), begins with a section called "Memory," and in *All Souls: New and Selected Poems* (1997), which won the American Book Award, she soars with her theme to yet greater heights, most notably in the tour de force, "Faubourg Study No. 3 The

Seven Sisters of New Orleans," in which we come to see the "madness" and "spirit possession" of so many of the female characters in her poetry as, in reality, a profoundest working through of memory, a transformation, most particularly, of mourning into the visionary arts of song.

In commenting on her work, Tracy Watts says that Osbey's poetry hinges on a crucial distinction between history and memory: history is an intellectual, secular, and prosaic tool of the masters, who are liars, evil and cruel. Memory, in contrast, is lived in the body, sacred, poetic, a tool of healing, a practice of love by which the dead are kept alive to strengthen and hold together, in turn, particular communities.[100] Though Osbey's most recent collection of verse is called *History* (2013), her poetry is rooted deeply, in Watts's terms, in the opposite. In "A Peculiar Fascination with the Dead," Osbey begins with a list of things one can and must do to venerate the dead by way of "marrying memory to them." In "House of the Dead Remembering (House of Mercies Variation 2)," she writes,

> ... *my grandmother insisted*
> *that as children we learn*
> *the many proper ways*
> *to honor our dead*
> *because memory is everything*

Coda: Woodfox's Return to Tremé

Osbey's verse, particularly on the theme of honoring the dead, may offer a helpful framework for trying to come to terms with one of the city's highest literary achievements of the post-Katrina era – and, arguably, one of the most extraordinary stories of the city's entire 300-year history. This book is the memoir published in 2019 by Tremé native Albert Woodfox called *Solitary*. It is a dazzling feat of remembering, of remembering indeed the yet more dazzling feat of surviving for forty-three years in solitary confinement at the infamous Louisiana State Penitentiary at Angola. A finalist for the National Book Award and the Pulitzer Prize, it won at least a half-dozen other major awards.

The first word of the book is "Echoes," appearing as the title to a poem Woodfox wrote about the memory of his mother. The greatest pain Woodfox experienced in his life came when he learned that his mother was dying and that he wouldn't be allowed a temporary release to attend her funeral. This agony, he says, was the only instance during his forty-three years in solitary confinement that presented a genuine challenge to his sanity. It nearly broke him.[101] He began to suffer acute attacks of claustrophobia, a sense that he was suffocating, for the opportunity to form memories, and to cultivate the memory of his humanity was what kept him alive – and the ceremony of his mother's funeral would have been thus crucial to him. In that poem, "Echoes," that begins his astounding memoir, Woodfox begins every other line with the phrase "Echoes of ...", and the final couplet of the poem reads, "Echoes of motherhood gentle and near / echoes of a lost mother I will always hear." These echoes are a kind of music that connects Woodfox to the past and, in turn, to his humanity, despite overwhelming odds.

Woodfox had a tough upbringing. He writes of hitchhiking 170 miles a day as a 10-year-old to work a job in the Carolinas, when his family briefly lived there, coming home only to witness his mother victimized by an abusive spouse. She finally ran away, back home to New Orleans, with Albert and a few of his siblings, to raise them in the two rooms at the rear of her sister's house in Tremé at 918 N. Villere. Growing up in Tremé in the 1950s, Woodfox had almost no contact with white people, other than tourists in the Quarter. He spent a lot of time hanging out at the corner of Dumaine and Robertson, gradually drifting into trouble with the law, until he was sentenced to a first, relatively short stint in Angola.

Writing of Angola in the mid 1960s, he says that "sexual slavery was the culture." Once one was raped, one became the possession of one's rapist, to be pimped or sold to others, used repeatedly, and beaten mercilessly. One's only way out was to manage somehow to kill one's rapist – and, though one could regain some dignity and autonomy thereby, one would also likely be condemned to spend the rest of one's life inside Angola. In this period, there were four stabbings a week inside the prison.[102]

Upon Woodfox's release after that first, brief stay, he was soon arrested again, but escaped to Harlem, where he was arrested yet one more time and sentenced to a few years in the Tombs, Manhattan's municipal jail, where he met some members of the Black Panther Party. Through the Panthers, Woodfox began to learn about Black history and, perhaps even more important, about the implications of his having been deprived of opportunities to learn it until now. These conversations would plant the seed of his salvation, for, soon back in Angola, he was sentenced to life in prison for the alleged killing of a guard. Woodfox's trial for the murder of the prison guard was a grotesque charade even by Louisiana standards, the case against him riddled with holes and contradictions. And yet, despite an absolute absence of credible testimony, evidence, and even logic, the all-white jury returned a verdict, in less than an hour, of guilty.

He and his comrades who had also been convicted in that stabbing came to understand that the struggle to survive would be the meaning of their lives. Specifically, Woodfox faced the agonizing, repetitive sameness of the days, each one tortuously echoing all the others, by choosing to cultivate a sense of his humanity.[103] What's more, "What they didn't realize was that with every action they took against us, the stronger we became; the more united it made us … that knowledge gave us a new determination, a new strength, and a new sense of dedication to our cause."[104] He drew deep inspiration from other prisoners who used their time in prison to come to ever more refined understandings of the necessity of remembering that one is human, reading over and over again the work of Malcolm X, George Jackson, and Nelson Mandela. He writes, "By age 40, I had learned that to be human is to grow, to create, to contribute, and that fear stops growth."[105]

In order to contribute, Woodfox dedicated himself to advancing the ideals of the Panthers, organizing his fellow prisoners, for example, to end the practices of strip searches and the serving of meals on the floor. He even taught a fellow inmate to read. Perhaps most important, he drew on his conversations with Panthers to alter the culture of the prison in ways that decreased significantly the rate of prison rape in the cellblocks where he lived. He is remembered today in a most material way in the daily life of those imprisoned at Angola: a special oversight board he helped to create is known popularly among them as the Woodfox Board.

On the evening of his release in February of 2016, he realized that he could no longer remember how to walk without leg irons; nonetheless, he managed to appear at a community event in Tremé at the Carver Theater on Orleans Avenue. He was brought on stage to cheers and applause. The next day he went to his mother's grave.

In the weeks following the publication of his memoir, which appeared a few years after his release from Angola, Woodfox gave a public talk at the main branch of the library in New Orleans. Someone in the audience asked Woodfox how he managed to stay sane during his forty-three years in solitary confinement. He said that he was able to keep himself together because he had a purpose. He said that he held himself together as a way to honor his ancestors. He said, "I did it for them."

1. Lillian Hellman's aunt's boarding houses – 1718 and 1463 Prytania
2. Hamett Kane's home – 5919 Freret
3. Memorial Hospital – corner of Claiborne and Napoleon
4. Grace King's home – 1749 Coliseum St.
5. George Cable's home – 1313 Eighth St.
6. Everette Maddox / F. Scott Fitzgerald apartments – 2900 Prytania
7. Girlhood home of Anne Rice – 2301 St. Charles
8. Teenage home of Anne Rice – 2524 St. Charles
9. Adult home of Anne Rice – SE corner of First and Chestnut
10. Saint Alphonus Church, heart of Irish Channel – 2029 Constance St
11. Boyhood home of John Kennedy Toole – 1128 Webster
12. Final home of John Kennedy Toole – 7632 Hampson
13. Hope House – Sister Helen Prejean's former office – 916 St. Andrew St.
14. Former site of Leland University – NE corner of Broad and St. Charles
15. Former site of New Orleans University – 5818 St. Charles
16. Maple Leaf Bar – 8316 Oak St

17. New Zion Baptist Church – 2319 Third St.
18. Robert Charles's apartment – 2023 Fourth St.
19. Robert Charles's initial scuffle with police – 2815 Dryades
20. Robert Charles's final showdown with mob – 1208 Saratoga
21. Former site of Howard Johnson's Hotel – 303 Loyola Ave
22. Mark Essex's apartment – 2619 Dryades
23. Club Tijuana – 1209 Saratoga
24. Professor Longhair's home – 1738 Terpsichore
25. The Dew Drop Inn – 2836 LaSalle
26. Lil Wayne's boyhood home – SE corner of Eagle and Apple
27. Where Mahalia Jackson spent her girlhood
28. Plymouth Rock Missionary Baptist Church, where Mahalia first sang in public- 233 Hillary St
29. Former site of the Magnolia Public Housing Projects
30. Former site of the Calliope Public Housing Project

Map of St. Charles corridor: Garden District, Irish Channel, University District, Central City.

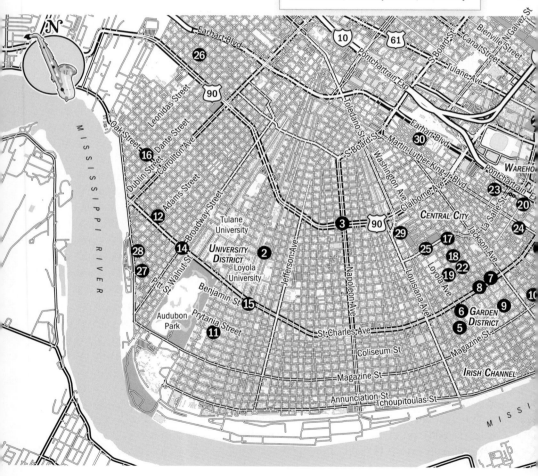

St. Charles Avenue — Blood and Money

The Garden District — the Irish Channel — the University District — Central City

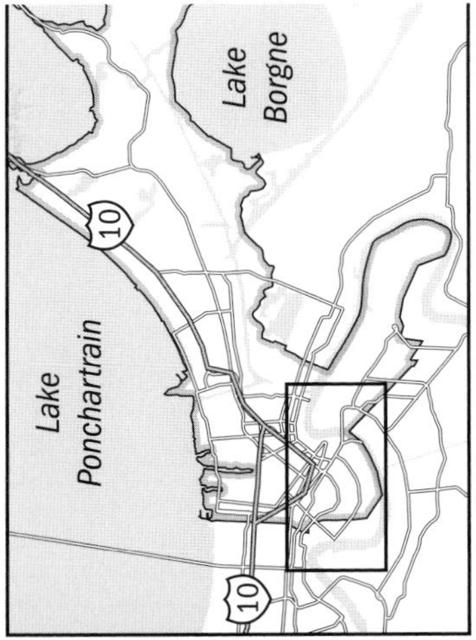

Lake Ponchartrain

Lake Borgne

10

10

Esplanade-Ave

90

90

RIVER

5

Lillian Hellman would live in many houses over the course of her life, but the boardinghouses run by her unmarried aunts at 1718 and 1463 Prytania were, together, "her first and most beloved home," for there was a fig tree in the yard of one of them that she would climb and use as a hideout when she skipped school. Secreted away in the high branches of that tree with a book, she learned to love to read.[1] A life of considerable adventure followed – she would visit Spain at the height of its civil war and travel to the Russian front during World War II – but her childhood adventures in New Orleans, detailed in her memoirs, were "the best times" of her life.[2]

Her earliest memories show signs of what would come, both in her character and in the plays she would write. Hellman describes the typical Sunday dinner of her childhood as essentially a "corporation meeting," at which an extended network of great-aunts and great-uncles would gather in "open ill will about who had the most money … or who would inherit what." These gatherings were chaired by her formidable Uncle Jake, who was the only person she knew who was not afraid of her grandmother. Like Hellman's grandmother, Uncle Jake was given "to breaking the spirit of people for the pleasure of the exercise."[3] For her high-school graduation at age 15, he gave her a ring, which she promptly pawned to buy more books. She told him what she had done and used the declaration to dissolve all connection to him. Hellman remembered his response the rest of her life: "He stared at me a long time, and then he laughed and said … 'So you've got spirit after all. Most of the rest of them are made of sugar water'."[4]

Hellman used this line twenty years later in her 1939 play *The Little Foxes*, her first major success. Set in a small town near the Gulf Coast at the dawn of the twentieth century, the play ran for 410 performances over the span of a year, and then embarked upon a two-season tour of the US.[5] It made her wealthy enough to buy a 130-acre farm in Westchester County, New York, which she shared with her partner of three decades, Dashiell Hammett. The play showcases a family much like the one she describes having grown up in, as a woman and her two brothers-in-law and a nephew scheme ruthlessly to get over on each other by way of dominating opportunities for greater and greater wealth. The woman, in the end, wins, but at the price of having alienated everyone else, even her daughter, who says she refuses to stand by and watch as her mother "eats the earth." The woman, richer now than ever, has destroyed the familial bonds that enabled her wealth.

The same theme of relationships dissolving and leaving characters to face loneliness is at the center of Hellman's greatest critical success, *The Autumn Garden*, which drew comparison to Ibsen and Chekhov. This play unfolds over the span of a week in September 1949 at a boardinghouse on the Gulf Coast, about a hundred miles from New Orleans, where nine characters, several of them New Orleanians, most of them middle-aged, find that the ties that join them have frayed, and grown tentative and confusing. During the play itself, these ties finally break altogether, leaving the characters to confront the loneliness that one of them casts as dangerous for those growing old. The play ends with the owner of the boardinghouse giving up on her love interest from the distant past, who has disgraced himself during his recent stay, and turning to a man who is so devoted to her that he has been visiting there for his annual vacation for decades. This man, however, tells her that he won't be coming back again and that he's no longer interested in her. Her response – "Nevermind" – evokes the muted violence of oblivion, a one-word microcosm of the fate that, this play suggests, awaits us all.

The play was probably written at the farm in Westchester County, where she lived with Hammett. She shared 15 percent of its royalties with him, for he had worked on it with her. Some twenty years earlier, when they first met, he mentored her, and he dedicated to her his final novel, *The Thin Man*, for its main female character, the hard-drinking, sharp-witted Nora, was based upon her. Their time together on the farm was idyllic, as both managed to stop drinking during significant intervals there, and, though they never married, these years must have cemented their bond and given them the strength to endure together what happened to them right after *The Autumn Garden* premiered in 1951.

Hellman was blacklisted for refusing to name names during the hearings led by Joe McCarthy and his House Un-American Activities Committee. Her beloved Hammett, despite having served in World War I and World War II, would fare even worse: he was sent to the federal prison in West Virginia, where he scrubbed toilets for five months, and his tuberculosis worsened. Perhaps he and Hellman were partly targeted by McCarthy and his goons for their portraits of capitalist alienation and amoralism – money, in Hellman's work, is nearly always ill-gotten and destroys human connections; and Hammett, in the years just before he and Hellman met, and for a few years after, had fashioned, out of the hardboiled pulp tradition in the detective fiction of the 1920s, a literary anti-hero who, in the iciest ways, always does what's best for business, no matter the cost in bloodshed. Hellman also may have been the victim of the larger currents of anti-Semitism flowing through US culture. The financial hardships that followed in the wake of their persecution cost them their Westchester farm.

After Hammett's release from prison, Hellman took care of him for what would be the final decade of his life, as he died the year after the 1960 premier of Hellman's *Toys in the Attic*, one of her greatest commercial successes. The play, set in New Orleans, draws closely from the circumstances of Hellman's girlhood at the Prytania Street boardinghouse, as two spinster

Lillian Hellman 1976 by Bill King. Public domain.

aunts struggle to process the sudden, extraordinary windfall of their ne'er-do-well brother. They assume he has won the fortune by gambling, probably in a poker game, but it turns out that the money came to him by even riskier means, and he's soon beaten up by the gangster whose wife gave it to him – and loses all the money back to the gangster. The lives of all of the characters, particularly in their relationships with each other, are soon plunged into chaos, and the play climaxes when, after his beating, the brother staggers, his money gone, back onto the stage, bleeding and covered in bruises.

A few years after Hammett's death in 1961, Hellman edited a collection of his short stories called *The Big Knockover*, and, in writing the foreword to the book, she embarked upon a process of memoir-writing that would yield three books and a second wave of legal troubles. The first, *An Unfinished Woman*, won the National Book Award in 1970, and the second, *Pentimento*, would be a finalist for the same award four years later. The latter led a woman to sue Hellman for appropriating without attribution her life story as an anti-Nazi activist; Hellman was already involved in a lawsuit against her literary rival and political adversary, Mary McCarthy, who had accused her of blurring fact and fiction in her memoirs. These feuds echo the kinds of antagonisms that drove her work as a playwright, and that she first studied as a girl during those Sunday dinners at the Prytania Street boardinghouses.

Hellman died in 1984, before these lawsuits could be settled. But her career, spanning some five decades, yielding more than a half-dozen plays, another half-dozen screen adaptations, three memoirs, and a novel, places her among the central figures in American literary culture of the middle twentieth century. As she remarked in her final book, however, uptown New Orleans has seemed to pretend, ever since she was blacklisted during the McCarthy hearings, that she never existed at all.[6] In refusing to name names before the House Un-American Activities Committee, her own name, at least in New Orleans, has faded, if not into oblivion, then surely from the forefront of the uptown literary canon.

But Hellman's strength and skill in handling Joe McCarthy, first developed when dealing with Uncle Jake and her grandmother, are a characteristic of much of the most historic literary achievement of uptown New Orleans: taking a courageous stand against dense networks of power and money, and calling out the forms of bullying and outright bloodlust upon which they're based.

Prominent among the uptown New Orleanians who have spoken truth to power was Harnett Kane of 5919 Freret Street, a contemporary of Lillian Hellman. He published reams of travel writing about south Louisiana in newspapers and magazines, as well as some two dozen books. His most important book, however, was his first. Called *Louisiana Hayride: The American Rehearsal for Dictatorship, 1928–1940*, it has the distinction of being the first book written about the phenomenon of Huey "the Kingfish" Long. A best seller, it brought him a national audience. In railing against the crude, lawless populism of what would become the Long Dynasty (a descendant would serve in the US Senate until 1987), Kane's first book offers important frameworks for grappling with similar political movements today, nearly a century after the Kingfish first rose to power. Kane's book was surely essential to Robert Penn Warren's research for his masterpiece, *All the King's Men*, which appeared five years later and won the Pulitzer Prize. Kane, however, is hardly the only journalist associated with uptown New Orleans whose best work follows the logic of David going after Goliath, nor is Warren the only chronicler of power in Louisiana to land a Pulitzer.

Sheri Fink is another. Her 2013 book about what transpired in the aftermath of Hurricane Katrina, called *Five Days at Memorial: Life and Death at a Storm Ravaged Hospital*, details the agonizing hour-by-hour efforts to triage and evacuate critically ill patients in the absence of electricity, plumbing, or food near the deeply flooded intersection of Claiborne and Napoleon Avenues. Those who worked at the hospital had to prioritize which patients at the hospital would be worth evacuating first and which ones should go last, given the patients' relative chances of surviving the ordeal; those making these decisions knew that they themselves couldn't leave the hellish conditions behind as long as there were any patients alive there. Of the forty-five patients who died at the hospital that week, about half of them were found during autopsy to have the same suspiciously high doses of morphine, for no clear medical reason, which led to accusations of euthanasia and questions about the race and class of those who were administered the lethal shots. One doctor and two nurses were charged with second-degree murder but were never convicted. The article Fink wrote about these events, which she later developed into a book, won the Pulitzer Prize, and amplified, through its exhaustive research, concerns about whether justice had prevailed.

The most historic achievement, however, in this mode is Jason Berry's. Like Harnett Kane, Berry has written a great deal about the city, particularly the musical and cultural traditions that he loves so dearly, and, again, like Kane, he has lived in uptown New Orleans for decades. As Kane did, Berry earned his place in history early in his career. Berry wrote the first book on the Catholic Church's efforts to cover up the problem of priests who sexually abuse minors. *Lead Us Not into Temptation: Catholic Priests and the Sexual Abuse of Children* appeared in 1992, growing out of Berry's article-length reportage on the issue in the 1980s, and, as several others wrote books on the subject after Berry's in the 1990s, the issue became, by the dawn of the twenty-first century, a national and then a global crisis for the Catholic Church. Since Berry's book appeared, the Church has paid out hundreds of millions of dollars in settlements and continues to reel from the forfeiture of its moral credibility. Berry has since followed that book with one focused on a different aspect of the Vatican, *Render unto Rome: The Secret Life of Money in the Catholic Church* (2012).

Another ambitious investigative reporter, Nathaniel Rich, the son of *New York Times* columnist Frank Rich, lives in this same part of the city. His work on the environmental crimes of the chemical manufacturer Dupont became the Todd Haynes film *Dark Waters* in 2019. He has also written a few novels, including *King Zeno*, based on the notorious serial killer known as the Jazz Butcher, who stalked New Orleans a century ago. But his most recent work is focused on the environment.

First, *Losing Earth: A Recent History* describes the political struggle over the last forty years to convince people of the urgency of climate change, and then *Second Nature: Scenes from a World Remade* explores the ways human beings have replaced the natural world with one that is almost entirely an artificial, human creation. The dangers implicit herein have captured the attention of another writer who lives off St. Charles – Tom Beller – whose most recent work is focused on lead poisoning, particularly as it comes from the paint on the gorgeous old houses of his uptown neighborhood.

New Orleans has long struggled to reshape its natural surroundings to make them livable, and the city, moreover, seems to adjudicate, even straddle, oppositions on an even greater scale than those that have focused the major investigative work of Kane, Fink, and Berry. As Ned Sublette suggests, when Royal Street in the French Quarter crosses Canal Street it becomes St. Charles Avenue, but far more changes than just the name. For Canal marks a kind of global caesura between two fundamentally distinct versions of reality, the divider between the cultural equivalent of two vast tectonic plates. Sublette suggests that what's above Canal Street – all the way to Hudson Bay in northernmost Canada – was originated and shaped by Anglo-Protestantism; and everything below Canal – all the way past Rio De Janeiro – by Catholicism. He notes that when Louisiana became a state, there were no Catholic churches in Boston, nor a single Protestant church in New Orleans.

As the neighborhoods upriver from Canal developed, they would do so with the significant imprint of the Protestants. But what's especially important, as Sublette notes, about the Catholicism that continued to dominate below Canal Street is that it is not solely the Catholicism of the French or Spanish. That is, it differs more dramatically from the Anglo-Protestantism above Canal in being shaped, in large part, by the Catholicism of the Kongo. Sublette explains that Kongo was Catholicized in 1491, before Columbus crossed the Atlantic; this European spiritual system, with its attendant rituals and symbols, fit more or less smoothly onto the Kongo cosmology to make a distinctive version, one that held onto the Kongo devotion to the spirits of the ancestors, whom one could venerate or even summon via the hand drum.[7]

In Anglo-Protestant America, the hand drum was prohibited. Downriver from Canal Street, it flourished, particularly, as we noted in

the last chapter, at Congo Square. Eventually, the traffic back and forth
across Canal led to the germination of new cultural forms. The most
obvious such new form, of course, was Jazz, which began to take shape
as uptown African Americans who were just two generations out from
plantation slavery brought their field-hollers, work chants, and the
ecstatic trances of sanctified Baptist spirituality into cultural dialogue
with the Catholic-Creole, conservatory-trained light opera of the world
below Canal.[8] The hybrid form, first taking shape on Sunday afternoons in Congo Square, became popular at the dance halls out Bayou
St. John in the latter decades of the nineteenth century, and then fully
exploded with the rise of Storyville at the turn of the century. After
Storyville was shut down in 1917, it migrated to Chicago, then New
York and, from there, seemingly, everywhere in the US and Europe, and
not necessarily stopping there.

But the tension between uptown and downtown endures. The Anglo-
Protestant world above Canal Street, often known in the nineteenth century as "the American Sector," developed in opposition to what had come
before. The French Quarter began as a fortified city itself, with gates
protected by armed guards at the foot of Esplanade, the foot of Canal,
and at the rear near Congo Square. The areas outside the fortifications
were called "faubourgs," from the Latin *foris* meaning "outside," a term
that today is loosely translated as "suburb."[9] When a fire in 1788 destroyed nearly 80 percent of the city's buildings, these faubourgs became
crucial to recovery and were well positioned for windfall profits. Just
upriver from the city, the Gravier family carved up their plantation into
smaller parcels, and thus was born Faubourg Ste. Marie, which Anglos
would call St. Mary and which today is known as the Central Business
District.[10] Other faubourgs soon followed – Faubourg Marigny in 1805,
Faubourg Tremé a few years later; but the most dramatic growth was
in an upriver direction, as, in the same moment, another four faubourgs
were added above Canal Street, named Duplantier, Saulet, La Course,
and Annunciation; and, in the decades that followed, in the same upriver
direction, there were added another *nine*.

The development of that first faubourg – St. Mary – began as a volatile flashpoint in national politics, as the Mississippi River's shiftiness
and overwhelming force made distinct boundaries a tricky business. As
Richard Campanella explains, because the river in the early decades
of the nineteenth century was gradually relocating its path toward
the west, a sizable beach, known then as a "batture," was expanding
between the natural levee and the water itself. The lucky landowners
of St. Mary were happy to watch their landholdings grow. Technically,

however, the beach was understood to be public land. The dispute over whether this expanding territory could be owned by private interests reached the desk of President Thomas Jefferson, who declared it should be open to public use and then sent federal marshals to evict the would-be owner. Litigation about the details would persist for decades, but an uneasy compromise was achieved by the 1820s, that included shoring up the natural levees to greater heights to protect against flood. Development in St. Mary could thereby boom, and it did, and continues to do so under its current name, the Central Business District.

As the population of the city swelled dramatically with more and more Americans in the first third of the nineteenth century, expanding in a predominantly upriver direction, another canal was dug, mostly by Irish immigrants. Called the New Basin Canal, it followed the path of today's I-10 Expressway from West End, through the cemeteries, past what is now the Superdome into the Central Business District. It soon eclipsed the old Carondelet Canal created a few decades earlier, as the turning basin of the latter became a relatively seedy backwater where, by the century's end, the world's oldest profession would be its primary business. The turning basin for the New Basin Canal, as Campanella notes, also gave rise to its own vice district, but that was hardly the only business being done there. On the upriver side of Canal, the spirit of commercial competition, innovation, and the need for constant upgrades would rule the area ever after, always consigning the older infrastructure to oblivion to make way for the new.[11] In the 1960s, for example, Poydras Street, which had been, as Campanella notes, a crowded, blue-collar cousin to glamorous Canal Street, underwent a bold makeover. Its decrepit nineteenth-century storefronts were razed and replaced with the gleaming towers of the oil industry that hoped to compete against Houston (Arthur Hailey's best-selling blockbuster of this same period, *Hotel*, is set in this same area and attuned to these same themes). In the aftermath of hosting the World's Fair in the 1980s, the nearby expanse of decaying warehouses was rebranded as the Warehouse District, home now to expensive art galleries and restaurants.[12] Ongoing development seems now to be a permanent feature of the area, as condominium towers continue to spring up and compete with each other with ever flashier amenities.

The faubourgs just upriver from what became the Central Business District were, for a while, a separate town named Lafayette City. This area was, first, a set of plantations where the enslaved worked indigo, rice, and sugar crops, but as the population in New Orleans soared in the first few decades after the Louisiana Purchase, pressure mounted to sell off those lands as a planned subdivision. As Campanella explains, Lafayette City's economy depended on the wharves up and down Tchoupitoulas Street, where livestock was delivered from upcountry. That economy grew hotter as the vast economic behemoth to the north came to capitalize more and more on the river in the steamboat era. Jobs were plentiful for Irish and German immigrants, both working the riverfront as well as among the variety of ambitious infrastructural projects – canals and railroads – a mile or two off the river toward the swampy rear of the city.

Between the bustling waterfront and the rapidly transforming but still flood-prone stretches to the rear, a significant expanse of prime real estate began to attract affluent Anglos. They were soon building their mansions on spacious lots, which, as Campanella explains, gave them more than enough room to pursue the fashionable hobby of ornamental horticulture. By the 1850s, the neighborhood at the center of the little town of Lafayette had picked up a nickname that stuck – "the Garden District."

The Garden District

A suburb of transplants, roughly 40 percent of the population of Lafayette City in 1850 had been born in Germany, 20 percent in Ireland, another 20 percent in the US but outside of Louisiana, and just under 10 percent had been born in France. Only 6 percent of the people in Lafayette City had been born in New Orleans. Among people of color, the enslaved outnumbered the free by a ratio of 3:1, the exact opposite of the ratio in the downtown Creole neighborhoods of that period.[13] In this sense, the world upriver from the Quarter resembled, in its racial logic, the antebellum, Anglo-Protestant South more closely than it did its downriver, Creole-Catholic counterpart.

Lafayette City was annexed by New Orleans in 1852, but the evolving power dynamics in the decades that followed suggests that the opposite happened: Lafayette City, in giving up only its name and accepting the hardly unflattering nickname for its opulent heart, annexed New Orleans. The annexation ended what had been a fifteen-year experiment in running the metropolitan area as three separate cities, two being governed by Francophone, downtown Creoles and, above Canal Street, one run by Anglophone Americans, each with its own police force, school system, newspapers, and so on.[14] The division of the two Creole municipalities paved the way for the American one to conquer them. The dissolution of these three autonomous entities into one was a turning point in the Americanization of New Orleans, as the newly surging power and wealth concentrated above Canal Street increasingly set the direction of the city's future.[15]

Symbolic of this moment in the history of uptown New Orleans, a tycoon who had made a staggering fortune by creating banks, railroads, and private utilities bought up the entire block that begins at 1200 Washington Avenue and built there in the early 1850s a colossal palazzo modeled upon those seen in paintings of the Italian countryside, replete with terraced gardens, galleries and verandas, marble steps and ornate iron railings, and spacious expanses inside for the display of his considerable art collection.[16] Only a few years after he completed it, he sold it; when the new owner passed away, a women's college moved in. This school, created by Josephine Louise Newcomb under the auspices of Tulane University to honor the memory of her daughter Sophie, had outgrown its original campus around what would become Lee Circle (and, in 2021, Égalité Circle). By educating thousands of young ladies on Washington Avenue, it became an anchor of the high society of the surrounding area. Twenty years later, Newcomb moved again, this time onto the campus it shares today with what had been its male counterpart, Tulane. The extraordinary building on Washington Avenue, after housing a Baptist seminary for a few decades, was demolished in the 1950s, about a century after it was built.[17] Nonetheless, in its time, it set the standard for the shock-and-awe architecture to which the Anglo elites of the St. Charles corridor would aspire, particularly in the Garden District.

By the end of the nineteenth century, as proud family lineages of Americans had taken root in the popular imagination and in the economy, conditions were ripe for a literature that would focus on them. This tradition probably begins when George Cable, as noted in the first chapter, sparked the ire of many by writing about the city's financial elites in unflattering ways. Cable lived at 1313 Eighth Street in the Garden District, where he wrote *The Grandissimes* and other works, but only for ten years, as the pushback against him drove him to live in New England. Cable's principal target had been Creoles in the French Quarter, but a key detractor was an uptown Anglo named Grace King, who lived around the corner from Cable at 1749 Coliseum Street, where she hosted for decades an influential weekly salon.

Beginning with her criticism of Cable, King became a prolific writer of fiction and history, though some of her detractors feel that her historical studies have a fictive quality: for example, her history of the city called *New Orleans: The Place and the People* makes almost no reference to slavery. A proud defender of the romance of antebellum Louisiana, King is sometimes credited with having feminized the subject of local history by framing it in terms of familial bloodlines, as in one of her last works, *Creole Families of New Orleans.* And though a master prose stylist, her ethos would seem an almost deliberate provocation to writers motivated by social justice, as when she compares New Orleans to the court ladies of Revolutionary France, who stepped toward the guillotine with "a firmness and composure that unnerved their executioners … for they at least knew the qualities of their defects."[18]

Nonetheless, King deserves credit for helping to spark a tradition of writers associated with uptown New Orleans whose scholarly engagement with the city's history and architecture has been an essential arm of the preservationist movement: Samuel Wilson, Jr., Richard Koch, Mary Louise Christovich, Roulhac Toledano, Sally Kittredge Evans Reeves, John Reeves, Robert Cangelosi, and others. King framed her devotion to the city's history as something like a spiritual calling. This tradition has reached extraordinary heights in the work of Rich Campanella, whose dozen or so books and countless articles have made him the leading public intellectual on the subject of New Orleans in this era.

At the same time that Grace King was at the height of her stature, F. Scott Fitzgerald, then a young and as yet unknown novelist, moved into a boardinghouse less than a mile away at 2900 Prytania Street, across from the Lafayette Cemetery and two blocks from the palazzo that filled the 1200 block of Washington. He stayed for only a month, working on the page proofs to his debut novel, *This Side of Paradise.* He seemed not to like the area much, and left town twice during his short stay to visit Zelda Sayre in Montgomery, Alabama. In April of that year, they married and, only a few months later, as his debut novel became an instant blockbuster, he was hailed as the voice of a generation. Today, a hundred years on, his name is now synonymous with the contemplation of the nuances of class and the excesses of wealth in the US.

Though Fitzgerald never wrote about New Orleans, another major figure – Tennessee Williams – chose to confront the Garden District explicitly and directly in what is perhaps his most horrifying play, *Suddenly Last Summer* (1958). The opening stage directions set the play in the steaming courtyard of a Garden District mansion in the 1930s, where someone has created and curated a surreal and spooky sort of jungle, where "Massive tree-flowers … suggest organs of a body ripped out, still glistening with undried blood." Williams adds, anticipating the *Jurassic Park* movies, that this garden calls to mind the "giant fern-forests" of the prehistoric age, for it is full of "harsh cries and sibilant hissings and thrashing sounds" as if the place were "inhabited by beasts, serpents, and birds, all of a savage nature."[19] We soon learn that a young man – a poet, recently dead, named Sebastian – was the garden's creator, as his elderly mother breathlessly explains to the handsome young doctor who is visiting to see about her willingness to endow his new lobotomy clinic. The elderly woman has a niece, a young woman living at a mental hospital since her cousin (the older woman's son, who created the exotic courtyard garden) died. When the young woman arrives, she is accompanied by a nurse from the hospital, as well as by her own mother and brother. This family – the sister of the elderly woman's deceased husband and that woman's son and incarcerated daughter – is poised to inherit a considerable fortune, just as the young doctor is poised to have his clinic endowed. But there's a catch: the old woman has let them all know that the niece must cease her ghoulish "babbling" about how Sebastian's life ended, even if that means – as it must – lobotomizing her. Another twist: her family must consent to the procedure, and the handsome young doctor must perform it. Otherwise, no money for any of them. The niece, however, stands her ground, and tells the story of how Sebastian took her travelling in Europe, where he would use her to attract teenaged boys, whom he would then exploit sexually – until finally a small mob of them organized, chased Sebastian down, killed him, and, in macabre parody of the oral sex he had likely coerced from them, ate him.

The play is structured and paced to a pitch of horrific perfection, from the slow opening in which we get to know the mother and the fictive vision she seeks to sustain about her prized son to the agonizing climax when, after her niece tells her story, the elderly woman screams "Cut this hideous story out of her brain." What is of paramount importance to the mother is upholding not simply the lie about her son's effete, hyper-spiritual aestheticism and ascetism, but, more to the point, her status in Garden District society.

Three years later, a similar, but more subtly drawn mother appears in Shirley Anne Grau's early novel of the same neighborhood, *The House on Coliseum Street* (1961). The central character of the novel is a sad young woman who has lived her entire life in a house in the Garden District, where her mother and half-sister have kept her from knowing and enjoying her full potential and worth. She has a fling with a Tulane professor, gets pregnant, and then, as per her mother's icy intervention, gets spirited out of town to have an abortion. In the aftermath of the abortion, she is plunged into a yet more excruciating loneliness and sense of her own worthlessness, hovering, it would seem, on the margins of oblivion.

Grau's debut collection a half-decade earlier had been nominated for the National Book Award, and the novel she wrote immediately after *The House on Coliseum Street*, set in Alabama, where she grew up, called *The Keepers of the House*, won the Pulitzer Prize. Though she would publish a half-dozen novels and some collections of short stories, none of them conjure the mid twentieth-century Garden District with greater resonance, delineating the ways privilege can be seamlessly intertwined with imprisonment and high social status with its opposite, so much so as to collapse the illusions that structure life in that place. Grau's achievement is considerable.

In the generation that came after hers, another writer – Ellen Gilchrest – has sought to mine the same territory, painting the uptown elites, however, in less subtle colors and harkening back, to a degree, to the Tennessee Williams of *Suddenly Last Summer*. Gilchrest made an abrupt and splashy arrival on the national literary scene in 1981 with her first collection of short stories, *In the Land of Dreamy Dreams*, a phrase culled from the Jazz standard, "Basin Street Blues." She followed this set of stories, most of them set in uptown New Orleans, with a novel about a woman who decides to leave her husband, a rich New Orleans lawyer, to immerse herself in the musical and academic-literary bohemia of Arkansas. Though that novel didn't do well, she then published another collection of short stories, some of which revisit the same characters from the first collection, called *Victory over Japan* (1984), which won the National Book Award. Since then, her work has been uneven, if bountiful: eight novels, and no fewer than ten collections of short stories, characterized by an infectious voice, but with characters that, as some have complained, can sometimes seem to blur together, a great many of them being highly privileged, white women of the urban South who take pleasure and pride in being demanding, if not altogether spoiled.

The first line of the first story in her first book signals the terrain she engages throughout her career: the story is called "Rich," and it begins, "Tom and Letty Wilson were rich in everything." This young couple, we soon learn, is rich in friends, houses, and a sense of belonging in their Garden District community. But in the end, the husband, unable to sustain this mythic perfection, succumbs to a sort of madness and unleashes a horrific bloodbath. Afterward, the family's neighbors believed "[I]t was some kind of mistake or accident."[20] Tom, however, is an unambiguous monster, and perhaps part of what drives him to this blood-splattered madness is the fact that he's surrounded by people whose minds are entirely organized around the denial of any such possibility, so committed are they to fostering their shared belief that they are fully deserving of all that they have.

The strains of Southern Gothic in this story are updated in ways appropriate to their setting in the 1980s, but another novelist – Sheila Bosworth – who engaged the same part of New Orleans in her debut novel harkens back yet more boldly to the lurid tones of *Suddenly Last Summer* and, as others have noted, to the Gothicism in Flannery O'Connor, Truman Capote, and Carson McCullers. Bosworth's first novel – *Almost Innocent* – appeared in 1984, the same year as Gilchrest's National Book Award winner. Like Grau's *House on Coliseum Street*, Bosworth's first novel is a woman's coming-of-age story; the main character has grown up on a more hardscrabble block of Camp Street, and is particularly focused on figuring out her mother, who came from a wealthy family but fell in love with and married a bohemian artist when she was quite young. The artist has a wealthy, but sinister-seeming younger brother whom the narrator knows as Uncle Baby, and who pays for her to go to an elite boarding school. The revelation that finally allows her to make some sense of the household wherein she grows up comes when she uncovers a secret about the relationships between the adults in her life – something that signals scandalous decadence and corruption. Bosworth's second and final novel – *Slow Poison* – appeared eight years later and is focused, with comic elements, on a wealthy, if star-crossed and decadent, family that lives across the lake from New Orleans. More recently, this sense of doom hovering over certain houses in the Garden District has been turned to yet more fully humorous ends in Julie Reed's Katrina-memoir, *The House on First Street*. Only in the Garden District does the money and sense of insularity run deep enough to cast Hurricane Katrina in comic terms.

A few writers of nonfiction who were raised along St. Charles Avenue within the orbit of the Garden District have produced important work more or less directly focused upon dynastic wealth. For example, Tom Sancton's investigative best seller *The Death of a Princess* (about the fatal automobile crash in Paris that killed Princess Diana, written with Scott

MacLeod) was recently reissued in a twentieth-anniversary edition; his memoir *Song for My Fathers* contemplates his relationship with his well-known father (a journalist who published widely on the Civil Rights struggle, as well as two novels set in Louisiana) while foregrounding Sancton's other, musical lineage among the royalty of traditional Jazz at Preservation Hall. And Nicholas Lemann, who was, for ten years, the dean of the School of Journalism at Columbia University and has been for four decades a contributor to leading national publications, has written books about the idea of a meritocracy in the US and also about the death of the American Dream. His history of the twilight of Reconstruction, titled *Redemption*, is particularly strong in explaining what happened in Louisiana in that era. Finally Michael Lewis's career took off in the late 1980s, when, as a young man, he walked away from his job at a Wall Street investment bank and wrote about his experiences there in the vertiginous aftermath of federal deregulation. The book – *Liar's Poker: Rising through the Wreckage of Wall Street* – went to the top of *The New York Times* best-seller list; since then, he has written nearly twenty popular nonfiction books, roughly half of them about economics and finance.

Setting aside the motif of outright dishonesty, the realm of fantasy – particularly fantasy about decadent sensuality – has been especially fruitful territory for writers interested in the Garden District, particularly those inclined to the spooky, Gothic atmospheres noted earlier in connection with Bosworth, Gilchrest, and Williams. In the horror genre, Poppy Z. Brite (also known as Billy Martin), a native of Kentucky, had some success in the 1990s with a series of horror novels that often feature gay male characters, and P. Curran's collection of short stories, *Stay out of New Orleans*, appeared in that same, pre-Katrina period to showcase the gritty side of a city sodden with disturbing paranormal forces.

Much subtler – and explicitly focused on the Garden District – is Truman Capote's essay "Dazzle" in *Music for Chameleons*, about his childhood fascination with an Irish-American laundress called Mrs. Ferguson, who worked in the Garden District. She was said to have supernatural powers – specifically, the power to make one's deepest wishes come true. Mrs. Ferguson had been publicly flogged at 15 by her own father in the small town in Texas where she grew up for having had a child by a Black man, after which she ran away to New Orleans with her son and became a domestic servant to a Catholic priest, who also sired a child with her. She then went through a succession of lovers, marrying none of them, but having four more children. That first son – Skeeter – would die in the electric chair at Texas State Prison for a murder he committed in Houston, but the main focus of Capote's story is how Skeeter persuaded an 8-year-old Capote to steal a piece of his grandmother's jewelry to bring to Mrs. Ferguson, who used it to hypnotize him. Capote did it and was tormented by guilt, but his dreams of living his life among movie stars did come true.

Later in this same collection of essays – which, incidentally, Capote dedicated to his close friend, Tennessee Williams, and which was the last work Capote published – he contemplates a New Orleans woman whose "house was famous for an exotic refreshment it offered – fresh cherries boiled in cream sweetened with absinthe and served stuffed inside the vagina of a reclining quadroon beauty."[21] This memory could well belong to the fictional world of Dean Paschal, whose debut collection of short stories, *By the Light of the Jukebox*, Joyce Carol Oates called the "most disturbing first collection of American short stories … published in recent decades." In the story "Python," for example, the narrator reminisces about her years in a sexually adventurous secret society in the Garden District. She is now in a cage in the zoo, for she has been reincarnated as a snake, perhaps for having offered her young son to the leader of the coven of sexual decadents to which she belongs. Another of Paschal's stories, called "Sautéing the Platygast," subtly implies that a strange professor, living on the edge of a swamp that reads as an enchanted garden of monsters, is fattening up his children in preparation for cooking and eating them, though the yet subtler implication is that this family may not be quite human at all but some creepy, human-reptile hybrid. In Paschal's "L'Annonciation," the narrator ruminates on the devotion and repulsion he feels toward a promiscuous woman who collects penises the way others collect pets. She has made millions in the stock market, but dismisses that part of her life as "all fakery." Their relationship is complex, to say the least, centered in alternating sado-masochistic roles with overtones of occult ritual, voyeurism, polyamory, and varieties of mutual – and very real – abuse. In the end, after installing a makeshift trapeze in her bedroom, the narrator thinks of killing her, placing, that is, "a series of shots, evenly spaced, along her cranium, like a halo." Paschal's work belongs to the tradition that runs through Kafka back to Poe, and, in his proclivity for cold scientific language (he studied zoology as an undergraduate, then worked for decades as an emergency room physician in New Orleans) and to iron-clad philosophic axioms, he would seem the contemporary

New Orleans descendant of the Marquis de Sade. However, like Brite and Curran and the scores of others who write spooky stories in New Orleans, his work belongs, to a degree, to the literary world that is ruled by another writer who is associated with the Garden District, Anne Rice.

She was born in 1941 in the nearby Irish Channel on Annunciation Street at Mercy Hospital. She was given the name Howard Allen Frances O'Brien but declared, in the first grade, that she would be called Anne. Her father, who had grown up in the Irish Channel, spent six years in the seminary, then joined the Merchant Marine for a time, but spent most of his life working at the post office near their home. Her mother's family, from the same neighborhood, had a history of alcohol troubles, as her grandfather on that side had been barred from the house by her grandmother for his drinking and died of complications from alcoholism at the age of 48. Anne's mother would follow suit – drinking and reading in bed all night, year after year, until, when Anne was 14, her drinking finally killed her. Rice's mother had been raising her family in a townhouse that was owned by a wealthy and generous friend at 2301 St. Charles Avenue, where her mother had been raised too, but, at a certain stage in her alcoholic disintegration, the family moved a block farther upriver to 2524 St. Charles to be closer to the church they hoped would somehow help them.[22] After her mother's death, Anne went to a medieval-looking boarding school then called St. Joseph's Academy on Ursulines Street in Tremé, and then moved to Dallas where her father had landed a better job. In Dallas, she met a man named Stan Rice, and the two were soon married and living in San Francisco on Ashbury Street, near the corner of Haight. The year was 1960, and Anne Rice was 19.

She and her husband both graduated from San Francisco State University four years later. Her husband developed quickly a reputation as a poet of the first rank. In 1969, they began to spend time at a 100-year-old cabin in Big Sur as guests of the good friend who owned it, and Anne committed herself to a block of uninterrupted writing there every evening from 8:00 to 10:00 pm. On one of those evenings, she wrote a thirty-page short story about a vampire whose dandyism and cynicism called to mind Oscar Wilde. She didn't finish it. Meanwhile, she had given birth to a baby girl named Michelle, who developed, at age 5, a terminal blood disorder and soon died. The loss sent both Anne and her husband reeling into a booze-sodden tailspin, but, as she began to pull through it, she showed her unfinished vampire story from a few years earlier to a friend, who suggested that it be expanded.[23] As she worked through her grief, Anne devoted herself to the story all night, every night, for five weeks, gave it the title *Interview with the Vampire*, and handed it to her husband to read. After finishing it, his first words were "Our lives have changed."[24] The book's success would lead her to write some 35 books over the next 40 years, her body of work eventually selling an estimated 150 million copies.

Anne Rice's novels are often shaped in part as genealogy, tracing generations of vampire families across continents and centuries, but with contemporary New Orleans figuring prominently in much of the work. Some suggest that Rice's fixation on family lineages is parodic of dysfunctional modern families, the motif of incest in particular suggestive of the stereotypical elites' leeriness toward outsiders and racist obsession with the purity of their own bloodlines. Others suggest that what's most important in her work is her drawing to the fore the homoerotic elements that had long been latent in the tradition of vampire lore. Her vampires, in short, are often in relationships that echo patterns in queer culture, and she did so at a time – the 1970s and 80s – when an openly queer identity was associated with the courage of political pioneers.[25] Rice had long been interested in gay culture, because she thought that gay men, in particular, managed to retain all of the beauty of masculinity with none of its toxic qualities, and their interactions, being interactions of perfect equals, were thus the supreme erotic ideal.[26]

But the homoerotic dimensions of her vampires are not their only characteristic, for when the main character in *Interview*, for example, first becomes a vampire, he undergoes a profound transformation in his capacity for sensory perception, which Rice adapted from her keen interest in Carlos Casteneda's then enormously popular books of peyote mysticism.[27] Rice is also interested in history and mythology, for she followed *Interview* with two historical novels, one about free people of color in 1840s New Orleans, the other about castrated opera singers in Italy, neither of which garnered much attention. She then wrote a trilogy of sadomasochistic erotica based on the Sleeping

> **Real Vampires** In New Orleans today, there are at least fifty individuals who believe they have a medical condition that requires them to drink fresh blood. They have formed a support network, according to a 2015 *Washington Post* article, called the New Orleans Vampire Association. Estimates suggest another 5,000 such people around the country. Some wear prosthetic fangs and Gothic attire, but many, perhaps in a bid for yet greater authenticity, disavow what they see as the sensationalist stereotypes of Rice and her imitators. A number of academic studies have been published about today's real vampires by John Edgar Browning, Joseph Laycock, DJ Williams, and John Morehead.

Beauty fairy-tale, and an erotic fantasy novel about an island in the Caribbean where the very rich could go to recreate the considerable sexual privilege of plantation slave-owners. But like the two historical novels, these also failed to garner a significant mainstream audience. Meanwhile, however, the readership for *Interview* had come to seem an endlessly expanding cult. She then wrote the first of several sequels to *Interview*, a novel called *The Vampire Lestat*, which *The New York Times* called "brilliant" and leaped up the best-seller list. A few years later, however, another sequel, *Queen of the Damned*, outpaced *Lestat*'s considerable sales by a ratio of 4:1.[28] From there, she accepted a massive advance on what would be the next novel in the series, *The Witching Hour*, and used it to buy a mansion in the Garden District, where she would write – and set – that novel, and which would have a significant autobiographical dimension.

By the early 1990s, living in New Orleans for the first time in thirty years, Rice was soon wealthy enough to become a collector of Garden District mansions, owning at one time or another at least a half-dozen of them. She would live in the neighborhood for about fifteen years. The house at the downriver, riverside corner of First and Chestnut is the one most associated with her, and serves as the setting for the *Mayfair Witches* series. These works, which intersect her vampire novels, are about generations of a family of witches.

A grinning Anne Rice stages her own Jazz funeral to deliver her to a book signing in New Orleans in the early 1990s. Photo by Elliott Kamenitz, courtesy of Capital City Press.

Rice's influence on mass culture is hard to overstate. Beginning in the 1970s, as the popular imagination began to hunger for new myths, she delivered. The publication of her first novel was, by any definition, an event in the industry of mass-market fiction and an intervention in the centuries-long tradition of vampire lore.[29] Following her lead, other members of her family have had success in the same industry: her older sister, Alice Borchardt, has published a series of werewolf novels, and her son, Christopher, who spent his first ten years in the Castro section of San Francisco during the AIDS epidemic, has become a best-selling author of gay romances and thrillers, with more than a dozen titles to his credit. The Rice family today lives in very different financial circumstances from when Anne was born in the Irish Channel.

The Irish Channel
Between the Garden District and the Mississippi River lies the Irish Channel. The story of the Irish in New Orleans is well told in Laura D. Kelley's comprehensive book of that name, wherein she notes that the precise boundaries of the Irish Channel have long been debated, as have the particular dates that it came into existence. She explains that the National Register of Historic Places situates the Irish Channel between Jackson Avenue and Aline, and between Magazine Street and Tchoupitoulas, but that the Irish of nineteenth-century New Orleans would have insisted that the heart of this ethnic enclave was actually outside of this area, between Jackson and Felicity, with St. Alphonsus Church at 2029 Constance Street being its focal point.[30] In another twist, the City Planning Commission locates the upriver boundary of the Irish Channel all the way up to Napoleon Avenue. Whatever its precise origins and parameters, this close-knit community of large families began, by the 1930s, to disperse, roughly a century after it first began to take shape, as a significant influx of African Americans from the rural South began to compete for low-paying waterfront jobs, and the Irish Americans who preceded them ascended to better positions in the local workforce.

Well within the City Planning Commission's idea of the Irish Channel is the home on Constantinople Street of one Ignatius Reilly. He first lived only in the imagination of his creator, John Kennedy Toole; now, of course, he lives in the imagination of readers everywhere, especially in the Spanish-speaking world, who love Toole's novel, *A Confederacy of Dunces*.[31] So iconic has Toole's creation become that a statue of Ignatius stands on Canal Street, in front of the old D. H. Holmes Department Store, where, in the opening lines of the novel, he waits for his mother.

In the sentences that follow, Ignatius falls into an altercation with a police officer, and, no sooner than he and his mother flee around the corner into the French Quarter, she accidentally rams her car into one of the iron-lace columns that hold up a gallery, which comes crashing down. Faced now with a huge expense, poor Ignatius must find a job — and thus the action of the novel gets underway.

The statue of Ignatius is on the downriver, Catholic side of Canal Street, facing uptown, as if Ignatius, from within his medieval Catholic world-view, is aiming his haughty opprobrium at the modern, materialist, American side of his hometown, where he lives with his mother. Like Ignatius, Toole grew up uptown, but his family's roots are downtown. Both his father and his mother grew up on Elysian Fields, only a block apart, very near the apartment where Stanley, Stella, and Blanche live in *Streetcar*. They were married at St. Peter and Paul Church, a block off Elysian Fields on Burgundy, which is where Toole's funeral would be held in the spring of 1969, the day after he took his life at the age of 31.[32]

Toole's mother was a strong woman, and quite controlling. When someone approached her toward the end of her life to discuss working on a biography of her son, she replied, "You would have to live in my house for several months, perhaps a year, perhaps more" and only after that interval of sifting many boxes of memorabilia and ephemera could the collaboration with her begin. Perhaps worried that the would-be biographer might agree to these terms, she reconsidered, before he could reply, and withdrew the offer.[33] One of her ancestors was a French Creole who had been an associate of the legendary pirate Jean Lafitte, and, like her husband, she had several ancestors among the Irish who came to New Orleans in the nineteenth century.[34] She was married for ten years before her only son was born, whom she would call "Kenny" and raise at 1128 Webster Street, near Loyola University and Tulane University. She surely chose the location based on its proximity to these schools, for she was grooming her son to take a place in the city's high-culture circles, far above her own hardscrabble upbringing. The proximity to Loyola might have inspired Toole in *Dunces* to name the protagonist Ignatius (though Toole had also been devoted to George Herriman's *Krazy Kat* cartoons as a kid, which featured a character named Ignatz, the German form of Ignatius).[35]

During his boyhood, Toole's mother created and ran a youth theater group, working tirelessly to bring off productions that often featured her only child in the starring role. She believed her little Kenny to be a

A typical cartoon John Kennedy Toole created for Tulane's student newspaper, *The Tulane Hullabaloo*. Courtesy of *The Tulane Hullabaloo*.

I TOLD YOU NOT TO SLAM THAT DOOR!

genius, and he was soon skipping grades in elementary school, enrolling on a full scholarship at Tulane at 16 in 1954.[36] He loved to contribute satirical cartoons to the student newspaper, *The Tulane Hullabaloo*, and other artwork to the campus literary magazine, *Carnival*, where he eventually became an editor. So promising was Toole that the faculty in the English Department allowed him to take graduate seminars before he graduated, a rare arrangement.[37] As an undergraduate, he lived at home with his parents in a second-floor apartment at 390 Audubon Street, just across Audubon Park from the house on Webster Street where he spent his childhood, and a short walk from the English Department at Tulane.

After finishing at Tulane, Toole was probably excited to get out of the cramped apartment he shared with his parents, for his father's mental health had begun to falter and give way to increasing paranoia and depression. Toole soon moved to New York City to get a master's degree at Columbia University. He then spent a year teaching at Southwestern Louisiana Institute (now UL-Lafayette) from 1959 to 1960, where he shared an office with Bobby Byrne, a former Tulane doctoral student in English, who became the model for Ignatius. Like Ignatius, a scholar of medieval thought with a large mustache, Byrne loved to practice his harp, read Boethius, and eat hot dogs; he was fond of saying that certain people had "their theology and geometry all wrong"; he lived his life firm in the conviction that humanity had peaked several centuries ago and that, since then, nothing of much consequence could possibly happen. He was legendary too for his ill-timed and prodigious flatulence.[38]

Toole returned to Columbia after only a year, surely carrying uproarious memories of his office mate, but soon decided against pursuing the Ph.D. and was drafted. He rose to the rank of sergeant and was stationed in Puerto Rico when, in the autumn of 1963, he wrote *A Confederacy of Dunces* in just a few months. He later said, "The [writing of the] book went along [well] until President Kennedy's assassination. Then I couldn't write anything more. Nothing seemed funny to me."[39] No longer able to continue tinkering with the manuscript, he decided at the dawn of 1964 to start looking for a publisher and was soon getting a close look from high-powered New York editors, all of whom ultimately decided against it. By the end of that year, Toole had returned to New Orleans and was teaching at Dominican (now the campus of Loyola's law school on St. Charles). Moving back in with his parents, at a small apartment in the duplex at 7632 Hampson, he seemed, according to those who knew him, a deflated person.[40] He made some attempts to revise his novel, but soon gave up and stashed the manuscript in a box. He then re-enrolled at Tulane to work toward a doctorate in English. It was then that he began to lose his mind.[41]

By 1968, friends, colleagues, and students were noting that he was becoming a very different person. Just as his father had, Toole suddenly seemed depressed, anxious, and paranoid, and then steadily more so. Some faculty in the English Department at Tulane recommended to their chair that he be required to undergo a psychiatric evaluation, for he had declared publicly that some of them were plotting against him. On January 19, 1969, he abruptly resigned from his teaching post at Dominican, withdrew from the doctoral program at Tulane, left his parents with no means of support – and vanished. He apparently drove around the country for a few months, ultimately going as far as California to tour the castle of William Randolph Hearst. During this time, there's no record of his having any contact with anyone who knew him. In the spring, he headed back in the direction of New Orleans, but never came all the way home. At the end of March, in some woods outside Biloxi, he put one end of a garden hose in his car's exhaust pipe and put the other end at the top of the rolled-up driver's side window. He left a note for his parents, which his mother would destroy.[42] He died having no inkling of how famous he would be.

Toole's father died a few years later; alone in the Hampson Street apartment, his mother found, a few months later, the manuscript of *Dunces* in a cedar box and started mailing this sole existing version to publishers. Over the next few years, she would send it to eight of them, all of whom would reject it.[43] Finally, she took it to Walker Percy in his office at Loyola, who, in turn, asked his wife to have a look at it. She read it, and told him he should read it too; he liked it, and shared it with some friends, some of whom liked it, while others shook their head against it. He then passed it along to LSU Press, who published it to very positive reviews. The following year – 1981, some dozen years after its author's suicide – it won the Pulitzer. Toole's mother died a few years later at her home on Elysian Fields, in the same neighborhood where she had grown up. She was surely very pleased to have made her dream of her son's genius come true in the eyes of the world.

Those who love the novel probably experience it as a satirical cartoon of the sort Toole created for *The Tulane Hullabaloo* in his late teens. Others point out that it should be understood according to the early literary form of the picaresque, because it takes a central figure through a series of social situations that allow a portrait of a society to emerge, a portrait loaded with moral instruction and sociological observation.[44] Others add that it is also built around the form of the pilgrimage and the heroic quest, or that it follows the logic of chivalric romance and allegory, that it can be read as an updating of *Don Quixote*, as Ignatius's mystical devotion forever butts heads with the practical demands of contemporary society. Still others point out the novel seeks to situate itself in partial dialogue with works by Henry David Thoreau, Mark Twain, or Walker Percy.

Whatever its precedents and purposes, most discussions of *Dunces* begin, however, by glossing the point that, though wildly popular, the book, for many, is unreadable – silly, sophomoric, crude, bigoted, plotless, meandering, and brimming with clunky prose and even worse dialogue. Of course, to turn up one's nose at it is to adopt the signature attitude of the grotesque anti-hero at its center, who finds that modern life itself is beneath his dignity. In short, in the act of snapping the book shut and pushing it aside, the eye-rolling, dismissive readers can't help but glimpse in it a mirror-image of themselves. As recently as January of 2021, the controversy over the merits of *Dunces* was still alive and well – and featured in *The New Yorker*, where Tom Bissell opined that while Ignatius had seemed too strange in the mid 1960s when Toole was struggling to publish his novel, and had come to seem, to a vast audience in the 1980s, a lovable, clownish counterweight to the bur-geoning yuppie phenomenon, we must recognize today that Ignatius is a precursor and archetype of the internet troll. No longer harmless and hilarious, he thinks the problems of the modern world will simply go away if we could just install some form of medieval theocracy. One can readily see him lumbering up the Capitol steps on that fateful January 6, the day after Bissell's article appeared, a flabby and flatulent history buff who lives with his mother, hoisting a placard that says "Death to the Infidels" – and not joking at all.[45]

The Irish Channel was also home to a figure who constitutes the ulti-mate contrast to Ignatius, a real-life figure who lived there around the same time that *Dunces* burst on the international scene and whose idealism and choice to inhabit a medieval social order has had very real political consequences in the world – Sister Helen Prejean. Raised on the outskirts of Baton Rouge as the daughter of a successful attorney, Prejean joined the Sisters of Saint Joseph in the late 1950s; after becom-ing a nun, she taught at Cabrini, then a junior high, on Esplanade Avenue, from 1962 to 1964. She began keeping a journal there, inspired to do so by the oratory of President Kennedy. She took her writ-ing more seriously in 1966, when she moved to Ontario for a year to continue her education. In the years that followed, she would learn, through various opportunities to continue her training, the ideas asso-ciated with liberation theology and the ways the Church was grow-ing more interested in social justice. By 1981, she began working at Hope House, a Catholic service ministry next to the St. Thomas Public Housing Project, in the Irish Channel, in what had by then become one of the poorest and most crime-ridden parts of New Orleans. Here, she came to know Civil Rights activists and lawyers and educators who were focused on the problems faced by those who lived there. Upon taking up her residence at Hope House, she befriended her next-door neighbor, who, two weeks later, was shot to death.[46] In the months that followed, together with Bill Quigley, Sister Barbara Breaud, and Jim Hodge, she founded a newspaper called *Flambeau: A Catholic Voice for Justice*.

Perhaps because of her interest in writing, a priest approached her in January of 1982 to tell her of a man who was on death row at the Angola Penitentiary and who wanted a pen pal. She began to correspond with him. The writing that went back and forth between her and the con-demned man continued for two years. The correspondence changed her life, for it led her to accompany him to his execution.

During her correspondence with the condemned man, she had come to see human institutions – governments, courts, prisons – as imperfect, and thus not as a credible authority on the question of whether someone should be put to death. After the execution, she knew ever after that God had called her to witness this horror and to devote her life to ending this practice. When she first arrived at the penitentiary to walk her pen pal into the death chamber and witness his killing, she passed out. Afterward, as she was leaving, she began to vomit.[47] As she talked about her experience with friends, she warmed to their suggestion that she write a book about it. She began by writing an essay for a magazine called *Saint Anthony Messenger* about her experience of praying alongside the family of the victim of her pen pal. She had been friends with Bill McKibben, who was becoming a well-known writer about environmental issues, and he showed the article to his agent.[48]

Thus began her book, which she would call *Dead Man Walking: An Eyewitness Account of the Death Penalty in the United States*, the title borrowed from the phrase prison guards call out as they escort a man to his execution.[49] By 1993, a little more than a decade after her correspondence with the condemned man began, the book was published and hailed as a milestone that would transform the conversation on the death penalty.[50] Its most famous observation hinges on the Christian theme of forgiveness: "People are more than the worst thing they have ever done." The book reached the top position in *The New York Times* best-seller list and stayed there for thirty-one weeks. It was nominated for a Pulitzer, and when it was turned into a movie, it won four Oscars. A decade later, she published *The Death of Innocents: An Eyewitness Account of Wrongful Executions*, and then a memoir *River of Fire: On Becoming an Activist* (2020), which tells the story of her life up to *Dead Man Walking*. Since that first execution, she has accompanied a half-dozen people as they walked into the death chamber to be killed. She has come to be known at Angola as Death Row's Nun.

The University District
The expansion of the city in an upriver direction didn't end in the mid nineteenth century with the Garden District and the Irish Channel. It kept going in the same direction, all the way to the uppermost end of St. Charles Avenue. That neighborhood was originally settled as the Macarty Plantation, but, anticipating the area becoming a hub of rail and canal infrastructure for the expanding population, the family sold it in the 1830s. The new town was named Carrollton, after a Kaintuck militia leader whose troops camped there during the War of 1812.[51]

Some three decades after Carrollton was founded, in the immediate aftermath of the Civil War, the police of the little town fell into conflict with those of New Orleans, who had jurisdiction of the entire area, but were racially integrated and thus an affront to Carrolltonians. A similar conflict had turned violent in the neighboring community of Jefferson City, which sat between the Garden District and Carrollton, and so the governor of Louisiana eradicated Jefferson City, merging it with New Orleans in 1870.[52] This was a kind of warning shot to Carrollton, and in 1874 all agreed to bring the little town into New Orleans, where it became the uprivermost neighborhood of the city proper.

The following decade, the area between Carrollton and the former Jefferson City now known as Audubon Park hosted the World's Fair and Cotton Exposition of 1884–85, and, after the event, the campuses of both Loyola University and Tulane University were relocated to that same stretch of land in 1889 and 1894 respectively. They were following the lead of Leland University at what is now Newcomb Boulevard. Leland's charter declared that it was a co-educational institution that aimed to serve students "irrespective of race, color, or previous condition of servitude" – meaning it would educate the formerly enslaved.[53] Leland had an uneasy relationship with its all-white neighbor, Tulane, and so when Leland's campus was badly damaged in the major hurricane in 1915, the university's administrators decided to sell it and move the school just north of Baton Rouge.[54] Tulane and Loyola stayed, and the area is now known as the University District. What's just upriver from the University District is still sometimes called Carrollton, and often Riverbend, but given how much of the writing of this part of town, and that of the old Jefferson City too, is connected to Tulane and Loyola, it can all be discussed together in terms of the University District, as a set of literary family lineages, beginning with two quite different figures, Margaret Walker and James Feibleman.

Walker was born in Birmingham in 1915 to a mother and father who were both prominent Black intellectuals. When she was around 10 years old, her parents accepted professorships at New Orleans University at 5318 St. Charles at the corner of Jefferson. This university was connected to an auxiliary preparatory school named Gilbert Academy, and so Walker's parents would thus be within walking distance not only of their own classrooms, but from the most elite school for children of African descent in the area. Margaret was enrolled, and, at her parents' urging, she began to fill notebooks with poetry as a daily practice, publishing some of it in the school newspaper.

NEW ORLEANS UNIVERSITY,

New Orleans University, seen here in 1888, operated on St. Charles Avenue near Jefferson Avenue from 1873 to 1934, when it merged with Straight University to form Dillard University. Wikimedia Commons – Public Domain.

By 1932, as a 17-year-old student at the university where her mother and father taught, she began to beg her parents to bring Langston Hughes, her hero, to campus for a poetry reading. University officials worried that no one would show up and that they couldn't afford Hughes's 100-dollar fee, so Margaret Walker, together with a small group, wrote some 800 personal letters to leaders in the community of color in New Orleans to encourage them to come. The event ended up drawing an extraordinary crowd. Over the course of the evening, Walker tried several times to approach Hughes to give him some of her poems, but she was too star-struck to speak. Her mother intervened, and the poems made their way into Hughes's hands, who read them and praised them. Walker's career had begun.

Months later, she left New Orleans for the Chicago area to become a student at Northwestern University, and from there she was hired by the Federal Writers Program and came to know many of the major literary figures in Chicago of that period, striking up an especially strong friendship with Richard Wright. In 1939, she enrolled in the Iowa Creative Writers' Workshop, and three years later became the first African-American poet to win the Yale Younger Poets Prize for her debut collection called *For My People*. During three decades of teaching at Jackson State in Mississippi, she worked for twenty years on what would become her masterpiece – the novel, *Jubilee*. Based on the life of her great-grandmother, who had been enslaved, the novel became an essential text of the Black Arts Movement. She happened to be out of town, in residency at the Iowa Creative Writers' Workshop in June of

1963, when her friend and neighbor, Medgar Evers, was murdered in his driveway by white supremacists. A handful of years later, she would be a key advisor to the student group at Jackson State that, on May 15, 1970, lost two of its members to murderous police. In the years that followed, she created an institute at Jackson State for collecting, interpreting, and disseminating African-American culture, which, after her death, was renamed the Margaret Walker Center.

A contemporary of Walker, James K. Feibleman, chaired the Department of Philosophy at Tulane for two decades. His father had been a self-made millionaire, and, like Walker, he came to prominence as a poet at an early age, publishing his self-consciously Modernist poetry in *The Double Dealer* and hobnobbing in the Quarter with William Faulkner and Sherwood Anderson when he was barely out of his teens. He would go on to publish dozens of books of various literary kinds, but his major achievement was what he wrote as a philosopher, for he published in 1951 a totalizing system of thought that encompassed poetry, politics, religion, history, and science.[55] He called this magnum opus *Ontology*. A few years later, Feibleman married the soon-to-be-famous novelist Shirley Anne Grau, and then his son by a prior marriage, Peter, published what would be his own best novel, *A Place without Twilight*. This novel is about a Black family and narrated by the daughter, Lucille; the family's mother is extremely overbearing, crushing her husband and two sons. Lucille, however, manages to escape. The younger Feibleman produced a few other novels during the 1960s and into the 70s, one called *Daughter of Necessity*, an allegorical work about family, and *Charlie Boy*, about a serial killer in New Orleans. In the early 1980s, he moved in with Lillian Hellman, whom he had come to know in New Orleans when he was a child and she a young woman, and they lived together during the final years of her life, during which time they co-authored a cookbook filled with reminiscences called *Eating Together*.

The sixty-year weave of literary celebrity around the senior Feibleman, from partying with Faulkner in the 1920s, to marrying Grau in the 50s, to seeing his son publish to acclaim in the 60s, and then make a home with Lillian Hellman in the 80s, anticipates another writer who taught at Tulane University for forty years, Peter Cooley, who saw a considerable number of his students launch writing careers. Over that span of decades, Cooley published ten books of verse rooted in religious devotion and rapture, bringing to life in recognizable, contemporary, often familial settings terms like prayer, saint, angel, miracle, soul, blessing, heaven, eternity, spirit, and so on. The titles of his books signal this focus, among them: *Sacred Conversations, Nightbus to the Afterlife, The Astonished Hours, Divine Margins,* and *Miracles, Miracles.* In addition to being a sort of literary father to a cohort of local poets who came of age, artistically, around the dawn of the twenty-first century, his biological daughter, Nicole Cooley, has published a half-dozen books of poetry too. Like her father's work, her poetry often situates itself in familial relationships (she has written three non-fiction books about motherhood). Her first book of poetry, *Resurrection* (1996), shows the influence of her father, and her second one, about the Salem witch trials, titled *The Afflicted Girls* (2004), calls to mind Brenda Marie Osbey and Irna Brodber's history-consumed work of the preceding decades on "mad" women. Since then, she has come increasingly into her own poetic vision with a book of poetry on the experience of Hurricane Katrina (*Breach*, 2010), on the collecting of objects (*Girl after Girl after Girl*, 2017), and most recently in a collection called *Of Marriage* (2018).

In the late 1990s, Cooley contacted fellow poet Brad Richard about starting a workshop group of peers that flourishes to this day. The poetry that has emerged from this group is formidable, for in addition to Cooley and Richard (whose father is the celebrated painter and studio-art professor at the University of New Orleans, Jim Richard), this circle has included a stunning list of poets with major, national reputations: Katy Balma, Allison Campbell, Melissa Dickey, Toi Derrecotte, Tonya Foster, Carolyn Hembree, Jessica Henrickson, Major Jackson, Rodney Jones, Laura Mullen, Ed Skoog, Andy Stallings, Elizabeth Thomas, and Andy Young.

Brad Richard's 2018 collection *Parasite Kingdom*, which emerged from this group, is a vision of an authoritarian, totalitarian hellscape, where destroyed palaces and bombed schools serve as a backdrop for contemplating themes of torture, surveillance, interrogation, and capitalist technocracy. Richard has written a number of other books of poetry: *Butcher's Sugar* (2012) explores queer male embodiment from boyhood through adolescence to adulthood, middle age, and beyond, articulating in each of these registers the always vexed experience of self-discovery and desire, with some scenes of devastating violence; and *Motion Studies* (2011) contemplates to great effect how visual art serves as a tool for locating one's self in the movement of history. But *Parasite Kingdom* distills the agonies of the Trump era into an abstract stream of night-terrors that serve as a benchmark for contemplating this chapter in our history. In a related vein, Carolyn Hembree begins her first book of poetry, *Skinny* (2012), with an epigraph that reads, in part, "you know what people will do to one another." Heavily spondaic, with challenging syntax, the book asks "who wrung the necks of your hopes?" Hembree's next collection, *Rigging a Chevy into a Time Machine and Other Ways to Escape a Plague* (2016), is even more explicitly apocalyptic, with the titles of the book's major sections being "Safety Restraints" and "Roadside Emergencies" and "Warning Lights and Gauges."

There are many other poets in the University District. Laura Mullen lived nearby for eight years and several of her books – notably, *The Tale of Horror* (1999), *After I Was Dead* (1999), and *Dark Archive* (2011) – anticipate the territory that characterize the most recent poetry of Richard and Hembree. Also Sarah Dorries, who taught briefly at Tulane, died suddenly of an aneurism at age 44; her posthumous collection, *Watch Your Trees*, appeared in 2018, and meditates on her beloved New Orleans, on travel, and on nude portraiture, among other themes.

At the level of the local and the purely literary, no hero looms larger in the lore of the uppermost end of St. Charles Avenue than Everette Maddox. He arrived in the city in 1976, the same year as Peter Cooley, and lived for a time at 2900 Prytania, the same boardinghouse where F. Scott Fitzgerald spent a few weeks in 1920. His acute alcoholism, however, meant he was often homeless and used the Maple Leaf Bar on Oak Street as a kind of unofficial headquarters. As his friend Ralph Adamo noted in the introduction to the first locally produced collection of Maddox's poetry, most writers, indeed most people, are steered through life by a desire for success, or at least survival, but Maddox simply was not. He cared only about the creation of poetry.

By early 1989, barely a dozen years after arriving in New Orleans, Maddox was dead. He only wrote regularly for the first third of that short tenure in the city, and then again in the last few years; during the middle years, he drank and read – read, specifically, in ways that enabled him to recite from memory long passages of Joyce and Proust. But that first burst of creativity, which Adamo has culled and assembled into the beautiful collection of over a hundred exquisitely crafted gems of boozy whimsy called *I Hope It's Not Over and Goodbye: Selected Poems of Everette Maddox*, is the basis today of his popularity. A second collection, *American Waste*, was collected from the final phase of jottings (on bar napkins and coasters and other scraps of paper) at the end of his life, but the wit, craft, and range are markedly diminished. Comparable to a degree to Charles Bukowski, Maddox's quirky, lyrical, and droll poems about alcohol as a life-defining object of devotion and vehicle for transport into oblivion are finally warmer and more soft-spoken than Bukowski's, and have none of the latter's bitter anger and bile. Maddox often slept in the doorways of banks and churches along Carrollton Avenue, and, according to legend, once spent a cold winter night on a bench along the streetcar line, protected by some pages of the local newspaper that, coincidentally, featured an article about him.

Maddox founded the tradition of Sunday afternoon poetry readings at the Maple Leaf Bar in 1979, where he would have regularly crossed paths with another of the bar's fixtures whose achievement is now considered historic – the pianist James Booker. Those Sunday poetry readings are still an important part of the literary culture of the city, and, since his passing, have been renamed in his honor. A number of luminaries in the regional poetry scene have been associated with that Sunday afternoon institution: Nancy Harris, who helped Maddox launch the series in 1979, edited in 2019 its anthology, called *40th Anniversary: Maple Leaf Poetry*; Julie Kane, who eventually served as poet laureate of Louisiana; Maxine Cassin, who founded *The New Orleans Poetry Journal* in the 1950s and played a key role in the Maple Leaf scene into the years that followed Hurricane Katrina; Megan Burns and Dave Brinks, who founded a downtown spin-off of the Maple Leaf series called "Seventeen Poets" at the Gold Mine Saloon in the Quarter; and Bob Borsodi, whose eponymous coffeehouse on Freret Street became

Everette Maddox in the 1980s at the Maple Leaf Bar, where he wrote much of his verse on bar napkins and founded the still vital Sunday afternoon tradition of poetry readings. Courtesy of the Historic New Orleans Collection.

known for similar sorts of poetry readings in roughly the same years that Maddox was in the area.

In the years just before the older Cooley and Maddox arrived, another important poet, Miller Williams, worked at Loyola University, where, in the late 1960s, he founded the still vital literary journal, *The New Orleans Review*. Williams would ultimately publish nearly forty books of poetry and prose, and serve as a mentor to many who have become major figures: Billy Collins, for example, calls Williams his "editorial father,"[56] and President Bill Clinton had Williams deliver a poem at his second inauguration. Williams's daughter, the celebrated singer-songwriter Lucinda Williams, invokes Louisiana in a number of songs and has set some of her father's verse to music, as on the lead-off track of her 2014 album, "Where the Spirit Meets the Bone."

Lucinda Williams is today the central figure in a genre known as country rock, and this part of New Orleans where her father lived and worked during her girlhood is the scene of important milestones in the life of the artist commonly known as the father of that genre, Gram Parsons. Parson's short life – he died at 26 – constitutes a blend of glamor, tragedy, genius, and horror that is itself one of the most astonishing stories of this part of town. Parsons's father, a veteran of World War II named Coon Dog Snively, committed suicide when Parsons was a boy, but his mother, the heiress to one of Florida's great citrus fortunes, steered him through an elite high school in Jacksonville, only to die of cirrhosis on the day he graduated. She had married a businessman from the University District in New Orleans a year after her first husband's suicide, and this man – Bob Parsons – became Gram's only parent as he set off, a few months later, to Harvard. Gram stayed at Harvard less than a full semester, and drifted, on his considerable inheritance, from there to Los Angeles, where he met a member of the Byrds as they stood in line at a bank. As they began to work together, he pulled the Byrds away from the psychedelic rock that had been their primary style and led them in the creation of their masterpiece, *Sweetheart of the Rodeo* (1968), an early instance of country music emerging from and being embraced by the hip, young elites of the counterculture. He then formed his own band, the Flying Burrito Brothers, to create two albums that have become iconic, *The Gilded Palace of Sin* and *Burrito Deluxe*, and then recorded a few more equally strong albums under his own name, *GP*, *Grievous Angel*, and *No More Sleepless Nights*. He also worked with the Rolling Stones while they recorded their magnum opus, *Exile on Main Street*, writing the song "Country Honk" for them and arranging their major hit, "Honky Tonk Woman," as they would write "Wild Horses" for him.

In the midst of this extraordinary set of creative and professional adventures, Gram Parsons flew to New Orleans in 1971 to marry Gretchen Burrell at his stepfather's mansion on Audubon Place, next door to Tulane. Gram asked the man who had briefly been his mentor at Harvard, Jet Thomas, to perform the ceremony. Thomas later said that he had felt very uncomfortable there, as most of the guests at the wedding were friends of Bob's, and seemed to him to be "psychic vampires."[57] The bride, Gretchen Burrell, later observed that Bob was "an evil man."[58] Shortly after Gram's mother died, Bob had married the family's babysitter, and when Gram himself overdosed and died in 1973, Bob understood that he needed to have Gram's corpse buried in Louisiana in order to inherit the fortune that Gram had inherited from his mother, to say nothing of the potential long-term royalties from his catalogue of recordings.[59] He had already had Gram's younger sister locked away in a mental hospital where she could cause him no trouble.

Bob Dylan The Nobel Laureate, who has been a central figure in American culture for more than a half-century, rented a house next door to Tulane University on Audubon Circle in 1987, close to the home where Gram Parsons was married. He was feeling burnt out and, at age 48, considering retirement. He had been talking to Bono, who introduced him to producer Daniel Lanois, then based in New Orleans. Together, they made the album *Oh, Mercy!* Dylan noted in his memoir, *Chronicles*, that he took to tooling around New Orleans late at night on a motorcycle and listening to WWOZ 90.7 FM. Not long after, his slump ended, and, from 1992 to 2001, he made his most successful records since the mid 1970s.

When Gram Parsons died, some of his friends, believing that they were carrying out his wishes, stole his corpse from the Los Angeles airport, drove it out to Joshua Tree National Forest, and set it on fire. Not to be denied, Bob retrieved about 35 pounds of the charred remains, managed to bring them back to Louisiana, and used them to claim his stepson's fortune. Only two years after getting what was left of Gram's body into the ground near New Orleans, Bob himself died of cirrhosis.

In recent decades, literary work that has emerged from the University District has continued to focus on families. A particular example is the three-play sequence that John Biguenet published as *The Rising Water Trilogy*. The productions of these works were a major event in New Orleans in the years right after Hurricane Katrina. Biguenet taught for many years at Loyola University, identifying himself first as a poet, then as a fiction writer, and finally as a playwright. His short-story collection *The Torturer's Apprentice* (2001) explores moral quandaries in various kinds of relationships, while in *Oyster* (2003) two Cajun families in the

1950s fall into an escalating conflict with each other, leading to murder and vengeance. His dramatic trilogy hinges on the notion of home as the place where familial bonds are challenged and then actualized more deeply by the overwhelming pressures of catastrophe.

In the realm of prose, another key work of the period right after Hurricane Katrina is Dave Eggers's *Zeitoun*, which recounts the ostensibly true story of a Syrian-American who had lived the American Dream near the upriver end of St. Charles Avenue by building a successful house-painting business from scratch. In the days after the storm and levee failure, he was helping to rescue the elderly around his flooded neighborhood, only to be arrested as a suspected terrorist because he had a large amount of cash with him. Eggers's book portrays Zeitoun as the quintessential American and also a selfless Good Samaritan who became the hapless victim of Islamophobia. However, a few years after the book's release, Zeitoun's marriage deteriorated badly, perhaps because his wife threatened to expose a different version of his activities in the aftermath of the storm, and he eventually attacked her in the middle of Prytania Street with a tire iron. He was later accused of plotting, from within prison, to have her killed.

In contrast to Eggers's incomplete portrait of his subject, some work directly affiliated with the universities has taken up the notion of disaster in more comprehensive ways to reach a wide audience. John M. Barry's *Rising Tide*, a book on the great flood of 1927 and efforts to contain the Mississippi River, has been invaluable in informing large numbers of people about the sheer precarity of the city's position vis-à-vis water, and his book *The Great Influenza: The Story of the Deadliest Plague in History*, though published in 2004, has seen a surge of new interest in the context of Covid-19. Kevin Rabalais, a Louisiana native who lived in Australia for nearly a decade and now teaches at Loyola, published a novel in 2008 called *Landscape of Desire*, set against the backdrop of the disastrous, gold rush–driven expedition of Burke and Wills across the deserts of central Australia. And Randy Fertel, whose mother founded the Ruth's Chris Steakhouse empire and who has taught at Tulane and a number of prestigious universities, has written a memoir about his parents that's loaded with colorful local history, as well as a book about the quintessentially New Orleans theme of improvisation – a human necessity in the absence of reliable, sustainable structures. Still another writer who has taught at Tulane, uptown native Walter Isaacson – who has been the editor of *Time* and the president of CNN – has written a number of widely read biographies about figures powerful enough to have changed the world: Albert Einstein, Steve Jobs, Benjamin Franklin, and Leonardo da

Vinci, among others. And another Tulane professor, Bernice McFadden, has written more than a dozen novels, among them *The Book of Harlan*, *Praise Song for Butterflies*, and *Gathering of Waters*, that situate fictional characters within cataclysmic national histories, from World War II, for example, to the murder of Emmett Till.

But the most powerful voice to emerge from this part of the city belongs to a woman who made a point, her whole life, of turning away from worldly events to devote her artistic craft, as Peter Cooley has, to the subject of God: Mahalia Jackson. She was born at 7015 Water Street (now Constance Street), a building that abutted the railroad tracks at Leake Street.[60] Commonly recognized as the greatest gospel singer of the recorded era, she became friends with the Reverend Doctor Martin Luther King. She was his favorite singer.

Before King took the stage at the Lincoln Memorial in Washington DC, on August 28, 1963, as the culmination of the March on Washington for Jobs and Freedom, before an audience of a quarter of a million people, she warmed up the crowd for him. He had asked her to sing his favorite, "I Been 'Buked and I Been Scorned," and then, after she stepped back to give him the podium, she began to prompt him, repeating "Tell them about your dream, Martin, tell them about your dream."[61] What followed, of course, is now widely recognized as the very summit of American oratory.

Central City
The New Zion Baptist Church on Third Street, under the leadership of the Reverend A. L. Davis, hosted a conference in 1957 that featured Martin Luther King, who used the occasion to coalesce the Southern Christian Leadership Conference, which would be at the center of the struggle to end Jim Crow. Surely inspired by King,

Mahalia Jackson, born in a deeply religious three-room household where twelve other people lived on what is now Leake Street next to the levee. Wikimedia Commons – Public Domain.

a particular, local protest movement developed in the neighborhood in the years that followed as white business owners who no longer lived in the area continued to make money off the African Americans there but refused to hire them. A boycott was organized. Some background: when a rail line was proposed in the 1830s to connect New Orleans to the small community of Carrollton some 5 miles upriver, the landowners on the opposite side of St. Charles from what would soon become the Garden District began to sell off small parcels to working-class immigrants; a neighborhood began to emerge, particularly along Dryades Street, where Orthodox Jewish immigrants from Russia and Poland opened businesses in the years after the Civil War. It flourished this way for nearly a century, then followed the same pattern that unfolded in the Irish Channel, whereby most of the people of European descent moved out of the area by the 1950s and were replaced by African Americans, a process that involved mounting tensions around commerce. By the time the boycott got underway in 1960, African Americans constituted a vast majority in the area.

Through the boycott, a woman named Oretha Castle emerged as a leader. She was arrested and charged with "conspiracy to commit criminal anarchy." Her case went to the Supreme Court, and she won, a milestone victory in the Civil Rights Movement. In 1989, a twelve-block stretch of Dryades was renamed to honor her legacy.

The strength she demonstrated through this process was demonstrated in another, even more astonishing struggle of a Central City native, Gregory Bright. In 1975, at the age of 20, Bright, who had never been taught to read or write, was convicted of a murder based on the testimony of a single eyewitness, a paranoid schizophrenic who self-medicated with heroin and sold information to police for cash under a variety of different names. As further revealed in later years, this woman had no sight line between her window, where she claimed to have been standing, and the spot where the killing occurred. Bright was sentenced to life with no chance of parole in the state penitentiary at Angola, where, over the course of twenty-seven years, he taught himself to read, and then to practice law; he then pursued his own case all the way to the Louisiana Supreme Court, which overturned his conviction and set him free. He then, with Laura Naughton, wrote the one-man play *Never Fight a Shark in Water*, which he regularly performs before live audiences around the US.

Both Castle and Bright were drawing on a long tradition of courageous activism in the neighborhood, reaching back to the dawn of the twentieth century, when a particular Black activist triggered an historic episode of white rage, an event first etched into the historical record when Ida B. Wells of Chicago published, a month afterward, *Mob Rule in New Orleans: Robert Charles and His Fight to the Death, the Story of His Life, Burning Human Beings Alive, and Other Lynching Statistics.* In this work, she chronicles the bloodthirsty swarm of white people in New Orleans in late July of 1900, who sought vengeance against Charles, an African American, for his having shot a policeman. "Despising all law," wrote Wells, the mob "roamed the streets day and night, searching for colored men and women, whom they beat, shot, and killed at will."

In *Mob Rule*, she rails against the role of the popular press in fomenting the white riot that terrorized New Orleans. The most prominent such voice was surely Major Henry James Hearsey, who founded the *New Orleans Daily States* – the unofficial organ of the city's government and the leading afternoon daily in the city in the final decades of the nineteenth century. A strong advocate of lynching whenever a Black person was accused of any crime against whites, he said that, in mob rule, he could see the "divine impulse," and the "highest law known on earth, because it is the law written on the human heart by the Lord God Almighty Himself." He was especially unnerved by Robert Charles's courage in fighting against the police and assumed that many African Americans were privately celebrating him as a hero. Within days of the riots' end, he wrote an editorial that declared that the only solution to "the negro problem" was the "extermination" of the race.[62]

According to those who knew him, Robert Charles was "a stylish type of Negro" and "well educated."[63] When the police raided his apartment after the shootout, they found boxes of notebooks and other evidence of him seeking intellectual self-improvement. His neighbors thought he was some kind of scholar, and said there was an air of elegance about him.[64] He had been born in the immediate aftermath of the Civil War in Copiah County, Mississippi, the same area where the iconic blues legend Robert Johnson would be born around the same time that Charles was killed in New Orleans. During the summer and fall of 1865, Copiah County was briefly occupied by Black troops who fought for the Union, which surely shaped the racial dynamics of Charles's boyhood. When Charles was in his teens, the elections of the mid 1880s were wracked with obvious corruption and violent terror against Blacks; in fact, between 1882 and 1903 there were 334 lynchings in Mississippi, the worst year of them all being 1891, when Charles would have been in his mid twenties, when there were twenty lynchings in the state.[65] Around this time, he became interested in the national anti-lynching campaign led by Ida B. Wells, who would soon chronicle his death.

In this era, African Americans from the nearby rural areas were streaming into New Orleans, probably hoping for safety in numbers, and increasing the city's population by some 20 percent, despite low wages, substandard housing, high mortality rates, and police brutality. Robert Charles was among them. A vast supply of inexpensive labor, they posed a threat to working-class whites. Given that the city's population at the dawn of the twentieth century was around 300,000, with a police force of only 193 officers, the circumstances were a veritable powder keg awaiting a spark.

In the middle of the summer of 1900, Robert Charles became that spark. He was living in apartment #4 at 2023 Fourth Street, between Rampart and Saratoga, with a roommate named Lenard Pierce. Toward evening on Monday, July 23, Pierce came back to the apartment to find Robert in some of his finest clothes, sitting at his desk, writing.[66] Robert told him to put on some nice clothes too, for they were "going to meet some ladies" – Robert's girlfriend and her roommate, who lived nearby. Soon, they were sitting on a stoop at 2815 Dryades, near the corner of Washington, waiting for the ladies' landlord to go to bed so they could be slipped in for a visit.

Around 10:15 that night, two policemen approached the pair. Robert Charles stood up, an act which one of the cops interpreted as a threat and began to hit him with his night-stick. Charles knocked it away and ran down the street. The cop fired at him, and Charles returned fire, both wounding each other. The second cop held Charles's roommate at gunpoint, then arrested him. Soon, large numbers of police began to converge on the area, but Charles was back at his apartment, dressing his wound, and loading his Winchester. He knew that, having shot at a cop, chances were slim that he could escape being lynched.

Soon, a police captain came with a few officers to Charles's apartment just as Charles was leaving (his roommate had given them the address soon after being arrested). Charles shot the captain and killed him instantly, then killed one more. The other officers fled. More cops approached later, Charles shot at them, and again they scattered. Charles also ran, for, as he rightly anticipated, a massive crowd began to arrive at his apartment around dawn to tear it apart. At some point, a rumor swept through the crowd that he was hiding in a nearby privy, which promptly triggered an orgy of gunfire into the structure, which the mob then ripped off its foundations. Some members of the mob leaped into the narrow pit beneath it to splash around together in the dark muck in the hope of rousing the "fiend" from its reeking depths and thereby becoming the city's saviors. They didn't catch him there, probably clutching instead only at each other's arms and ankles in a jumble of elation, terror, and disappointment that distilled the mindset that drove the larger mob.

Within hours, the crowd of whites that gathered in front of Charles's apartment swelled to fully 5,000. The most dangerous situation emerged around sundown at what was then the still fairly new statue of Robert E. Lee on St. Charles Avenue, an area still often called Lee Circle despite the recent removal of the statue: a large lynch mob was mobilizing there for a night of blood. Around the city, several African Americans were severely beaten, and three died, while six others suffered severe injury; five whites were taken to the hospital as well, two of them having been shot by drunken fellow-travellers, the others likely beaten for having dissented. Meanwhile, the president of nearby Tangipahoa Parish offered to send enough armed white men to "annihilate the Negroes of New Orleans."[67] By the end of the week, three more Black people were fatally shot, and another fifteen severely injured by white rioters.[68]

Charles was hiding out not far from the scene of the initial encounter with the police in a ramshackle set of slave quarters behind the house at 1208 Saratoga Street, where some old acquaintances from Mississippi took him in. He hid there from early morning on Tuesday all the way to his death on Friday afternoon. Hiding in the large closet under the staircase, Charles had access to several pounds of lead pipe and a miniature portable charcoal furnace – with which he began frantically to manufacture his own bullets for the inevitable showdown.

Acting on a tip, two policemen approached Charles's hideout. He shot and killed them both. Word spread all but instantly that cops were getting shot at 1208 Saratoga. Large mobs headed that way. By 5:00 pm that Friday afternoon, the crowd had swelled to as many as 15,000. The volume of gunfire aimed at the slave quarters in back, where Charles had moved upstairs for a better view, was a veritable storm. Robert Charles stood his ground and returned fire. From here, he shot twenty-four white people, including four more cops. As afternoon tilted toward evening, kerosene was poured on a mattress then ignited on the staircase in an attempt to smoke him out. At last, his brown derby hat pulled low on his head, Charles dashed the 20 feet across the courtyard toward the main house, but there a bullet fired by a Tulane student stopped him.

Chaos ensued, as everyone wanted to take a turn emptying their gun into the corpse, which was soon unrecognizable. Random assaults on African Americans continued all through the night. Charles's remains were secretly buried in an unmarked spot in Holt Cemetery just before dawn to prevent more frenzied theatrics and gunplay around what was left of his body. Typical of the mood of many of the white people in the city, a carnival owner tried to buy the corpse so he could pickle it, take it around the country, and charge people money to see it. Spurred by the events in New Orleans, violence erupted around the US, particularly in Houston and Chicago. In Baton Rouge, an African-American man named Melby Dotson was so upset about the fate of Robert Charles that he began to complain of constant nightmares in which he himself was being lynched; and then, dozing off on a train a few weeks later, he began to struggle with an imaginary rope around his neck. When a conductor tried to calm him, Dotson woke up in befuddlement and panic, and shot him. Dotson was arrested and, the next day, dragged from his prison cell in Baton Rouge and lynched.[69]

Robert Charles is remembered in the city in curious and conflicted ways. Louis Armstrong, for example, who was born on August 4, 1901, claimed for much of his public life that he was born on July 4, 1900 – an act of self-fashioning probably aimed at linking himself to an idea of "the American century," but that Black audiences in his hometown might equate instead with the legend of the quintessentially American martyr who was killed that month. And Jelly Roll Morton, who would have been on the cusp of his teens during the riots, if not a bit older, spoke at some length about the event in the 1930s to Alan Lomax, noting that a song had been written about Robert Charles – but saying that the police, along with many others, had squashed the song, for it was known to be a "trouble breeder." Morton continues by saying that he once knew the song, but had made a point of forgetting it "in order to go along with the world on the peaceful side."[70] No one has ever found any sheet music, or a recording, or any other trace of the song's existence.[71] Buddy Bolden, who lived most of his life at 2309 First Street, in the immediate vicinity of all of this mayhem, is not known to have said a word about it, and Kid Ory, another musical leader of the period who lived nearby at 2135 Jackson Avenue, kept the same silence.

The long-standing silence about this event was first foreshadowed just a week after the riots ended, when Major Henry Hearsey announced, in the same editorial in which he called for genocide, that his newspaper would never publish another word about Robert Charles, a prohibition meant to pre-empt Charles's potential rise to a posthumous, symbolic power. After dominating headlines for several days, the story would be largely erased from public discourse, though, within the city's African-American lore, it has never been forgotten. A monument to Robert Charles was recently unveiled at the corner of Martin Luther King Boulevard and Oretha Castle Haley Boulevard in Central City.

An event oddly parallel to the so-called Robert Charles Riot unfolded not far away on January 7, 1973. A young man from the Emporia, Kansas, named Mark Essex set himself up as a sniper in the Howard Johnson's Hotel (now the Holiday Inn) at 303 Loyola Avenue that faces Duncan Plaza, between the main branch of the New Orleans Public Library and City Hall. For a little less than twelve hours, Essex fired on white people, mostly policemen below, ultimately killing nine, including five cops, and wounding twelve others, the rampage ending only when a Marine helicopter gunship made multiple passes to strafe his position on the roof. The sharp-shooters in the helicopter eventually killed him, the inquiry afterward showing 200 bullet wounds to his body, and only two bullets left in his possession – those two bullets some have interpreted as evidence that he allowed himself, having essentially run out of ammunition, to be hit – a choice of suicide rather than surrender. This event contrasts that of Robert Charles in a number of ways, perhaps most pointedly in that it has inspired a considerable body of rhetoric and literature, whereas the event of 1900 has been, until recently, met with relative silence beyond the level of lore.

In the days after Essex was killed, Eldridge Cleaver sent a wreath and a message of condolence and praise from the Black Panthers to the funeral back in Kansas, and Stokely Carmichael, speaking to a group of high-school students in Newark, sang his praises thus, "We should study and learn from the actions of Brother Mark Essex. We should understand that Brother Essex took our struggle to its next quantitative level."[72] A leading playwright of the Black Arts Movement, Adrienne Kennedy, wrote a play called *An Evening with Dead Essex* that was performed less than a year after the event by the Yale Repertory Theater and then made a successful run off-Broadway. Before the end of that year, James Brown would release what many see

The Black Liberation Army Several months after the chaos unleashed by Mark Essex and white vigilantes, Herman Bell of the Black Liberation Army was arrested in New Orleans, near where he was living at 820 Second Street, for the murder two years earlier of two police officers in New York City. Bell's presence in New Orleans fuels speculation that Essex, during his time in New York, had been further radicalized by the BLA, perhaps even that the BLA were in New Orleans to work with Essex in carrying out his mission.

as his final masterpiece, the double album called *The Payback*. The poet Alvin Aubert, who grew up just outside New Orleans, wrote a poem called "Remember Mark Robert James Essex." References to the event would appear in two quite different movies of that period, Mel Brooks's *Blazing Saddles* and Sidney Lumet's *Dog Day Afternoon*. In the decades that followed, the shooter's mother, Nellie Essex, wrote a book called *Blacks in Emporia*, apparently to create a sense of context for her son's actions, showing that the Kansas town he grew up in was, on one hand, an ordinary African-American community no different from countless others, and that, on the other, his murderous rage might also be understood as a pervasive and understandable aspect of African-American experience. A true-crime book called *A Terrible Thunder: The Story of the New Orleans Sniper* by Pete Hernon appeared in the late 1970s, and Gil Scott Heron released three separate recordings about the event. In his version of the Marvin Gaye classic, "Inner City Blues," he ends by inserting his own lyrics:

Did you ever hear about Mark Essex
and the things that made him choose
to fight the inner-city blues?

Yeah, Essex took to rooftops guerrilla style
and watched while all the crackers went wild
Brought in six hundred troops, I hear,
Brand new to see them crushed with fear

Essex fought back with a thousand rounds
And New Orleans was a changing town
And Rat-a-tat-tat-tat-tat-tat was the only sound

Yeah bring on the stone rifles
To knock down walls
Bring on the elephant guns
Bring on the helicopters
to block out the sun

Yeah, made the devil wanna holler
Cos eight was dead and a dozen was down
Cries for freedom – brand new sound
New York, Chicago, Frisco, LA
Justice was served and the unjust were afraid
Because in spite of all the years and all the fears
Brothers were alive to courage found

Perhaps inspired by Gil Scott Heron, the hip-hop artist DeJoshua "Almightydollar" Williams, originally from New Orleans, released an album called *Mark Essex* in 2020, nearly fifty years after the shootings, that features a portrait of the shooter as the cover image. The response to the event from the white establishment is encapsulated in Congress's taking up for discussion in the weeks that followed the possibility of legislation that would require the death penalty for anyone who killed a cop.[73]

The story of Mark Essex is loaded with interesting coincidences with that of Robert Charles. Around the time the latter was born in Copiah County, Mississippi, in the 1870s, hundreds of Black people were fleeing the area and heading for Kansas in the hopes of creating their own community with other recently emancipated people from Kentucky and Tennessee. Known as "Exodusters," Robert Charles likely had relatives among them – and Mark Essex was probably a descendant of this same community. When he left there to come to New Orleans, he took an apartment at 2619 Dryades, just two blocks from where Robert Charles first scuffled with police.

Unlike Robert Charles, however, there is some suggestion of a mental break in Essex in the years before he came to New Orleans. Right around his twenty-first birthday, in August 1970, he would have been well aware of events that unfolded some 500 miles to the north of the military base in San Diego where he was undergoing basic training (and enduring racist bullying): the younger brother of Black revolutionary writer George Jackson got into a shoot-out with police at the Marin County Courthouse, using weapons registered to another leading Black revolutionary, Angela Davis. A few weeks later, Essex assaulted a superior officer, a white man, even jumping on his chest. He then went AWOL and got on a bus for New Orleans, where the Black Panthers' conflict with the police in the Desire Projects would soon peak. He never arrived to participate in that showdown, stepping off the New Orleans-bound bus somewhere out west and boarding another that would take him to his hometown in Kansas instead. A few months later, he was in New York City, where a group calling itself the Black Liberation Army would take credit for shooting some policemen in the spring of 1971. The man eventually charged with those killings, Herman Bell, would be arrested in New Orleans in September of 1973. Essex seems likely to have been in contact with the Black Liberation Army during his time in New York, and his landlord told police investigators that, in the weeks before he started shooting, he had hosted some mysterious visitors from New York. But when the New York police killings for which the group took credit occurred in May of 1971, he was already back at his parents' house in Kansas, bent on cultivating an ever purer and more absolute relationship to the vision of Black uprising, telling his sister, for example, that a revolution was coming to the US and he intended to play a part in starting it – to be the spark that, as Chairman Mao said, would start the prairie fire.

More clues about Essex's mental health were provided by photos depicting the walls of his apartment on Dryades Street in Central City, which were covered floor-to-ceiling in writing. Some of it was perfectly sensible, as Essex had painted in giant, block letters the word "AFRICA" across one wall and then, around it, a set of proclamations: "My destiny lies in the bloody death of racist pigs" and "Shoot the devil like you shoot a dog" and "Revolutionary Justice is Blood Justice." But the walls are also filled with schizoid nonsense: lists of what appear to be mis-spelled Swahili words and the names of African animals, in particular the pangolin, a large rodent-like creature covered in a heavy armor of scales that can roll up into an impenetrable ball when attacked.

A few months after Essex moved to New Orleans in August of 1972, some police in Baton Rouge opened fire on student protestors at the histori-cally Black university there named Southern, killing two. A few weeks later, Essex wrote to the local TV station in New Orleans to declare

Walls of Mark Essex's Apartment at 2619 Dryades Street. Courtesy of Getty Images.

that he would avenge their deaths. From the upper floors of the hotel, he shot policemen (and a few hotel guests), and, as he did so, a larger and larger crowd of vigilantes began to assemble, firing fairly randomly at the roof of the hotel. The shots echoed through the concrete canyon of Central Business District, creating the illusion of far more shooting, and whipping up the hysteria in the white mob yet further to shoot still more and to encourage more whites to join them. Given the relatively random positioning of the vigilantes, they often inadvertently shot in the direction of each other. Finally, as the sun went down, Essex was killed. As in the case with Robert Charles, several hours would pass before the white mob would calm down and stop assaulting random African Americans who, in their paranoid fantasy, were accomplices to the sniper.

Essex probably hoped to provoke the police in a way that would, in turn, lead them to provoke an uprising in the several nearby housing projects of the sort that had occurred in the Desire Projects a little over two years earlier. What stymied Essex's scheme, however, was a sudden turn in the weather: that morning temperatures had been in the low 70s in New Orleans, and the streets would naturally have filled with the revelers, as they do every Sunday that time of year, especially in nice weather, but by the time the sun went down the temperature had plummeted over 30 degrees, with some precipitation, driving any potential followers indoors. Nonetheless, the day-long stand-off between Essex and the crowds below him in the surrounding streets was televised around the country, for it unfolded on the Sunday between the final NFL play-offs and the Superbowl, when there was nothing else on TV. That Sunday was also the day after Twelfth Night, the official first day, therefore, of carnival season: Essex would have known from Herbert Aptheker's *American Negro Slave Revolts*, a book published in 1943 that was popular with Black revolutionary leaders in the decades that followed, that the day after Twelfth Night was also the anniversary of the 1811 uprising in which a group of enslaved people just upriver from New Orleans had organized, slain their masters, and begun liberating plantation after plantation, as they made their way to the city.

The Central City neighborhood where Essex lived did see, however, two major uprisings of a purely cultural sort, one in the decades before and the other in the decades just after that event. The first came with the golden era of New Orleans R & B, the second with Hip Hop.

Directly across the street from the house at 1208 Saratoga where Robert Charles made his last stand in the summer of 1900, there arose at 1209, a half-century later, a musical hub known as the Club Tijuana. Both a hotel and a restaurant, as well as a performance venue and bar, the clientele skewed toward the working class, and was known as the place where musicians would go to listen to each other. Little Richard had a weekly gig there through most of 1953, just before he exploded onto the national scene with "Tutti Frutti" two years later. That song first got attention when, after a lackluster recording session one afternoon at Cosimo Matassa's studio on Rampart Street, he started playing it that evening at another club in Central City called the Dew Drop Inn. A producer thought it had potential, if the raunchy lyrics could be rewritten, and decided to record it back on Rampart Street at Matassa's, whereupon it soared immediately to the #2 position on the Billboard R & B charts and launched Little Richard as a national star.

The Club Tijuana was bulldozed in the late 1980s, but the Dew Drop Inn is poised to reopen soon as a version of its former self, with its original combination of hotel rooms, a restaurant, and a nightclub. Commonly known in its heyday simply as "the Drop," it began when Frank Painia opened a barbershop at 2836 LaSalle Street in 1935.[74] In less than a decade, it had grown into a fixture of the regional and national circuit for Black entertainers, part of the same system that included the Apollo in Harlem, the Barrel House in Watts, the Bronze Peacock in Houston, and Club DeLisa in Chicago.[75] Everyone from Duke Ellington to James Brown stayed there and played there, and, when the touring superstars of Black music in the 1940s and 50s weren't on stage, the locals were: not only musicians playing regular gigs and all-night jam sessions, but also drag queens, dancers, and comedians.

In 1953, the same year that Little Richard had a weekly gig at the Club Tijuana and Professor Longhair, who lived a dozen blocks away at 1738 Terpsichore, was reaching his creative peak, a relatively unknown 22-year-old, Georgia-born Ray Charles, moved into the neighborhood. He had been living in Dallas and trying to model himself upon Nat "King" Cole, but wasn't having much success. In December 1952, he had brought the house down at the Pelican Club on Rampart Street, and, after his mother died in the spring of 1953, he decided to go back to New Orleans, and try something new. He moved into the Hotel Foster, one block from the Drop, and soon had a regular gig there with Guitar Slim.[76] At an August 18 recording session, Ray Charles "went to church" for the first time in a studio. What he created – a gospel-blues hybrid that would soon be called "soul music" – was a key step in the musical direction that would make him one of the iconic figures of American music.[77]

Two months later, at another recording session for Guitar Slim on Rampart Street, he took over the session, writing horn-lines and arranging tunes. His growth over the summer had been significant. His work that day, particularly on Guitar Slim's "Things I Used to Do," paid off – less than four months later, it reached the top spot on the R & B charts, remained there for six weeks, and ultimately became the best-selling R & B record of 1954.[78] During this first burst of success, he heard a gospel tune on the radio called "It Must Be Jesus" and built from it a new tune called "I Got a Woman," which he would play at most of his performances through the following year. He

> **Professor Longhair** Coming to local notoriety by playing the piano in the clubs along S. Rampart Street in Central City in the 1940s, he wrote and recorded, in the 1950s, what would become anthems of the city's R & B legacy, but saw little money. In the 1960s, he supported himself by gambling, but, in 1970, while working as a janitor at a record shop, he was rediscovered and swept to international fame. In 1977, an old banana warehouse at Napoleon and Tchoupitoulas was named after one of his songs – "Tipitina's" – and a statue of him was positioned just inside the front door, where it continues to greet music lovers night after night.

finally recorded it a little less than a year after he left New Orleans, and it quickly rose to #1 on the R & B charts, the first time his name had arrived there, as it would again many times in the years that followed.

Three decades later, another commercial music phenomenon arose from the public housing projects of Central City: Bounce music. In *Bounce: Rap Music and Local Identity in New Orleans*, Matt Miller explains that, in the mid 1980s, DJ Slick Leo and Captain Charles were the first in New Orleans to begin intersecting rap, the contemporary party sound of the Bronx, with local traditions like the chanted call-and-response of the Mardi Gras Indians and the Black church. As they did this, mixing it in real time in disco clubs, they created something new.[79] The primary locales for this creative breakthrough and cultural turning point were downtown, some distance from the Central City housing projects where it became a mass phenomenon: Famous Theater Disco at the corner of Claiborne and Elysian Fields (now Melba's Poboys) and Club Discovery (at 2831 St. Claude, by the railroad tracks). The first major instance of that particular sound, says Miller, appeared in 1991 on a single entitled "Where Dey At" by MC T Tucker and DJ Irv, which was built around what came to be known as the "triggerman" beat and features as a melodic motif the opening theme to the old TV show *Dragnet*: dom da dom dom.[80] From these starting points, the new sound became a favorite feature of block parties, particularly around the public housing projects.

Miller explains why this art form can be challenging for traditional literary cultures to absorb: the vocal performance is not linear, much less inclined to narrative, but is rather constructed out of a short, simple, single cell that gets repeated, over and over, the voice becoming as much a percussion instrument as a source of anything like text-based meaning.[81] Miller continues, "by improvising rhythmic patterns consisting of repeated phrases … [the] vocal performance [enters] into dynamic interaction with the backing track and with the audience's verbal and physical response," particularly as the vocalist begins to "shout out" different housing projects, neighborhoods, or streets, and invoke the oldest of all exchanges, sex and money.[82] A chant like "Make Dat Ass Clap" would bring to the center of everyone's attention a wave of female (and later a queer male) dancers whose hard, highly-stylized pelvic shaking drove a new dance craze, the dances themselves given names like the Pussy Pop, the Wobble, the Twerk, and of course Bounce.[83] In the late 1990s, this cultural phenomenon made New Orleans the epicenter of a new chapter in the history of Hip Hop, with Mystikal, a combat veteran from the Gulf War, being its first major star.

Among those who first capitalized on this phenomenon was Master P. He made nearly 50 million dollars on his first album, and, after directing and playing himself in the direct-to-video biopic, *I'm Bout It*, shot on location in the Calliope Projects where he grew up, he moved in 1998 into a gated community in Baton Rouge, close to the plantation where his ancestors had been enslaved.[84] His record label soon signed Snoop Dogg, as well as several others, including Mystikal and Master P's brother, C-Murder, and all four of them lived in the Baton Rouge mansion, from which Master P reigned for about two years as among the most successful Black businessmen in America,[85] making a vast fortune mostly from within the communities that his stars came from and wrote about. A key to his success: he kept as many aspects of his business as possible under the control of his immediate blood relatives.[86]

C-Murder, Master P's brother, was eventually convicted of murder, and, during his time in prison, has published a book of poems called *Red Beans and Dirty Rice for the Soul*, as well as two novels, one called *Death around the Corner*, about a rising Hip-Hop star from the housing projects in New Orleans, and another called *Bound for Loyalty*, about two young girls who have recently lost their wealthy sports-star father and are struggling to prevent their treacherous, extended family from scamming them out of their inheritance. Other works that engage the rise of New Orleans as a Hip-Hop epicenter in the 1990s are *The Meaning of Bounce* by 10th Ward Buck and Alison Fensterstock, and *Triksta* by Nik Cohn, which offers a compelling account of the rise,

murder, and funeral of Souljah Slim, the brightest star of the New
Orleans streets of the 1990s.

No writer from this community, however, has achieved anything quite
like the cachet of Lil Wayne. Growing up near the corner of Eagle and
Apple in the uppermost end of uptown New Orleans, he was signed at
age 11 to the Cash Money label, which was based in the Central City
housing projects known as the Magnolia and built around the legendary beat-making of Mannie Fresh. Around the same time Lil Wayne
signed with Cash Money, he was playing in front of a mirror, stoned,
with his mother's Glock when the weapon discharged and sent a bullet
through his chest, just missing his heart. His father would be murdered
soon thereafter. At 15, in 1999, he would have his first major hit – "The
Block Is Hot" – and was known always to have a notebook open and a
pen in his hand, writing.[87]

When he signed with Cash Money, he essentially found a second family,
for the Williams brothers who owned it, Slim and Baby (aka Birdman),
used the same business model as Master P: run the business with family members, and those who weren't actual blood relatives must come
to see themselves that way. Lil Wayne was soon referring to Baby
Williams as "daddy," and in fact Baby has numerous tattoos of portraits of family members,[88] part of his meticulously constructed self-
presentation as a criminal kingpin.[89] In fact, the Williams's younger
half-brother, Terrance "Gangsta" Williams, who worked as an assassin
while building his own financial empire, claims to have killed more
than forty people,[90] earning him a prison sentence in 1999 of just
under two-and-a-half centuries. Gangsta Williams's prison writings
can be read at terrencewilliams.blogspot.com (note the slightly different spelling); he is working on a novel called *The Other Side of Bourban
Street* [*sic*].

Cash Money became one the most successful independent labels in
the history of the American music industry, enlisting its audience in
realizing the dream at the heart of the operation: that kids from the
slums could rhyme their way to endless wealth.[91] By the end of the
first decade of the twenty-first century, as Ben Westhoff notes, that
was the essential theme of much Hip Hop, and Cash Money, having
pioneered the concept, led the way in making it a reality: in 2008, Lil
Wayne outsold the entire genre of Jazz, and his Cash Money spin-off
imprint, Young Money, would sign two unknowns who became mega
stars, Nicki Minaj and Drake.[92]

Hurricane Katrina ended the major phase of this cultural phenomenon as anchored locally in New Orleans, for this music had been rooted in the public housing projects, most of which, whether flooded or not, were bulldozed in the aftermath of the storm. Lil Wayne and Cash Money relocated to Miami. But soon a second wave of New Orleans stars emerged on the national scene, as their adaptation of the original sound – known as Sissy Bounce – took off, largely through the charisma of Big Freedia.

Growing up in Josephine Street, near Danneel, in Central City, Big Freedia loved church as a child – the choir, the pageantry – and was 13 in the early 1990s when the first Bounce tune ("Where Dey At") swept the city. Freedia identifies as a gay man, but prefers she/her pronouns. In high school, she became friends with Katey Redd, "the original sissy."[93] Katey first strode onto a stage in October of 1998 at a block party, and became an instant sensation, the streets buzzing about her. Freedia was inspired. Soon thereafter, at age 20, she writes,

> My cousin Trisha and I were driving to a block party at the corner of Magnolia and Washington Streets when the light turned red. Waiting for the light to turn, I heard a dirty old beat blasting from the porch. I don't know what got to me, but suddenly I shot out of the car, bent over, and shook my ass off the back of that car like my life depended on it. The party was packed and all of them bitches went wild, clapping and screaming. When the light turned green, Trisha blew the horn which got everyone more juiced. I jumped back in the car and we tore down the street. My shake display became legendary. That night at the party, everyone was giving me props, high-fives, and bumps.[94]

After that, Freedia began to appear regularly at the Focus and Sam's, the two main clubs in Central City where the new Sissy-Bounce scene was exploding.

Freedia says, "I had grown up with death all around me,"[95] but nothing could have prepared her for the near total collapse of the social world from which she sprang in the aftermath of Hurricane Katrina. Freedia began to live in a house with her family some 30 miles outside the city in LaPlace, but soon discovered that "This queen ain't no country boy."[96] Freedia and Katey Redd then began driving all over Texas to perform, mostly in Houston and Austin, logging hundreds of miles every weekend, but returning to the family cottage in LaPlace during the week. In the following years, DJ Rusty Lazer began to organize performances for the Sissy-Bounce sensations in Brooklyn and Los

Angeles. As Freedia notes, by 2013, thanks to Miley Cyrus's performance at the MTV Video Music Awards, the particular dance form that she had popularized at some of the toughest housing-project block parties in Central City – "Twerking" – had entered the Merriam-Webster Dictionary and was known to every suburbanite in the US.[97] The same year that Miley Cyrus appropriated Freedia's signature move, Freedia's reality TV show began and ran for six seasons, but Freedia canceled it when her brother was murdered in the streets of Central City, an event too painful to be shared in that format.

Putting this broad cultural phenomenon of the last thirty years in the wider context of the city's long musical legacy, Ned Sublette, one of the keenest observers of both, writes that "[Hip Hop is] the youngest part of the New Orleans musical family, but it's family."[98] His comment too on the proclivity of artists recording for Master P's No Limit label to weave the sound of gunshots onto their tracks captures what he elsewhere quotes a long-time resident as calling the "murdery" atmosphere of the crack era as a whole in Central City: when you're on the street late at night, sitting at a stop light, and the guy who pulls up next to you, invisible behind tinted windows, is blasting that music at block-party levels, you can't help but wonder, were those shots real? Where did they come from? And where did they go?

Coda: Gwendolyn Midlo Hall's Database

Gwendolyn Midlo Hall grew up in a racially mixed area at the uppermost end of Central City near the corner of Peniston and South Robertson in the 1930s and 40s. She spent much of her adult life on the run, followed by the FBI, who got her fired from job after job and evicted from apartments. She lived in New York, Paris, North Carolina, Detroit, Mississippi, and Mexico. She taught at Rutgers for twenty years and has kept a home in recent decades near the uppermost end of St. Charles Avenue on Plum Street. In her recent memoir, *Haunted by Slavery*, she reports that "I always felt like New Orleans was home,"[99] but adds, "I was horrified by the society I grew up in."[100]

Although her father was a misogynist who regularly beat her, his work as a lawyer deeply inspired her. Long before the Civil Rights Era, he argued cases involving racist labor practices and police brutality, becoming known as the best lawyer in the state for freeing the wrongfully imprisoned. He battled the arch-segregationist Leander Perez and befriended A. P. Tureaud, the attorney for the NAACP in New Orleans.[101] Her parents immigrated to New Orleans in 1914 from what was then czarist Russia and "viewed the world from the perspective of the internationalist, wandering, persecuted Jews who identified with the poor and oppressed wherever they lived."[102] There are other important writers in uptown New Orleans whose Jewish identity is central to their work – Patty Friedmann, for example, has published at least eight books in a mostly sardonic vein, among them *Too Jewish*; and Rodger Kamenetz has drawn great acclaim for *The Missing Jew* and *The Jew and the Lotus*. But Gwendolyn Midlo Hall's sense of her cultural heritage has mobilized her in the work of social justice like no other.

When her father was a baby, the family hid revolutionary pamphlets in his diapers, and his oldest brother, as a teenager, fought in the streets to overthrow the czar. Upon arriving in New Orleans, her father's family opened Universal Tailors in the 500 block of South Rampart, every tailoring shop in the area being run by a relative.[103] She attended Newman for elementary and high school, but reports that she has no memory of ever talking to any of her classmates there.[104] Instead, she became a member of the American-Soviet Friendship Committee in her teens and began to receive in the mail the regular USSR Information Bulletin, where, through an article about the 1941 Nazi massacre of some 30,000 Jews at Babi Yar on the outskirts of Kiev, she first came to know about the Holocaust.[105] She was hanging out in this period too at interracial parties in the French Quarter bohemian community, listening to Woody Guthrie and Leadbelly and Paul Robeson, and forming life-long friendships through the South's only interracial youth organization.[106] She wrote all of the leaflets for the group, known as the New Orleans Youth Council, which she casts the youth arm of the Communist Party.[107] She got her education in communism talking to dockworkers on the New Orleans waterfront. (The Communist Party was a significant presence among the dockworkers of 1940s New Orleans, especially through the various unions that were active there.)[108] At 17, she dropped out of high school to devote herself to radical politics and joined the Communist Party in 1946.[109] She was soon being monitored by FBI agents, as she would be for the next several decades, who, again, would regularly meet with her employers and landlords to arrange her firing and eviction.[110] Soon after she joined the Communist Party, the Red Scare was underway,[111] and all of her associates in New Orleans – some 250 people, many of them Black leaders of waterfront unions – were instructed to leave town, change their names, and go underground.

Around this same time, she met Harry Haywood in Paris, whose *Negro Liberation* (1948) is a classic of Black Marxism. He was thirty years her senior, had worked as a Pullman porter, and fought in World War I. A self-educated worker-intellectual, he had handled a machine gun in the fight against white terrorists on the streets of Chicago during the Red Summer riots there in 1919.[112] He believed that there could be no successful advancement for Blacks without a communist revolution. She helped him to write.[113]

As they endured continuous harassment from the FBI, they began to spend more and more time in Mexico in the late 1950s, where her closest friend was the African-American artist, Elizabeth Catlett, who would soon become famous, and her husband, Francisco Mora. Within a few years, she would begin publishing a series of some half-dozen essays in *Negro Digest* and *Black World*, as well as a book with her husband called *Towards a Revolutionary Program for Negro Freedom*. It is dedicated to Robert F. Williams, who wrote *Negroes with Guns* (1962), among the seminal texts of the Black Power era, and whose wife, Mabel Williams, was Hall's close friend for four decades. A few years later, inspired by Williams's work in using a paramilitary approach to combatting Klan terrorism in North Carolina, she encouraged her students at a small, historically Black college in the northeast corner of North Carolina to take up arms to defend themselves the same way from the same group. She later said that this was the proudest moment of her life.[114]

Her first book was a comparative study of slavery in Haiti and Cuba, but she followed it in 1992 with the book for which she is most widely celebrated, *Africans in Colonial Louisiana*. But very important too is *Slavery and African Ethnicities in the Americas: Restoring the Links* (2005). These latter two works grew out of the work she did during a roughly fifteen-year period that began in the early 1980s, going through old courthouse files around Louisiana and Texas, and archives in Spain and France, to gather all records of the sales of individual slaves and enter them into what people were beginning to call a "database." She was able to amass a record of 100,000 enslaved people – by far the largest assemblage of information about the enslaved that anyone had ever created; she identified not only their names, but their birthplaces and skills, and passed along some few adjectives about their personalities and degree of rebelliousness. Through cross-referencing, something like a life story could begin to emerge for those who were otherwise assumed to be totally unknowable.

The database enables, moreover, the fleshing out of family bloodlines, even narratives made of actual names and dates, and, as more scholars follow in her footsteps to create an ever thicker web of connectedness, what had heretofore been understood as realm of pure oblivion, a spur to deep alienation, is potentially transformed into highest treasure.

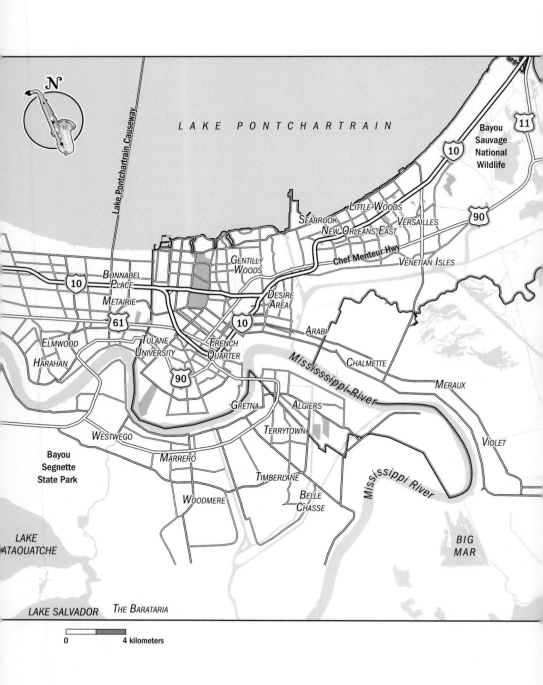

LAKE PONTCHARTRAIN

Bayou Sauvage National Wildlife

Lake Pontchartrain Causeway

SEABROOK
LITTLE WOODS
VERSAILLES
NEW ORLEANS EAST
GENTILLY WOODS
Chef Menteur Hwy
VENETIAN ISLES

BONNABEL PLACE
METAIRIE
DESIRE AREA
ARABI

ELMWOOD
TULANE UNIVERSITY
FRENCH QUARTER
CHALMETTE
MERAUX

HARAHAN

Mississippi River

GRETNA
ALGIERS

WESTWEGO
TERRYTOWN
VIOLET

Bayou Segnette State Park
MARRERO
TIMBERLANE
Mississippi River

WOODMERE
BELLE CHASSE

LAKE CATAQUATCHE
BIG MAR

LAKE SALVADOR   THE BARATARIA

0   4 kilometers

Map of the outskirts of New Orleans.

90

LAKE BORGNE

Outskirts – Writing through Loss
Gentilly – the Westbank – Versailles – the East

6

When Paul Chan, a video and installation artist, came to New Orleans in the spring of 2006 in the aftermath of Hurricane Katrina to teach for free at the University of New Orleans, what struck him first was the silence.[1] Born in Hong Kong and raised in Nebraska, he had first connected with the city through his lawyer, the New Orleans-based activist Bill Quigley, who defended him when he was charged with bringing food and medicine without permission to Iraq during the US invasion. During Chan's visits to the city (some of his animations were being exhibited that same spring at Tulane), the then 23-year-old became preoccupied with the sense of a population that was essentially "waiting for anything and everything." He continues, "I thought that this palpable sense of waiting needed a form."

That spring, on a street corner just off Claiborne Avenue, overwhelmed by the scale of the wreckage, Chan had suffered an hallucination, believing that he was seeing the two main characters from Samuel Beckett's *Waiting for Godot*, bantering back and forth.[2] The play, which he notes is the "most emblematic play of waiting that we have," had been staged at San Quentin State Prison in California, and Susan Sontag had produced a version of it in Sarajevo during the siege of Sarajevo.[3] Why not, thought Chan, do it amidst the carnage of post-Katrina New Orleans?

Hurricane Katrina Well over a thousand books have been written about the storm and the failure of the levees, a flood of stories, arguments, reportage, analysis, and rhetoric, intended for a wide range of audiences. There is no single archive that houses all of this material. However, a powerful memorial has been installed at the end of Canal Street farthest from the river, in the Charity Hospital Cemetery. A series of mausoleums house the unclaimed, unidentified remains of those who died in the storm, arranged around a spiraling walkway that symbolizes the hurricane.

By the following year, the Classical Theater of Harlem was rehearsing the play at a school on Chef Menteur Highway, where at least one of the classrooms had become a makeshift home for someone who had lost everything in the storm. The production would star J. Kyle Manzay, and also a New Orleans native, Wendell Pierce. It premiered in November of 2007, a little over two years after the catastrophic storm and levee failure, in a street intersection in the Lower 9th Ward, then did a second run directly afterward in front of a destroyed building in the Gentilly neighborhood, out Elysian Fields Avenue near the lake, where Pierce had grown up. These two neighborhoods had been quite distinct before Katrina, but in 2007 were part of the same undifferentiated abyss of desolation and ruin that stretched some 150 miles from New Orleans to Mobile.

In the months before the premier, there began to appear all over town signs tacked up on telephone poles that read: "A Country Road. A Tree.

Evening." These words – the opening set directions for *Waiting for Godot* – stirred curiosity and anticipation, small bursts of almost carnivalesque surrealism in a landscape that had already become entirely unmoored from the familiar and that a much reduced population, after word spread as to what the signs meant, was ready to read as a kind of invitation. While Chan and his colleagues had worried that no one would come to these productions, instead thousands came – and, in fact, thousands had to be turned away who couldn't be accommodated.

In the book that Chan assembled a few years later to commemorate the event, *Waiting for Godot in New Orleans: A Field Guide*, Gavin Kroeber, one of the producers, described people coming in lawn chairs with coolers, as if tailgating at a college football game, vast crowds who "had come not so much to see it as to make it work." Everyone in the arts communities who had managed to return to the city seemed to want to do their part in making something happen in a place where the sense of the void had been, for over two years, overwhelming. Kroeber continues, "The willingness to sit in the dirt, to stand at the periphery when the risers were full, to cramp together to let one more person in, to abide the cold or the bad sight lines – all these discomforts and compromises were contributions, simple gestures through which we all completed the symbol of *Godot*."[4] He continues, "Most hauntingly I remember the cries of 'thank you' from the crowd those first nights as the cast, in an unforgettable curtain call, walked side by side into the darkness, receding into the night."[5]

A number of radically surreal site-specific performances would be produced in the few years that followed, among them *Sweaty City* and *Rinse & Repeat* from Goat in the Road Productions, *Sea of Common Catastrophe* and *Cry You One* from Artspot Productions, and the solo performance from José Torres-Tama called *Aliens, Immigrants, and Evil-Doers*. One year after Godot's premier, Prospect New Orleans, the largest biennial of international, contemporary art ever organized in the US, was installed at dozens of sites around the city, ultimately drawing some 90,000 visitors, who pumped 25 million dollars into the local economy. Since then, every three years, another edition of Prospect fills the city with contemporary art for a few months, drawing visitors far from the traditional tourist circuitry to areas where the ravages of Katrina are still easy to discern.

Well before Katrina delivered New Orleans to the cutting edge of experimental theater and contemporary art, the poet Mackie Blanton, a native of the city who lived for decades at its northernmost edge near Lake Pontchartrain, was producing reams of verse, much of it enacting, in the manner of Wallace Stevens, the mind's abstract adventures in mapping its own potentials and hovering near its limits. Blanton moved to the far side of Lake Pontchartrain after Hurricane Katrina, and recently published a collection of nearly 200 poems called *The Casual Presence of Borders*. Another poet who shares Blanton's interest in consciousness, its limits, and what might lie beyond its limits is Dennis Formento, also a native New Orleanian, living, since Katrina, across the lake. Formento published a few years ago a collection called *Looking for an Out Place*, which proceeds as a "reclamation of the shadow / forms rejected by public discourse."[6] Like Bob Kaufman, Formento is self-consciously bohemian, celebrating Borsodi's coffee house, for example, and linking his work to the outer limits of improvisational Jazz, which he celebrates as "another way of knowing / providing you don't know what / providing / you don't take all the guesswork out." In Formento's poem for local percussionist Dave Capello, he notes that Capello doesn't play the beat, but rather invokes it in phantom outline by playing freely around it.

The notion of the outskirts of New Orleans as what Formento might call an "out" place has an important history that long precedes Katrina, and, since the storm, this "nowhere," relative to the city it surrounds, has been the scene of the most significant literary achievement in the entire region.

The masterpiece that inaugurates this emergent tradition is Walker Percy's novel *The Moviegoer* (1960). The main character – Binx Bolling – has chosen to live in the new, generic suburbs out near the lake, at the opposite end of Elysian Fields Avenue from the old, much mythologized neighborhoods along the river, because he has committed himself to what he calls a Search. What exactly he's searching for cannot be named, but it seems to involve a sense of absolute singularity, of authenticity, of freedom. To live in a wholly indistinct suburb, interchangeable with countless others around the country, he feels, is a good first step, for it has delivered him from the clichéd, tourist-clogged avenues of the more famous parts of the city, and which, as such, cannot deliver him to the pure originality he's trying to reach.

Binx is probably suffering from post-traumatic stress disorder, for he was nearly killed a few years earlier in the Korean War. The secondary character in the novel, a young woman named Kate, is probably also suffering from it, after having survived a car wreck that killed her fiancé. Binx and Kate are technically not blood relatives, but they were raised together as virtual siblings, and so their eventual marriage is precisely the bold overthrow of convention that would mean the completion of the main character's search, and the fact that he has managed to tell his story (the novel is his first-person narrative throughout) signals too that he has gone a long way to recovering from the post-traumatic stress disorder that undergirds his self-marginalization. In the end, he seems to have won for himself a happy home, though redolent with absurdist farce, in what Formento would call an "out" place.

Although Percy lived briefly in New Orleans in the 1940s, he spent most of his life across the lake, for it freed him, he felt, from the distractions of the city. The same kind of imaginative freedom from the old city marks another novelist's career – John Gregory Brown – who grew up in the same neighborhood where the protagonist of *The Moviegoer* has chosen to live. Brown's first two novels – *Decorations in a Ruined Cemetery* and *The Wrecked, Blessed Body of Shelton Lefleur* – are both well-crafted excavations into the racially charged secrets of difficult family histories. Brown has published two other novels in which characters revisit difficulties from earlier phases of their lives, one an historical novel about John James Audubon's experiences on a plantation on the outskirts of New Orleans and another about a Katrina evacuee who lands in a hotel in Virginia. Though Brown hasn't lived in New Orleans since his upbringing in the modern suburbs near the lake, he has described himself as feeling both sufficiently at home in the city, and, like the protagonist of *The Moviegoer*, distant enough from the epicenters of its age-old mystique to set aside significant concerns about geographic and historical accuracy, and thus to use the city as a setting with considerable imaginative freedom.[7]

The notion of New Orleans as a city of the imagination is predicated at least tacitly on the experience of New Orleans as a city that has been lost. This notion has most readily taken root in the outskirts of the city, where the city ends and gives way to the same sorts of generic suburbs that during the middle decades of the twentieth century began to spring up all over the US. These suburbs to the north and to the east of the old city bore the brunt of the apocalypse, and thus have become the places where the future of the city – its full destruction – is most easy to envision.

The story of Katrina, as Andy Horowitz argues, begins in 1915, when a major hurricane rolled over the city. New Orleans weathered that storm fairly well. With the advent of new pumps that could drain the cypress swamps that had surrounded the old city, and thereby make those former swamps viable land for modern development, and with surging confidence in the aftermath of that 1915 hurricane, the city began to expand very quickly in ways that, to earlier generations, would have seemed highly inadvisable. Over the decades that followed, a pattern took root familiar to all those who live in regions that, as Horowitz mordantly puts it, are cursed with a wealth of natural resources, south Louisiana's being oil: as the city recklessly expanded, the machinery of extraction, driven by the demons of greed, trumped all other infrastructural considerations, like, for instance, flood protection, even as it destroyed the coastal wetlands that had long been the city's primary defense against hurricanes. And thus, in 2005, while nearly everything built in New Orleans before the dawn of the twentieth century came through relatively unscathed, nearly everything built afterward was deeply flooded.[8] The old city, albeit in skeletal form, was up and running within a few weeks of the levee failure, the strip clubs of Bourbon Street bragging that they were the very first places in the city to re-open; but the farther one went from these blocks, the more unthinkable became any hope of a future, particularly for people of color and those without significant financial resources.

Katrina Displacement More than a million residents of the Gulf Coast were displaced by the hurricane, and New Orleans, which had a population of 480,000 before the storm, had, a year later, only 254,000. Now, over fifteen years since Katrina, the population has climbed to 390,000, still nearly 100,000 short of its pre-storm count. About 40 percent of the displaced never returned to the city, meaning that much of the current population has little direct knowledge of pre-Katrina New Orleans.

The neighborhood of Gentilly, decimated in the storm, however, might soon offer at least a glimpse of the kind of changes that the rest of the city should also soon undertake to handle heavy inundation from rain, if not the coastal surges from major hurricanes. Planning is underway to build through Gentilly a labyrinth of bayous, lakes, and lagoons – a web of water infrastructure that might call to mind the canals of Amsterdam or Venice, rather than the generic suburb that Gentilly has been for most of its existence. Or perhaps this new version of Gentilly will suggest a partial return through a series of open spaces to something like the swamps from which the neighborhood came, especially if what are known as rain gardens are widely adopted, whereby the standard suburban lawn is replaced by terraced spaces meant to catch and hold run off, and filled with plants that thrive in water. An elaborate network of these sorts of miniature bogs, a fine-grained version of the system of larger waterways, would ease the burden on the pumps, by letting Gentilly become a kind of hybrid of modern suburb and primordial swamp. The politics of this process of transformation would be, of course, unimaginably fraught.

Speculation about the future of the city, particularly as it will be forced to recalibrate its relation to the natural world, has driven significant writing associated with the outskirts of New Orleans. Perhaps the most famous is *The Saga of the Swamp Thing*. The original idea began in 1970, when Len Wein hit upon the notion of a scientist who is murdered by a friend, his body tossed in the swamp to rot; but the swamp somehow resurrects him, or at least comes to embody his bitter knowledge of the betrayal, and then organizes itself to embark on a project of revenge. Some ten years later, after the comic book's modest success, the horror-movie director Wes Craven decided to base a film on it. DC capitalized on the new interest in the story and pulled together a creative team to reboot the series, the leader of which would be a young man in England named Alan Moore. And thus *The Saga of the Swamp Thing* entered its classic phase and altered the course of comic-book history.

Moore had an uncanny ear for dialogue and for compressed but well-paced visual storytelling. He also had the requisite creativity to construct an original hybrid of the horror and superhero genres. He created forty issues between 1984 and 1987, stopping only to turn his full attention to his new project, *Watchmen*, which, alongside Art Spiegelman's *Maus* and Frank Miller's *Dark Knight Returns*, taught the world that the graphic novel (no longer merely known as the comic book, though Moore prefers the latter term) could be a vehicle of the most serious literary and artistic achievement and study. Under Moore's creative leadership, *The Saga of the Swamp Thing* offers a radical vision rooted in what today has become known as eco-critical theory, a vision of humanity's naïve, imperious goal to know, control, and exploit the natural world finally getting its comeuppance, as the swamp, in particular, organizes itself for vengeance. The scene for this karmic blowback is south Louisiana, some two dozen miles below New Orleans in the wetlands around Houma.

Moore's issues were the first works that DC comics released without bothering to get the seal of approval from the censors at the Comics Code of Authority since that body was founded three decades earlier. The story, in his hands, became thick with allusions to a wide range of figures who inspired him, from Blake to Dante to the American Transcendentalists, for instance, as well as to Brian Eno's *Another*

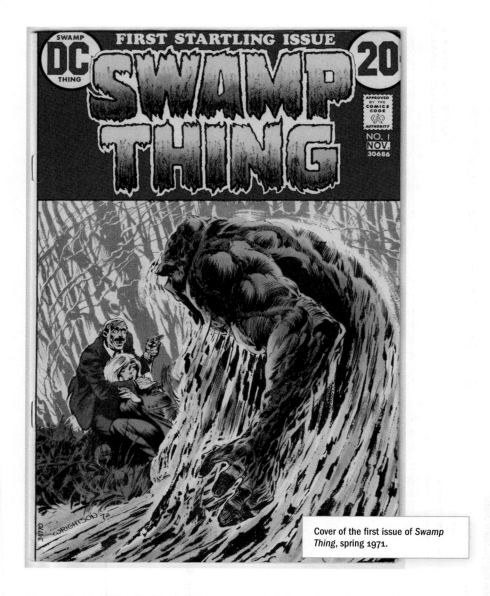

Cover of the first issue of *Swamp Thing*, spring 1971.

Green World, Billie Holiday's "Strange Fruit," Francisco Goya's *The Sleep of Reason Breeds Monsters*, Igor Stravinsky's *The Rite of Spring*, and Hieronymus Bosch's *The Garden of Earthly Delights*, among others. Each chapter of each issue constitutes a self-contained prose-poem that builds on what came before and lays the groundwork for what

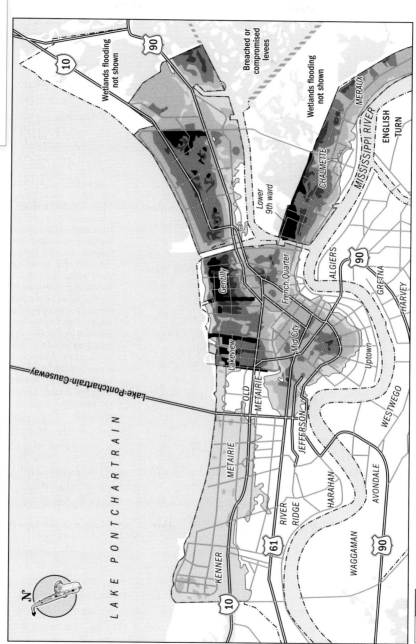

Federal Levee Failure/ Hurricane Katrina/ August 29, 2005

Map of the area flooded by Hurricane Katrina and subsequent levee failure.

Approximate Standing Floodwater Depths

- Over 10 feet
- 8–10 feet
- 6–8 feet
- 4–6 feet
- 2–4 feet
- 0–2 feet
- Levees/floodwalls
- Breached or compromisetd levees

Breached or compromised levees

Wetlands flooding not shown

Wetlands flooding not shown

LAKE PONTCHARTRAIN

Lake-Pontchartrain-Causeway

KENNER
METAIRIE
OLD METAIRIE
RIVER RIDGE
HARAHAN
WAGGAMAN
AVONDALE
WESTWEGO
JEFFERSON
Lakeview
Mid City
Gentilly
French Quarter
Uptown
ALGIERS
GRETNA
HARVEY
Lower 9th ward
CHALMETTE
MERAUX
ENGLISH TURN
MISSISSIPPI RIVER

10
90
10
61
90
90

N

0   4 kilometers

will happen next, in a visual style that one of the illustrators, Steven Bisette, calls "hallucinatory baroque," and in a literary mode that the cover of each issue announced with the discreet label near the top that read "sophisticated suspense." Moore's *Swamp Thing* is not the only important comic book associated with New Orleans, as, in 2007, Brad Benischek published *Revacuation*, and, two years later, Josh Neufield's *AD: New Orleans after the Deluge* found a place on *The New York Times* best-seller list. Both projects owe a debt to Moore's *Swamp Thing* of twenty years earlier. In a related vein, a new videogame called *NORCO*, named after a town some 25 miles upriver from New Orleans, describes itself on its website as "a Southern Gothic point and click narrative adventure that explores the industrial swamp-lands and decaying suburbs of South Louisiana."

When Moore chose to set *The Saga of the Swamp Thing* in the wetlands just south of New Orleans, he was probably paying homage to H. P. Lovecraft, whose classic story of 1928, "The Call of Cthulhu," follows a New Orleans police detective into the same territory to investigate a cult that worships, in bloody rituals, a mon-ster. And Moore surely knew well the work of William S. Burroughs, who lived just across the river from the French Quarter in the neigh-borhood of Algiers for two very tumultuous years in the late 1940s. Burroughs had recently failed in his efforts to farm marijuana in Texas, and brought his wife and two small children to New Orleans, where, as a corrupt port city, he anticipated a plentiful supply of heroin and easy-to-access queer underground. The Burroughs household at 509 Wagner Street, as described in a chapter of Jack Kerouac's *On the Road*, was a whirlpool of squalor and addiction, where the family was fast approaching a free fall that could only end in tragedy.

> **Coastal Erosion** As sea levels rise and the levees along the Mississippi River prevent ongoing sedimentation, coastal Louisiana loses wetlands at a rate of one football field an hour. An endless network of canals dredged by oil companies has further destabilized these wetlands, which are the primary buffer between the city and the storms that come from the ever warmer and more volatile Gulf of Mexico. Diverting the Mississippi River will likely prove too costly, too politically unpopular, and too slow to save the collapsing ecosystem, so many artists and cultural leaders in the city speak not of fixing the problem but of preparing the population in the area for the inevitable.

In Burroughs's own memoir, *Junky*, he describes New Orleans, in what was at least partly a projection of his own state, as a "stratified series of ruins," and fell in with a colorful cast of underworld characters around the corner of Exchange Place and Canal Street in the French Quarter.[9] Burroughs himself was soon arrested on Carondelet near the corner of Julia, but, rather than face the charges, he slipped out of town to Mexico City, where he would inadvertently shoot and kill his wife. Ten years later, this experience of running from the New Orleans cops would form the primary plotline of his masterpiece, *Naked Lunch* (1959). In that book, the various outlaw figures he met on the street in New Orleans – pimps, dealers, addicts, some of whom are also police informants – become loose models for his monstrous, insect-like figures who allegorize, in different ways, the grotesque aspect of humanity, always compromised and enslaved by abject needs and addictions that mire them in a natural world that is thoroughly polluted, even suffused with toxins.

Naked Lunch, in these terms, is part of what made *Swamp Thing* possible and, if only indirectly, it might have inspired two recent works of speculative fiction that have garnered significant attention. Both are preoccupied with looming environmental catastrophe and are situated in the much-transformed region around New Orleans. In Moira Crone's *The Not Yet* (2012), New Orleans has become a chaotic set of islands off the Gulf Coast, to which the novel's 20-year-old protagonist must travel in order to sort out a question of his inheritance and his right to ascend in a radically stratified society, at the top of which is a caste that has the biomedical means to escape the aging process and continue to enjoy the lower castes who exist only for their amusement. In the prophetic plot of Sherri L. Smith's *Orleans* (2013), an epidemic in the year 2020 identified as "Delta Fever" has shut down New Orleans; the fever, along with a succession of hurricanes over three decades, has transformed the city into a fully walled-in dystopia that the young female protagonist seeks to escape with the baby of her recently deceased friend, as a young doctor enters in the hopes of studying the deadly virus.

The work in this territory that has reached the widest audience, however, is Beyoncé's "Formation." The most frequently googled song, worldwide, for 2016, several magazines listed it as *the* song of that year, and others eventually identified it as the song of the decade. The video, which won the Grammy for best video, is built around exterior passages of contemporary New Orleans as a militarized, flooded dystopia, juxtaposed with sections in which the singer, in nineteenth-century clothing, filmed against opulent interiors of the same period, seems to suggest, with her light skin and hair, the age-old tradition of the quadroon (Beyoncé's mother's family has lived some two-dozen miles south of New Orleans around Houma for several generations, in the same area where *Swamp Thing* and "The Call of Cthulhu" take place). The video seems to offer these two modes – Beyoncé as nineteenth-century quadroon, New Orleans as militarized, flooded dystopia – as metaphors for each other. The mechanical rhythms of its electronic dance music suggest an especially dire and pessimistic strain of Afro-Futurism, particularly at the video's end, when Beyoncé, perched atop a New Orleans Police squad car, sinks beneath the water, perhaps suggesting a baptism, but more directly a drowning.

The implicit horror of the drowning at the video's end was nearly lived in the most literal way by the Nigerian poet Niyi Osundare in the days after Hurricane Katrina. Trapped in the attic of his Gentilly home with his wife, the water rising up to their necks, and then pressing their heads against the roof, and keeping them there for more than twenty-four hours, the couple was finally rescued when they heard a neighbor pass by in a boat and began to scream for help. The neighbor used an axe to open their roof and lift them out. A prolific poet, essayist, and dramatist whose long shelf's worth of work is rooted in the oral performance traditions of the Yoruban culture in which he was raised, Osundare published *City without People: The Katrina Poems* in 2011 after a lengthy exile from New Orleans. He describes the transformation of the city – where "roads lose their names / streets lose their memories" and "famous boulevards / dissolve into nameless pools" – as having been carried out by a kind of monster, impossibly vast, powerful, and cruel, that took the form of the lake and proceeded to toss houses from their foundations and send them searching for their roofs; the monster even snatched someone's baby from its bed to deliver it to "the hungry sea." In the aftermath, dogs sniff out an endless succession of corpses from the mud-caked rubble. In a related vein, the performance poet Patricia Smith also casts the storm as a monster in *Blood Dazzler* (2008). A finalist for the National Book Award, it was later adapted as a theatrical dance production at Harlem Stage. Some of Smith's poems are spoken from the persona of the Hurricane itself.

Hurricane Ida On August 29, 2021, the sixteenth anniversary of Katrina, the most powerful storm to impact New Orleans since that event made landfall just west of New Orleans. Despite Hurricane Ida's power, the levees held, and no one drowned, so some have called it a win. But the sheer frequency of storms in recent years tells a different story. In 2020, the storm season was the most active in Louisiana's recorded history, with insurance claims totaling over 10 billion dollars. While New Orleans is surely more prepared for big storms than it was when Katrina landed, concern that their sheer frequency could overwhelm the population's resources is mounting.

Another poet, Jerika Marchan, has taken an even more destabilizing approach to the question of voice in her debut collection called *Swole* (2018) about her experience of loss and displacement when Katrina upended her early adolescence in the suburbs on the eastern edge of the city. Born in the Philippines and raised in New Orleans, her mother worked, in the pre-Katrina period, as an emergency-medical first responder – and Marchan had no contact with her for the first five days after the levees failed. Marchan describes the months that followed as a kind of coma, in which her mind rejected the possibility of forming memories of what was happening. Her debut book is a multi-voiced collage that pulls together a wide variety of fragmentary snatches of language, juxtaposing and stringing them along with each other to enact and preserve something of the deep sense of confusion and dislocation that Katrina delivered. A kind of verbal scrapbook to take the place of the memories that, at the time, she wouldn't allow herself to form, the book is described by her as "a Greek chorus or a play or a libretto or a playlist or a score or a mash-up of all of those things," crafted out of snippets of radio broadcasts, fund-raising testimonials, stories from neighbors, signs people had posted on what was left of their homes, and the voices of the kids from her school.[10] In a related vein, Tonya Foster, who also grew up in the eastern edge of the city, now holds an endowed chair in poetry at San Francisco State University and is an editor at *The African American Review*. Her latest book, *A Mathematics of Chaos: Thingification*, is a multi-genre meditation on New Orleans that, like Marchan's book, defies traditional form.

Farther east, the neighborhood called Versailles is home to one of the largest concentrations of Vietnamese Americans in the US, a proud community near Bayou Sauvage that endured some of the worst of Katrina's power. This community was the subject of Robert Olen Butler's controversial short-story collection that won the Pulitzer Prize in 1993, and earlier this year saw the publication of the first novel by a Vietnamese American set in this particular community, Eric Nguyen's *Things We Lost to the Water* (2021). Like Margaret Wilkerson Sexton's *A Kind of Freedom*, it follows a family over a long arc of local history, tracing the process by which a mother and her two sons, after arriving in the area as war refugees in the late 1970s, slowly create a sense of home and a sense of identity in the city. It ends amidst the chaos and horror of Katrina. Nguyen's debut novel has garnered considerable attention and praise, particularly for showcasing a dimension of New Orleans on its most remote outskirts that, heretofore, has not been the subject of long-form narrative.

This particular pattern of inattention that defines this part of the city is part of what spurred Kelly DeBerry (long-time partner of newspaper editorialist Jarvis DeBerry) to form The MelaNated Writers Collective, a workshop that met regularly on Franklin Avenue in Gentilly for years to give a sense of audience to young Black writers who otherwise might feel invisible and silenced. The sense of invisibility experienced by those who write from within these relatively new suburbs at the outskirts of the city is at the center of Sarah Broom's National Book Award–winning memoir of 2019, *The Yellow House*. Broom narrates a full century of her family's history, finding their way in New Orleans in the aftermath of enslavement, contending with the scattering forces of the Jim Crow era, and finally finding a focal point in the early 1960s in a small cottage on the outskirts of town, in an area that was, in those days, expected to prosper. Her mother bought the house and raised a dozen children there, and did so, throughout the author's upbringing, as a single mother. The social history of this area in the final decades of the twentieth century is vividly drawn, blended as it is with the most heartfelt personal memories, and framed in tension, every step of the way, with the area's near total invisibility within the larger culture and tourist economy of the region. The titular yellow house, a nexus of memory and bonding for everyone in Broom's expansive family, was destroyed by Katrina, cast to the oblivion that, when her mother first bought it a half-century earlier, its whole purpose was to overcome.

This sense of struggle against oblivion is implicit in the title of the debut collection by the young African-American poet, Skye Jackson, called *A Faster Grave*. In the poem "I Remember" she writes about the way her people have been displaced not by Hurricane Katrina but rather by white newcomers who have flooded the city's traditional centers of Black culture: "A chilling realization: / gentrification is just / another word for *revenge*." Jackson has a law degree and works by day in that profession. Similarly, Maurice Carlos Ruffin, who grew up not far from Broom and Jackson, has also been a lawyer, but recently stopped practicing law to devote himself full-time to writing. He released in 2019 his debut novel, *We Cast a Shadow*, which is haunted by the same anxiety about the looming possibility of oblivion. He drew on his experiences as a lawyer in this novel, set some half-century into the future, in which racial divisions have become only more entrenched and extreme, as the main character, a young African-American father, eyes his biracial son's birthmark, which is expanding. Worried that being engulfed in darkness will consign him to a life of few options, even an early grave, or, as in the case of his own father, a long prison term, the lawyer tries a variety of solutions to lighten the boy's skin, even considering a new medical procedure that will reverse the terms of John Howard Griffin's *Black Like Me* and allow the boy to pass, the rest of his life, as white. Ruffin followed this debut novel with a collection of short stories called *The*

Ones Who Don't Say They Love You (2021), in which gentrification is the force most urgently seeking to erase the Black culture that has thrived for so many decades in the neighborhoods of New Orleans. Characters find the prices of homes skyrocketing, new neighbors everywhere, most of whom, Ruffin says, look like someone they used to work for, and struggle to imagine how to hang on to the legacies that give their life meaning. The hardest edge of this concern takes the spectrous form of mass incarceration, as a number of Ruffin's characters are driven to crime to make ends meet.

This territory is the particular focus of Zachary Lazar's *Vengeance* (2018), which begins when the narrator visits the state penitentiary at Angola to watch an Easter pageant and gets interested in the case of an inmate who is serving a life sentence for a drug murder that unfolded about a decade earlier in the working-class suburbs across the river from New Orleans. Lazar's novel avoids all the familiar markers of New Orleans – music, carnival, cuisine – to trace in detail the lives of those whom the tourist industry and gentrifiers avoid, ultimately to mull ambiguities in the inmate's case that expand until Truth itself seems to recede from reach, leaving the narrator and the audience adrift in an unresolvable agony of unreality. The sort of rage that can begin to roar in such environments is voiced in *Sleeper Cell* (2016) by Michael Moore (aka A Scribe Called Quess?). Some of Moore's poetry is a call to arms to extend the historic uprisings of the enslaved into the present and future, at least symbolically, as when Moore played a significant role in the work of having the Confederate monuments removed from the city in 2017. In a related vein, Rickey Laurentiis's 2015 collection of poetry, *Boy with Thorns*, has drawn considerable acclaim for exploring the psychic afterlife of long histories of racial and sexual violence. And yet another writer from the outskirts of the city, Clint Smith, has come to wide recognition not only for his performance poetry (he won the national poetry slam competition while a graduate student at Harvard), but also as a staff writer for *The Atlantic* and for his focus on mass incarceration. His book of poetry, *Counting Descent*, has won awards; his book on the history of slavery, *How the Word Is Passed*, reached the top of *The New York Times* best-seller list; and his TED talks have been viewed more than 7 million times. One of them, *How to Raise a Black Son in America*, anticipates themes in a recent work of nonfiction, *Across the River: Life, Death, and Football in an American City*, by Kent Babb, which profiles a high-school football program across the river from the French Quarter in the neighborhood of Algiers. The team has won the state championship a few times in the last several years and seen a good number of its players embark on professional football careers but struggles mightily against the forces of drugs, violence, and despair that stalk its surrounding community. Analogous struggles are at the heart of Dedra Johnson's *Sandrine's Letters to Tomorrow*, a young girl's coming-of-age story. Set in the same eastern edge of the city where Broom, Jackson, Laurentiis, and Ruffin grew up, it chronicles a brutal arc of abuse, rejection, and neglect – and also the dawning determination to value one's self – that has been compared to Morrison's *The Bluest Eye* and Angelou's *I Know Why the Caged Bird Sings*.

The struggle against oblivion also defines a stunning new 'zine called *Bulbancha Is Still a Place*, Bulbancha being the name that indigenous peoples use to refer to the stretch of land otherwise known as New Orleans. Bulbancha means "place of many tongues," a term that is turning up with increasing frequency in graffiti around the city. Jeffrey S. Darensbourg, a "contributing-editor-who-is-not-a-chief," points out in an interview in *Anti-Gravity Magazine* that, long before Congo Square was a dancing ground for people of African descent, it served the same purpose for indigenous groups who continued to inhabit the area long after Europeans and Africans arrived, and who likely therefore influenced the music that developed in Congo Square well beyond just the earliest iterations of the Mardi Gras Indian tradition. Darensbourg notes that indigenous heritage is particularly present today, though often unwittingly, in people who are mistakenly assumed to be of either purely African or European descent and identified as Cajun and Creole. *Bulbancha Is Still a Place* is noteworthy for its especially powerful visual layout, the work of an artist known only as Ozone504, who operates through Antennae Gallery. It is helping to make an aspect of New Orleans's remote past that had been all but erased newly visible within the cultural politics of the city.

The work of overturning oblivion and the dread that such efforts will always ultimately fall short, particularly in the context of climate change, drive the poetry of Karisma Price to singular heights. She was 10 years old when Katrina hit, her family's uptown home destroyed by floodwaters. She evacuated first to Meridian, Mississippi, for a few weeks, then spent a year in Dallas; from there, she returned to New Orleans only to spend a year with her family in a hotel room.[11] Soon thereafter, as a 7th grader in a poetry workshop, a poem by Pablo Neruda electrified her; several years later, she began to study poetry with Terrance Hayes in New York. Her debut collection, *I'm Always So Serious* (2023), grapples with the prospect of loss in the boldest terms.

In one poem, a father is diagnosed with cancer, and, in another, after police come to the door, "he is taken from the house in flip flops," the poem then concluding, "You pray for another flood, something to strip the house and leave you stranded / the way Lent bulldozes its way into your city and strips / the beads from the necks of drunk tourists." Later in the book, she writes "The police will not break the door … we will sing arrows into them." She notes, "I've had panic attacks since I was five," but then observes that "everything you fear keeps you alive." In another poem, she writes, "Breathing / is a tender type of breaking," and yet another ruminates on how the legendary pianist James Booker lost his eye.

These visions of loss go to the heart of contemporary New Orleans, as anxieties about what climate change will mean for this low-lying city grow ever sharper. And, as gentrification pushes more Black people toward the outskirts of the city, they find themselves not simply distanced from these home neighborhoods but living in places that, as Hurricane Katrina showed us, will suffer the most and the soonest from the larger and more frequent storms that are surely coming. Price has said she sometimes finds it difficult to imagine a future for New Orleans that includes her people. As the menace of hurricanes hangs over her world with the ever-present prospect of losing everything to the water, she thinks of her elders, writing, "This is the type of weather we lose matriarchs to." She then continues,

We will unfurl
the rollers from her hair when we find her,
stroke the blue suede of the casket …
There will be no headstone.
There will be nowhere to sing.

Want More?
Histories, Mysteries, and Movies

Anyone who is curious about the cultural history of the city and wants to create thicker context for thinking about its most important writing has quite a few options, for the years since Katrina, in particular, have seen an outpouring of excellent books aimed at understanding New Orleans. What follows is a brief survey of what's out there, beyond what I've already mentioned, as well as a glance at some genre-writing and some movies.

Jason Berry's *City of a Million Dreams: A History of New Orleans at 300* is an excellent general history of the city for non-specialists. And James B. Borders IV recently created the invaluable *Marking Time, Making Place: An Essential Chronology of Blacks in New Orleans since 1718* that traces key moments, over those same three centuries, of what his book describes as "one of the most Africanized spaces" in the US.

The early history of New Orleans has been an especially rich subject over the last two decades. Lawrence Powell's *Accidental City: Improvising New Orleans* is a gem and tells the story of the city from the earliest European settlement in the first decades of the eighteenth century up to the War of 1812. Powell is rumored to be working on a second volume that will pick up where the first left off and continue the narrative up to the assassination of Huey P. Long in the early 1930s. Another excellent study of early New Orleans can be found in Shannon Lee Dawdy's *Building the Devil's Empire: French Colonial New Orleans*. It follows only the first fifty years of the European presence in south Louisiana, stopping in 1768 with local resistance to the Spanish takeover of the erstwhile French project. For those who want the story of the area before the Europeans arrived and how indigenous peoples handled that arrival, the book is Elizabeth Ellis's forthcoming *Power on the Margins: The Petites Nations and the Lower Mississippi Valley, 1650–1800*.

For those particularly interested in the rise of Creole society through the eighteenth and early nineteenth centuries, Nathalie Dessens's two books are essential: *Creole City: A Chronicle of Early American New Orleans* and *From Saint-Domingue to New Orleans: Migration and Influences*. And, as a side note, when considering a crucial event that shaped nineteenth-century New Orleans at its core, one must go to Laurent Dubois's *Avengers of the New World: The Story of the Haitian Revolution*, and, on that same uprising of the enslaved, Michel-Rolph Trouillot's *Silencing the Past: Power and the Production of History*. To further situate early New Orleans in the cultural dynamics of the surrounding hemisphere, particularly the music and religion of the African diaspora and the colonial projects of Western Europe, one should go to Ned Sublette's *The World That Made New Orleans: From Spanish Silver to Congo Square*. And for the particular presence of Africa in the city's origins, the key source is Gwendolyn Midlo Hall's *Africans in Colonial Louisiana: The Development of Afro-Creole Culture in the 18th Century*. If one seeks to sort out the complexities of race in New Orleans in the decades around the Civil War, Angel Adams Parham's *American Routes: Racial Palimpsests and the Transformation of Race* is essential, as is Shirley Thompson's *Exiles at Home: The Struggle to Become American in Creole New Orleans*. In thinking about another dimension of race in the nineteenth century, one would do well to read Richard Campanella's *Lincoln in New Orleans: The 1828 and 1831 Flatboat Journeys and Their Place in History* to see how the spectacle of the auctions of the enslaved transformed one particular white outsider, with broad implications for the nation's history. The classic study of the experience of slave markets in New Orleans is Walter Johnson's *Soul by Soul: Life inside the Antebellum Slave Markets*, a book he followed with *River of Dark Dreams: Slavery and Empire in the Cotton Kingdom*, that sorts out the role of these slave markets and the labor of the enslaved in the larger economy of the Western world. To understand the years that followed the Civil War in New Orleans, three books are particularly helpful: James K. Hogue's *Uncivil War: Five New Orleans Street Battles and the Rise and Fall of Radical Reconstruction*; John DeSantis's *The Thibodaux Massacre: Racial Violence and the 1887 Sugar Cane Labor Strike*; and John Blassingame's classic *Black New Orleans: 1860–1880*.

Three major themes of New Orleans – sex and religion and music – have also yielded excellent books. On the subject of sex, one would do well to start with Emily Clark's *The Strange History of the American Quadroon in the Revolutionary Atlantic World*, Jessica Marie Johnson's *Wicked Flesh: Black Women, Intimacy, and Freedom in the Atlantic World*, and Emily Epstein Landau's *Spectacular Wickedness: Sex, Race, and Memory in Storyville, New Orleans*. On the theme of religion, Emily Clark, again, provides an essential starting point with *Masterless Mistresses: The New Orleans Ursulines and the Development of a New World Society, 1727 to 1834*. Another scholar, Emily Suzanne Clark, recently published a fine study titled *A Luminous Brotherhood: Afro-Creole Spiritualism in Nineteenth-Century New Orleans*. An excellent ethnography can be found in *The Spiritual Churches of New Orleans: Origins, Beliefs, and Rituals of an African-American Religion* by Claude F. Jacobs and Andrew J. Kaslow, with dazzling photographs by Michael P. Smith. Yet another essential book on religion in New Orleans is Jason Berry's *The Spirit of Blackhawk: A Mystery of Africans and Indians.*

Books about the music of the city abound, but a particularly great one is *Louis Armstrong's New Orleans* by Thomas Brothers, which tells the story of the city through a singular young trumpeter, and vice versa, to capture, as well as any book can, how Jazz was born. To consider all the other musical splendors of New Orleans, one should read *Up from the Cradle of Jazz: New Orleans Music since World War II* by Jason Berry, Jonathan Foose, and Tad Jones. Matt Sakakeeny's *Roll with It: Brass Bands in the Streets of New Orleans* is the definitive study of the music of the second-line parade tradition, revitalized by the Dirty Dozen around 1980 and still flourishing today. The particular topic of Hip Hop is handled well in Ned Sublette's *The Year before the Flood: A Story of New Orleans*, and one can do no better on the subject of Bounce than read *The Definition of Bounce* by 10th Ward Buck and Alison Fensterstock, and also Matt Miller's *Bounce*.

Those interested in histories of the twentieth century would do well to look at books by Richard Campanella. As noted earlier, Campanella has become the premier public intellectual on the subject of New Orleans in this era, having authored, for non-specialists, a dozen books and countless articles. To browse his website is to get an invaluable introduction to the city. His book *Bourbon Street: A History* is a great way to gather the backstory on what the French Quarter has become. His recent book on *The West Bank of New Orleans* succeeds on the same scale in discussing a cultural world that most tourists never see, and his forthcoming book on the history of efforts to solve New Orleans's drainage problems will deliver a world that, in turn, almost no one ever sees, except in weather emergencies – the network of pipes and canals that is the very basis of the city's existence.

Those interested in the particular politics of race over the last half-century will want to read Kent Germany's *New Orleans after the Promises: Poverty, Citizenship, and the Search for the Great Society* and Leonard Moore's *Black Rage in New Orleans: Police Brutality and African-American Activism from World War II to Katrina*. The subject of Katrina has of course generated a considerable stack of books, much of it centered around the American experience of race. The best of them is Andy Horowitz's *Katrina: 1915 to 2015*, as it situates the event in a long historical arc of bad decisions, as real-estate developers and oil-industry executives have pressured government officials to think, decade after decade, in terms of quick money rather than environmental sustainability and racial justice. Michael Eric Dyson's *Come Hell or High Water: Hurricane Katrina and the Color of Disaster* sorts out the particular meaning of the storm and its aftermath in terms of the unequal distribution of terror, grief, and misery along racial lines. For a book about the physical phenomenon of what happened in August of 2005, Jed Horne's *Breach of Faith* is the book to read. Katrina has also been the subject of important documentaries. Spike Lee's *When the Levees Broke: A Requiem in Four Acts* is indispensable; and Carl Deal and Tia Lessin's *Trouble the Water* has won at least a dozen major awards. In the more general category of documentary, Roberto Minervini's *What You Gonna Do When the World's on Fire* is utterly overwhelming.

The troubles associated with the city have also generated no small appetite for escapist fare, typically in the form of murder mysteries and horror fiction. For those hankering for a fictional detective to follow through a multi-volume series as they sleuth their way around the city, here's a partial list to get you started: James Lee Burke's Dave Robichaux, Tony Fennelly's Matty Sinclair, David Fulmer's Valentin St. Cyr, Barbara Hamby's Benjamin January, Greg Herren's Scotty Bradley and Chanse McLeod, Bill Loehfelm's Maureen Coughlin, J. M. Redmann's Mickey Knight, James Sallis's Lew Griffin, Robert Skinner's Wesley Farrell, Julie Smith's Skip Langdon, and Michael Allen Zell's Bobby Delery, to name just the first dozen or so that come to mind.

Filmmakers too have been drawn to the city. The early ones include a 1934 Mae West vehicle called *Belle of the Nineties*, a Bette Davis and Henry Fonda love story from 1938 called *Jezebel*, and a John Wayne movie from 1941 called *Lady from Louisiana*. A particular favorite is *New Orleans* from 1947, featuring both Louis Armstrong and Billie Holiday. The first genuine classic of New Orleans movies is Elia Kazan's *Panic in the Streets* (1950), starring Richard Widmark, about the rush to catch a killer who is carrying an infectious disease before he can unleash a plague. Kazan would make the iconic version of *A Streetcar Named Desire* with Marlon Brando and Vivian Leigh just a few years later. In that same period – the mid1950s – three more movies were filmed with New Orleans settings: *My Forbidden Past*, a love story with Robert Mitchum and Ava Gardner, *Mississippi Gambler* with Tyrone Power, and a noir-ish Edward G. Robinson thriller called *Nightmare* about a New Orleans musician. The stand-out, though, of the mid 1950s is Douglas Sirk's *The Tarnished Angels*, adapted from Faulkner's novel, *Pylon*, the movie appearing the same year – 1957 – as the film adaptation of Robert Penn Warren's *Band of Angels*. By the end of the 1950s, Elvis Presley would star in *King Creole*, and Katherine Hepburn, Montgomery Clift, and Elizabeth Taylor would appear in an adaptation of Tennessee Williams's *Suddenly Last Summer*. In the 1960s, Steve McQueen would star in *The Cincinnati Kid*, and Jane Fonda and Barbara Stanwyck would team up for an adaptation of Nelson Algren's *A Walk on the Wild Side*. Finally, in the late 1960s, the counterculture classic *Easy Rider* climaxes in New Orleans with a psychedelic vision of Metairie Cemetery. In the 1970s, Charles Bronson would star in *Hard Times*, a boxing movie set along the New Orleans waterfront, Clint Eastwood would direct and star in a thriller called *Tightrope*, and Louis Malle would make a movie about Storyville called *Pretty Baby*. In the early 1980s, Nastassja Kinski would star in a re-make of the old B-grade horror movie, *Cat People*. Jim Jarmusch filmed one of his greatest movies, *Down by Law*, in the mid 1980s in New Orleans, and Mickey Rourke and Lisa Bonet would star, in this same period, in *Angel Heart*. Also in the late 1980s, Ellen Barkin and Dennis Quaid, who mastered a version of the local accent, starred in *The Big Easy*. In the early 1990s, an adaption of *Interview with a Vampire* would feature Brad Pitt and Tom Cruise. And Oliver Stone's *JFK* would adapt District Attorney Jim Garrison's *On the Trail of the Assassins* in a new kind of quasi-documentary, noir style. In 2008, Brad Pitt starred in a movie that begins and ends with Katrina – *The Curious Case of Benjamin Button*, based on a short story by F. Scott Fitzgerald, it follows the life a man who ages in reverse.

Finally, for those readers who are looking for a way to get a handle on the meaning of New Orleans as a whole and at the broadest level, a relatively recent few books provide essential tools for conceptualizing the city that way. The first of them is Joseph P. Roach's *Cities of the Dead: Circum-Atlantic Performance*, which advances a theory of the dynamics of memory and culture through Mardi Gras Indians and Storyville. In a more distinctly literary key, Robert Azzarello's *Three Hundred Years of*

Decadence: New Orleans Literature in the Transatlantic World uses the single concept in its title to organize the entire cultural history of the city in an international framework. Violet Harrington Bryan's *The Myth of New Orleans in Literature: Dialogues of Race and Gender* and Barbara Eckstein's *Sustaining New Orleans: Literature, Local Memory, and the Fate of a City* both build on a handful of canonical literary texts – in Bryan's case, to grapple with the city's function in the larger cultural imagination of the US in terms of identity, and, in the case of Eckstein, who was writing in the aftermath of Katrina, to unearth from the rubble questions about the meaning of the city's struggle for survival. Three collections of essays have emerged in the post-Katrina era, namely Rebecca Solnit and Rebecca Snedeker's *Unfathomable City: A New Orleans Atlas,* Teresa Toulouse and Barbara Ewell's *Sweet Spots: The In-Between Spaces in New Orleans,* and Thomas Adams and Matt Sakakeeny's *Remaking New Orleans: Beyond Exceptionalism and Authenticity.*

As New Orleans continues to change, there will surely be others.

Acknowledgments

Ray Ryan of Cambridge University Press suggested, in the spring of 2020, that I write this book. Ray had published, a few months earlier, a comprehensive collection of essays that I edited by a wide range of academics on the literary history of the city and thought my perspective on the city's most important literary activity of the last few generations would be worth bringing into the world. For that invitation and the unflagging support along the way, I thank Ray. The book, he told me, would be part of a series that focused on the literary culture of a number of great cities, and that Chris Morash would edit the series as a whole. When I saw Chris's proposal for the series and another for his book on Dublin, I was inspired. Chris has continued, every step of the way, to inspire me. His ambition for the series, his keen appreciation of the urban humanities, especially the literary, has made this great series possible. I'm proud to be part of it, and am grateful for Chris's guidance. There are other key figures at Cambridge University Press whom I am eager to thank, namely Senior Editorial Assistant Edgar Mendez, Content Manager Melissa Ward and Content Team Lead Ian McIver. Edgar has always given prompt, detailed answers to every question I've had about the publishing process, and Melissa and Ian have been ideal colleagues in leading the production process. I must also thank Chloe Bradley, Chris Burrows, Josh Hamel, Chris Jackson, Jasmine Short, and Tom Willshire for the time, energy, and considerable skill they brought to the work of turning my manuscript and collection of images into the actual book at hand and bringing it to the attention of the reading public. Thanks to David Prout as well for creating the book's index. I must also thank the wonderful cartographer, Joe LeMonnier, for creating this book's maps.

Other colleagues have played an indispensable role in the process of getting the book written. First, I must thank Lily Johnson, my research assistant, for her thorough critique of early drafts and her thoughts on a number of key books that I discuss. Also, Jane Pinzino, a research librarian at Tulane's Howard Tilton Memorial Library, has been an indefatigable resource in helping me locate useful images and the permission to publish them. Without her, this book would not look the same. Jane's colleague Anthony DelRosario also gave special assistance with two old photographs that enabled them to serve the book well. Ray Foye also helped me track down a rare image, and Matt Sakakeeny and Adam McKeown also connected me to essential resources.

I must thank as well Susan Larson, whose *A Booklover's Guide to New Orleans* was an essential starting point in getting me to think about the city's literature in spatial terms, neighborhood by neighborhood. Susan was also kind enough to feature me on her radio program, *The Reading Life*, at WWNO 89.9 FM in New Orleans, by way of stirring up interest in my first book about New Orleans. Other good friends did the same, hosting and leading discussions about that earlier book in ways that energized me to do this new one: Jane Wolfe of Melba's Poboys, Frank Relle of Frank Relle Photography, and Gwen Tompkins through Britton Trice's Garden District Bookshop. I'm so grateful to each of them.

The largest event connected to that first book and the one that did the most by way of spurring me to write this new one was held at Tulane University in January of 2020. Called *The Literary History of New Orleans: A Symposium*, this event was made possible by the generous support of Tulane's Department of English, Dean Brian Edwards, and the New Orleans Center for the Gulf South. It was organized in large measure by the Assistant Director of the New Orleans Center of the Gulf South, Denise Frazier, without whom it could never have come to be. I'm grateful to the two-dozen panelists who participated and the scores of readers who attended to discuss various topics over the course of the day. In many ways, this book began on that day, as Ray Ryan and I sat down over drinks afterward and he told me of the new series he was planning with Chris Morash.

I'm particularly grateful to Denise Frazier not only for coordinating that event, but also for being kind enough to read an early draft of the present volume and offer input that made it a better book. Other colleagues also gave me essential feedback on early drafts. First, Rich Campanella from Tulane's School of Architecture did a line-by-line reading of the manuscript and helped enormously with fine points of geography and history. His work on the city, as everyone interested in

New Orleans knows, has been extraordinary; no one teaches us more about it than he does. Ned Sublette, too, has been an essential guide and model for how to explore the cultural history of the city. He also helped to tighten the prose in this book at a number of key junctures. I also benefited from the line-by-line commentary that Brad Richard gave me. I'm lucky enough to have had still others give me careful responses, most notably Bryan Wagner, Matt Smith, and Kevin Rabalais. Beyond a careful reading of the book, Marguerite Nguyen has been a beloved supporter and sounding-board for more than a decade for much of my thinking about where and how I live. She has made all of my work smarter and easier. I am eternally grateful to her.

A number of friends and neighbors have also played a key role in helping me to navigate the city, to find and maintain my place in it, and I thank them: Beth Arroyo-Utterback, Dale Ashmun, Michele Baker, Sondra Bibb, Sally Bird, Ryan Blackwood, Jane Bleecker, Scott Borne, Douglas Bourgeois, Dwayne Brashears, Susan Danielson, Christine Day, Jamie Dell'Apa, Joel Dinerstein, Chris Dunn, Scott Farrin, Ricky Feather, Heather Fox, Jorge Fuentes, Jim Gabour, Michael Griffith, Mary Howell, Eric and Nikki Houghton, Brian Hubbard, Danielle King, David Kunian, Chris Lawson, Zach Lazar, Deb Luster, Leslie Millar, Steve O'Keefe, Tom Piazza, Nicholas Payton, Murf Reeves, Frank Relle, Ben Reiss, Mike Rousey, Matt Sakakeeny, James Singleton, Ed Skoog, Travis Tanner, Molly Travis, Rachel Weathers, Melissa Weber, and Les White. A number of friends who have recently passed away have also figured importantly in my experience of the city: David Averbuck, Dan Baum, Radford Brown, Suzanne Corley, Alex Cosby, Dale Firestone, Rebecca Metheny, Chili Rigot, Pat Walsh, and Albert Woodfox. I can't begin to express how grateful I am to have known them. I would also like to thank all my students at Tulane, too many to name here, who, over the last decade and a half, have taken my course on the literature of New Orleans and spurred me to dig ever deeper into the various arcs of meaning woven through the city's vast textual fabric and thereby to hear the range of New Orleans voices that, together, occasion this book. Finally, I must thank my mother, Julia Johnson, and my late father, Richard Johnson, for putting me on my path.

Notes

Introduction

1. Ed Folsom, "What New Orleans Meant to Walt Whitman" in *New Orleans: A Literary History*. Ed. by T. R. Johnson. New York: Cambridge University Press, 2019. p. 50.

2. Rebecca Solnit and Rebecca Snedeker, *Unfathomable City: A New Orleans Atas*. Oakland: University of California Press, 2013. p. 1.

3. Richard Campanella, "A City in Time" in *Unfathomable City: A New Orleans Atlas*. Rebecca Solnit and Rebecca Snedeker. Oakland: University of California Press, 2013. p. 13.

Royal Street – A Masked Ball

1. Howard Smead, *Blood Justice: The Lynching of Mack Charles Parker*. New York: Oxford University Press, 1988.

2. Bruce Watson, "Black Like Me, Fifty Years Later." *Smithsonian Magazine*, October 2011.

3. Folsom, "What New Orleans Meant," pp. 43–57.

4. Ibid., 51.

5. John Howard Griffin, *Black Like Me: 50ᵗʰ Anniversary Edition*. New York: Signet, 2010. pp. 10–12.

6. Ibid., p. 4.

7. Ibid., p. 99.

8. Ibid., p. 5.

9. Lawrence Powell, "Lyle Saxon and the New Orleans City Guide" in *New Orleans City Guide 1938*. New Orleans: Garrett County Press, 2009. p. 3.

10. Richard Campanella, *Bienville's Dilemma: A Historical Geography of New Orleans.* Lafayette: Center for Louisiana Studies, 2008. p. 293.

11. Richard Campanella, *Bourbon Street: A History.* Baton Rouge: Louisiana State University Press, 2014. p. 76.

12. Henry Schvey, "The Place I Was Made For: Tennessee Williams in New Orleans" in *New Orleans: A Literary History.* Ed. by T. R. Johnson. New York: Cambridge University Press, 2019. p. 232.

13. Campanella, *Bourbon,* p. 57.

14. Ibid., p. 59.

15. John S. Kendall, "Patti in New Orleans." *Southern Review,* 16.4, July 1931.

16. Patricia Brady, "Mollie Moore Davis: A Literary Life" in *Louisiana Women Writers: New Essays and a Comprehensive Bibliography.* Ed. by Barbara Ewell and Dorothy Brown. Baton Rouge: Louisiana State University Press, 1992.

17. Lyle Saxon, *New Orleans City Guide 1938.* Garrett County Press, 2009. pp. 254–55.

18. William Faulkner, *Absalom, Absalom!* New York: Vintage Books/ Random House, 1936/1986. p. 83.

19. Campanella, *Bourbon,* p. 46.

20. Campanella, *Bienville,* p. 138.

21. Ibid.

22. Malcolm Heard, *French Quarter Manual: An Architectural Guide to the Vieux Carré.* New Orleans: Tulane School of Architecture, 1997. p. 10.

23. Richard Campanella, *Geographies of New Orleans: Urban Fabrics before the Storm.* Lafayette: Center for Louisiana Studies, 2006. p. 110.

24. Faulkner, *Absalom, Absalom!,* p. 83.

25. Heard, *French Quarter Manual,* p. 11.

26. Campanella, *Geographies,* p. 136.

27. Marcus Christian, *Negro Ironworkers of Louisiana, 1718–1900.* Gretna: Pelican Publishing, 2002. p. 25.

28. Ibid., p. 34.

29. Megan Smolenyak. 7 Things You Didn't Know about Prince's Roots. June 7, 2018. https://smolenyak.medium.com/7-things-

you-didnt-know-about-prince-s-roots-77b0ec569a7c (accessed May 23, 2022).

30. Christian, *Negro Ironworkers*, pp. 19–20.

31. Richard Campanella, *Lincoln in New Orleans: The 1828–1831 Flatboat Journeys and Their Place in History*, Lafayette: Center for Louisiana Studies. 2011. p. 94.

32. Michael Allen, *Western Rivermen, 1763–1861: Ohio and Mississippi Boatmen and the Myth of the Alligator Horse*. Baton Rouge: Louisiana State University Press, 1990. p. 61.

33. Ibid., p. 9.

34. Ibid., p. 17.

35. Ibid., pp. 6–8.

36. Herbert Asbury, *The French Quarter*. New York: Basic Books, 1936/2003.

37. Ibid., p. 83.

38. Allen, *Western Rivermen*, pp. 16–19.

39. Ron Powers, *Mark Twain: A Life*. New York: Free Press, 2006. p. 94.

40. Gary Schanhorst, *The Life of Mark Twain: The Early Years, 1835– 1871*. Columbia: University of Missouri Press, 2018. p. 94.

41. Campanella, *Lincoln*, pp. 208–09.

42. Ibid.

43. Ibid., p. 237.

44. Ibid., p. 186.

45. Walter Johnson, *Soul by Soul: Life inside the Antebellum Slave-Markets*. Cambridge, MA: Harvard University Press, 2001. p. 68.

46. Ibid., p. 4.

47. Teresa Toulouse, "John Galsworthy's 'That Old Time Place': Nostalgia, Repetition, and Interstitial Space in the St. Louis 'Exchange' Hotel" in *Sweet Spots: In-Between Spaces in New Orleans*. Ed. by Teresa A. Toulouse and Barbara C. Ewell. Jackson: University Press of Mississippi, 1912.

48. Clint Bruce, *Afro-Creole Poetry in French from Louisiana's Radical Civil War Era Newspapers: A Bilingual Edition*. New Orleans: Historic New Orleans Collection, 2020. p. 11.

49. Nathalie Dessens, *From Saint-Domingue to New Orleans: Migration and Influences*. Gainesville: University Press of Florida, 2007. pp. 1–5.

50. Bruce, *Afro-Creole Poetry*, p. 13.

51. Ibid.

52. Ibid.

53. Shirley Elizabeth Thompson, *Exiles at Home: The Struggle to Become American in Creole New Orleans*. Cambridge, MA: Harvard University Press, 2009. p. 183.

54. Ibid., p. 222.

55. Angel Adams Parham, "Foreword" in *Afro-Creole Poetry in French from Louisiana's Radical Civil War Era Newspapers*. Ed. and trans. by Clint Bruce. New Orleans: Historic New Orleans Collection, 2020. p. xiv.

56. Bruce, *Afro-Creole Poetry*, p. 8.

57. Ibid., p. 21.

58. Jean-Charles Houzeau, *My Passage at the New Orleans Tribune: A Memoir of the Civil War*. Ed. by David C. Rankin, trans. by Gerard F. Denault. Baton Rouge: Louisiana State University Press, 1984. pp. 83–85.

59. Thompson, *Exiles at Home*, p. 233.

60. Ibid.

61. Ibid., p. 235.

62. Matthew Paul Smith, "The Civil War's Literary Aftershocks: George Washington Cable" in *New Orleans: A Literary History*. Ed. by T. R. Johnson. New York: Cambridge University Press, 2019. p. 82.

63. Saxon, *New Orleans City Guide*, p. 251.

64. George Washington Cable, *Old Creole Days*. Gretna: Pelican Publishing, 1997. p. 62.

65. Campanella, *Geographies*, pp. 319–21.

66. John Shelton Reed, *Dixie Bohemia: A French Quarter Circle in the 1920s*. Baton Rouge: Louisiana State University Press, 2012. p. 73.

67. Campanella, *Geographies*, p. 319.

68. www.neworleanshistorical.org/items/show/961 (accessed May 24, 2022).

69. Reed, *Dixie Bohemia*, p. 2.

70. Ibid., p. 39.

71. Ibid., p. 50.

72. Kirsten Greusz, "Converging Americas: New Orleans in Spanish Language and Latina/o/x Literary Culture" in *New Orleans: A Literary History*. Ed. by T. R. Johnson. New York; Cambridge University Press, 2019.

73. Thomas Bonner, Jr., "New Orleans, Modernism, and *The Double Dealer*, 1821–26" in *New Orleans: A Literary History*. Ed. by T. R. Johnson. New York: Cambridge University Press, 2019. p. 198.

74. Frances Jean Bowen, *The New Orleans Double Dealer, 1921–1926: A Critical History*. Nashville: Vanderbilt University Press, 1954.

75. Reed, *Dixie Bohemia*, pp. 20–21.

76. T. R. Johnson, "Swan Song?" in *New Orleans: A Literary History*. Ed. by T. R. Johnson. New York: Cambridge University Press, 2019. p. 358.

77. Christine Vella, "The World Brought Her Its Secrets" in *Louisiana Women: Their Lives and Times*. Ed. by Janet Allured and Judith F. Gentry. Athens, GA: University of Georgia Press, 2009. p. 197.

78. Ibid., p. 199.

79. Ibid., p. 202.

80. Ibid., p. 199.

81. Ibid., p. 202.

82. Ibid., p. 205.

83. Joseph Blotner, *Robert Penn Warren: A Biography*. New York: Random House, 1999. p. 147.

84. Bruce Lambert, "Albert R. Erskine, 81, an Editor for Faulkner and Other Authors." *The New York Times*, February 1993.

85. Elizabeth Lowry, "Tooloose Lowrytrek." *London Review of Books*, November 1, 2007, 14–15.

86. Gerald Clarke, *Capote: A Biography*. New York: Simon and Schuster, 1988. p. 100.

87. Roy S. Simmonds, *The Two Worlds of William March*. Tuscaloosa: University of Alabama Press, 1984. p. 230.

88. Schvey, "The Place I Was Made For," 227.

89. Ibid., 234, 238.

90. W. Adolph Roberts, *These Many Years: An Autobiography*. Kingston: The University of the West Indies Press, 2015. p. 305.

91. William Bedford Clark, "A Civil Rights Era Novel of the American Civil War: Robert Penn Warren's *A Band of Angels*" in *New Orleans: A Literary History*. Ed. by T. R. Johnson. New York; Cambridge University Press, 2019. p. 242.

92. Ibid.

93. Jeff Weddle, *Bohemian New Orleans: The Story of the Outsider and Loujon Press*. Oxford, MS: University Press of Mississippi, 2007. p. 21.

94. Ibid., pp. 9–10, 26.

95. Ibid., pp. 26–32.

96. Ibid., p. 53.

97. Ibid., pp. 60–77.

98. Ibid., p. 75.

99. Ibid., p. 169.

100. Charles Casillo, "Fifty Years of Rechy's *City of Night*." *Los Angeles Review of Books*, October 13, 2013.

101. Christine Wiltz, *The Last Madame: A Life in the New Orleans Underworld*. New York: Da Capo Press, 2001. p. 20.

102. Ibid., p. 7.

103. Ibid., p. 10.

104. Ibid., p. 36.

105. Frenchy Brouillette and Matthew Randazzo, *Mr. New Orleans: The Life of a Big Easy Underworld Legend*. Seattle: MRV Entertainment, LLC, 2014. pp. 121–22.

106. Doug McCash, "The Geography of an Assassin: Seeking Lee Harvey Oswald's New Orleans Homes." *The New Orleans Times-Picayune*, November 20, 2013.

107. Lamar Waldron, *The Hidden History of the JFK Assassination*. Berkeley: Citadel, 2013. p. 59.

108. Ibid., p. 467.

109. Reed, *Dixie Bohemia*, pp. 81–91.

110. Katherine Ramsland, *Prism of Night: A Biography of Anne Rice*. New York: Plume Press, 1994. p. 153.

111. Kirkus reivews: www.kirkusreviews.com/book-reviews/elise-blackwell/the-lower-quarter/ (accessed May 24, 2022).

112. Valerie Martin, *Property*. New York: Vintage, 2004. p. 181.

St. Claude Avenue – Hard Times and Good Children

1. Zora Neale Hurston, "Mother Catherine" in *The Complete Stories*. New York: Harper Perennial, 2008. p. 99.

2. Ibid., p. 100.

3. Ibid.

4. WWNO. Mother Catherine Seals and the Temple of the Innocent Blood. December 1, 2016. www.google.com/search?q=Mother+Catherine+Seals&oq=Mother+C&aqs=chrome.0.69i59j46i67i175i199i275j69i57j46i131i175i199i433j46j69i60l3.1167j0j7&sourceid=chrome&ie=UTF-8

5. Hurston, "Mother Catherine," p. 104.

6. WWNO, Mother Catherine Seals.

7. Hurston, "Mother Catherine," p. 102.

8. Ibid., p. 105.

9. Claude Jacobs and Andrew Kaslow, *The Spiritual Churches of New Orleans: Origins, Beliefs, Rituals of an African-American Religion*. Knoxville: University of Tennessee Press, 1992. p. 41.

10. S. Frederick Starr, *Une Belle Maison: The Lombard Plantation House in New Orleans's Bywater*. Jackson: University Press of Mississippi, 2013. pp. 3–4.

11. Ibid., p. 99.

12. Ibid., p. 104.

13. Ibid., p. 10.

14. Emily Clark, *Masterless Mistresses: The New Orleans Ursulines and the Development of a New World Society, 1727–1834*. Chapel Hill: University of North Carolina Press, 2007. p. 243.

15. Laine Kaplan-Levinson and Travis Lux, WWNO. NOLA vs. Nature: The Blessing and the Curse of the Wood Screw Pump. January 11, 2018. www.wwno.org/post/nola-vs-nature-blessing-and-curse-wood-screw-pump

16. John Pope, "Draining the Swamp: A. Baldwin Wood and the Pump That Built New Orleans." *The New Orleans Advocate and Times-Picayune*, July 22, 2019.

17. S. Derby Gisclair, *The Olympic Club of New Orleans: Epicenter of Professional Boxing, 1883–1897*. Jefferson, NC: MacFarland Publishing, 2018. p. 80.

18. Ibid., p. 103.

19. Ibid., p. 98.

20. Rick Coleman, *Fats Domino and the Lost Dawn of Rock'n'Roll.* Cambridge, MA: Da Capo Press, 2006. p. xiii.

21. Ibid., p. 6.

22. Ibid., pp. 6–7.

23. Ibid., p. xvi.

24. Ibid., p. xix.

25. Ibid., pp. 15–16.

26. Ibid., p. 21.

27. Ibid., pp. 33–34.

28. Ibid., p. 54.

29. Ibid., p. 55.

30. John Steinbeck, *Travels with Charley.* New York: Penguin, 1961. pp. 256–57.

31. Ibid., p. 249.

32. Ibid., pp. 258–59.

33. Ibid., p. 259.

34. Stephen Maloney, "John Waters on New Orleans." *Offbeat Magazine*, March 2015.

35. Tom Dent, "Marcus B. Christian: A Reminiscence and an Appreciation." *Black American Literature Forum*, 18:1, spring, 1984, 26.

36. Ibid., 24.

37. Kalamu Ya Salaam, "Tom Dent and the Development of Black Literature in New Orleans" in *New Orleans: A Literary History.* Ed. by T. R. Johnson. New York; Cambridge University Press, 2019. pp. 268–69.

38. www.wwno.org/post/desire-louisiana

39. Orissa Arend, *Showdown in Desire: The Black Panthers Take a Stand in New Orleans.* Fayetteville: University of Arkansas Press, 2010. pp. 5–6.

40. Ibid., pp. 5–6.

41. Ibid., p. 98.

42. www.wwno.org/post/desire-louisiana

43. www.youtube.com/watch?v=lU5jZ_3j4XQ

44. James Nagel, *Race and Culture in New Orleans Stories: Kate Chopin, Grace King, Alice Dunbar-Nelson, George Cable.* Tuscaloosa: University of Alabama Press, 2014. p. 99.

45. Ibid., p. 98.

46. Joanna Scutts, Feminize Your Canon: Alice Dunbar-Nelson. *Paris Review*, September 28, 2020. www.theparisreview.org/blog/2020/09/28/feminize-your-canon-alice-dunbar-nelson/

47. Ibid.

48. Ibid.

49. Susan Larson, *A Booklover's Guide to New Orleans.* Baton Rouge: Louisiana State University Press, 1999. p. 89.

Esplanade Avenue – Escape Routes

1. Devorah Major, "Foreward: Eternal Poet" in *Collected Poems of Bob Kaufman.* Ed. by Neeli Cherkovski, Raymond Foye, and Tate Swindell. San Franciso: City Lights, 2019.

2. Mona Lisa Saloy, "When I Die, I Won't Stay Dead: The Poetry of Bob Kaufman." Doctoral dissertation. Louisiana State University, 2005. pp. 21–24.

3. Ibid., p. 61.

4. Ibid., p. 74.

5. Cassie Pruyn, *Bayou St. John: A Brief History.* Harahan: The History Press/Arcadia Publishing, 2017. p. 29.

6. Ibid., p. 27.

7. Personal correspondence with Richard Campanella.

8. Pruyn, *Bayou St. John*, p. 14.

9. Ibid., p. 13.

10. Geoff Dyer, "Horizontal Drift" in *Yoga for People Who Can't Be Bothered to Do It.* New York: Vintage, 2004. p. 23.

11. Pruyn, *Bayou St. John*, p. 31.

12. The Library Company of Philadelphia. A Few of Our Favorite Things, Number 14: Antoine-Simon Le Page du Pratz's *History of Louisiana Or of the Western Parts of Virginia and Carolina.* https://librarycompany.org/2014/02/10/a-few-of-our-favorite-things-part-fourteen-antoine-simon-le-page-du-pratzs-the-history-of-louisiana-or-of-the-western-parts-of-virginia-and-carolina/

13. Lawrence Powell, *Accidental City: Improvising New Orleans.* Cambridge, MA: Harvard University Press, 2012. p. 84.

14. Ibid., pp. 93–95.

15. Pruyn, *Bayou St. John*, p. 40.

16. Mary Louise Christovich, Sally Kittredge Evans, and Roulhac Toledano, "Introduction" in *Vol. V: Esplanade Ridge.* Gretna: Pelican, 1995. p. 12.

17. Greg Lambousy, "The Mint at New Orleans." *The Numismatist,* March 2003, 36–39.

18. Greg Lambousy, "The US Mint at New Orleans." *Numismatist,* March, 2003, 36–43.

19. Christovich et al., "Introduction," 26.

20. Ibid., 27.

21. Powell, *Accidental City*, pp. 289–90.

22. Ibid., p. 279.

23. Ibid.

24. Emily Clark. Interviewed by Stacey Parker Lemelle, "Quadroons for Beginners: Discussing the Suppressed and Sexualized History of Free Women of Color with Emily Clark." *Huffington Post*, November 4, 2013.

25. William Faulkner, *Absalom, Absalom!* New York: Vintage Books / Random House, 1936/1986. p. 93.

26. Christovich et al., "Introduction," xvii.

27. Pruyn, *Bayou St. John*, p. 52.

28. Lyle Saxon. "Duelling Oaks" in *New Orleans City Park: Its First Fifty Years.* New Orleans: Gulf Printing Co, 1941.

29. Neil Roberts, *Freedom as Marronage.* Chicago: University of Chicago Press, 2015.

30. Bryan Wagner, "A Jazz Origin Myth: Bras Coupé in History, Folklore, and Literature" in *New Orleans: A Literary History.* Ed. by T. R. Johnson. New York: Cambridge University Press, 2019. p. 148.

31. Ibid., 152.

32. Ibid., 148.

33. Solomon Northup, *Twelve Years a Slave.* Ed. by Sue Eakin and Joseph Logsdon. Baton Rouge: Louisiana State University Press, 1968. p. 42.

34. Calvin Schermerhorn, "'As I Have Seen and Known It': Ex-Slave Autobiographers and the New Orleans Slave Market" in *New Orleans: A Literary History*. Ed. by T. R. Johnson. New York: Cambridge University Press, 2019. p. 36.

35. Northup, *Twelve Years a Slave*, p. 50.

36. Ibid., p. 57.

37. Ibid., p. 120.

38. Michael Schulman, "The Historian Who Unearthed *Twelve Years a Slave*." *The New Yorker*, March 7, 2014.

39. Todd Spangler, "Top 20 Most Pirated Movies of 2014 Led by 'Wolf of Wall Street,' 'Frozen,' 'Gravity'." *The Hollywood Reporter*. December 28, 2014.

40. Bernard Koloski, *Awakenings: The Story of the Kate Chopin Revival*. Baton Rouge: Louisiana State University Press, 2009. pp. 3–4.

41. Ibid., p. 4.

42. Ibid., p. 1.

43. Ibid., p. 6.

44. Emily Toth, "Is Edna Pontellier Stupid? The Problem of the Intellectual Woman in New Orleans" in *New Orleans: A Literary History*. Ed. by T. R. Johnson. New York; Cambridge University Press, 2019. pp. 122–36.

45. Kate Chopin, *The Awakening*. Ed. by Suzanne Disheroon, Barbara C. Ewell, Pamela Glenn Menke, and Susie Scifres. Buffalo: Broadview Press, 1899/2011. pp. 40–41.

46. Ibid., p. 156.

47. Ibid., p. 163.

48. Ibid., p. 90.

49. Martha Ward, *Voodoo Queen: The Spirited Lives of Marie Laveau*. Oxford, MS: University Press of Mississippi, 2004. p. 19.

50. S. Frederick Starr, "Illusion and Disillusion: The Making of Lafcadio Hearn" in *New Orleans: A Literary History*. Ed. by T. R. Johnson. New York: Cambridge University Press, 2019. pp. 96–112.

51. Christovich et al., "Introduction," xvi.

52. Lafcadio Hearn, *Inventing New Orleans: Writings of Lafcadio Hearn*. Ed. by S. Frederick Starr. Jackson: University Press of Mississippi, 2001. p. 70–72.

53. Ibid., pp. 66, 69.

54. Ward, *Voodoo Queen*, p. 76.

55. Ibid., p. 39.

56. Ibid., p. 32.

57. Ibid., p. 24.

58. Ibid., p. 72.

59. Zora Neale Hurston, *Mules and Men*. New York: Amistad, 1935/2008. p. 145.

60. Pruyn, *Bayou St. John*, p. 63.

61. Jack Rummel and Mac Rebennak, *Dr. John: Under a Hoodoo Moon: The Life of the Night Tripper*. New York: Saint Martin's Press, 1994. pp. 7–8.

62. Mark Twain, *Life on the Mississippi*. New York: American Classics Society, 1883/1977. p. 161.

63. Alan Lomax, *Mister Jelly Roll: The Fortunes of Jelly Roll Morton, New Orleans Creole and "Inventor of Jazz."* Oakland: University of California Press, 1950/2001. pp. 6–10.

64. Ibid., pp. 17–29.

65. Ibid., p. 223.

66. Ibid., p. ix.

67. Sidney Bechet, *Treat It Gentle: An Autobiography*. Cambridge, MA: Da Capo Press, 1960/2009. p. 46.

68. Ibid., p. 128.

69. Ibid., p.152.

70. Barney Birgard, *With Louis and Duke*. New York: Oxford University Press, 1986. p. 24.

71. Ibid., p. 40.

72. Louis Armstrong, *Satchmo: My Life in New Orleans*. New York: Da Capo Press, 1986. p. 96.

73. Virginia Spencer Carr, *Dos Passos: A Life*. New York: Doubleday, 1984. pp. 199–200.

74. Pruyn, *Bayou St. John*, p. 90.

75. Richard Campanella, *Geographies of New Orleans: Urban Fabrics before the Storm*. Lafayette: Center for Louisiana Studies, 2006. p. 19.

76. Paul Kappilla. Allen Toussaint. *64 Parishes*. https://64parishes .org/entry/allen-toussaint

77. Keith Spera, "Alex Chilton's Life in New Orleans Was a Mystery, and That's the Way He Wanted It." *The New Orleans Times-Picayune*, April 7, 2010.

78. J. Edward Keyes. Hurray for the Riff Raff. https://web.archive .org/web/20100315033742/http://www.emusic.com/features/ spotlight/20010_201002-qa-selects-riffraff.html

79. Carter Fowler. Frank before the Ocean: The Story of Lonnie Breaux. *Central Sauce.* March 28, 2018. https://centralsauce .com/lonny-breaux-frank-ocean

80. Nik Kyriokopoulos, conversation with the author.

81. Sarah Guggemos, conversation with the author.

82. Maya Phillips, "A Poetic Body of Work Grapples with the Body at Risk." *The New York Times*, April 2, 2019.

83. www.purewow.com/entertainment/tyler-perry-net-worth

84. Madeline Berg, "From Poor as Hell to Billionaire: How Tyler Perry Changed Show Business Forever." *Forbes*, September 1, 2020.

85. Ibid.

86. Rashida Z. Shaw McMahon, *The Black Circuit: Race, Performance, and Spectatorship in Black Popular Theater.* New York: Routledge, 2020. pp. 132–71.

87. Louis Armstrong, *Satchmo: My Life in New Orleans.* Cambridge, MA: Da Capo Press, 1986. p. 37.

88. Ibid., pp. 46–48.

Basin Street – Memory and Music

1. Carol Lawson, "Broadway: Book and Lyrics of New Musical by Toni Morrison." *The New York Times*, July 23, 1982.

2. Sidney Bechet, *Treat It Gentle: An Autobiography.* Cambridge, MA: Da Capo Press, 1960/2009. p. 13.

3. Ibid., p. 30.

4. Ibid., p. 202.

5. Edward Branley. NOLA History: Backatown and the Evolution of New Orleans Neighborhoods. http://gonola-wp.southleft .com/things-to-do-in-new-orleans/history/nola-history-backatown-and-the-evolution-of-new-orleans-neighborhoods (accessed June 8, 2022).

6. Freddi Evans, *Congo Square: African Roots in New Orleans.* Lafayette: University of Lousiana at Lafayette Press, 2011. p. 18.

7. Ibid., pp. 2, 43.

8. Jeroen DeWulf, *From the Kingdom of Kongo to Congo Square: Kongo Dances and the Origins of the Mardi Gras Indians.* Lafayette: University of Lousiana at Lafayette Press, 2017. p. xiv.

9. Evans, *Congo Square*, p. 20.

10. Ibid., p. 7.

11. Ibid., p. 6.

12. Ibid., pp. 47–48.

13. Ibid., p. 40.

14. Ibid., p. 38.

15. Ibid., pp. 38–39.

16. Lawrence Powell, *Accidental City: Improvising New Orleans.* Cambridge, MA: Harvard University Press, 2013. pp. 99–100.

17. Dewulf, *From the Kingdom*, pp. 11–12.

18. Evans, *Congo Square*, p. 36.

19. Dewulf, *From the Kingdom*, pp. 43.

20. Evans, *Congo Square*, p. 44.

21. Ibid., p. 44.

22. Ibid., p. 76.

23. Ibid., p. 117.

24. Richard Campanella, "Today's Lafitte Greenway Was Spanish New Orleans' Carondelet Canal" in *Cityscapes: A Geographer's View of the New Orleans Area.* https://richcampanella.com/wp-content/uploads/2020/02/Picayune_Cityscapes_2017_11_Before-the-Lafitte-Greenway_Carondelet-Canal.pdf

25. Emily Clark, *The Strange History of the American Quadroon: Free Women of Color in the Revolutionary Atlantic World.* Chapel Hill: University of North Carolina Press, 2013.

26. Ibid., pp. 45, 54.

27. Sublette, Ned. *From Spanish Silver to Congo Square: The World that Made New Orleans.* New York: Lawrence Erlbaum, 2008. 51–52

28. Clark, *The Strange History*, p. 48.

29. Ibid., p. 51.

30. Ibid.

31. Ibid., pp. 51–52.

32. Ibid., p. 51.

33. Ibid., pp. 54–55.

34. Ibid., p. 54.

35. Ibid., p. 133.

36. Ibid., p. 147.

37. Ibid., p. 133.

38. Ibid., p. 177.

39. Ibid., p. 178.

40. Ibid., p. 177.

41. Gary Krist, *Empire of Sin: A Story of Sex, Jazz, Murder, and the Battle for Modern New Orleans.* New York: Crown Publishing, 2015. p. 73.

42. Ibid., p. 116.

43. Ibid., p. 148.

44. Ibid., p. 112.

45. Ibid., p. 115.

46. Ibid.

47. Ibid., p. 55.

48. Ibid., p. 123.

49. Joseph Roach, *Cities of the Dead: Circum-Atlantic Performance.* New York: Columbia University Press, 1996. p. 227.

50. Ibid., p. 226.

51. Ibid., p. 227.

52. Ibid., p. 228.

53. Emily Epstein Landau, *Spectacular Wickedness: Sex, Race, and Memory in Storyville, New Orleans.* Baton Rouge: Louisiana State University Press, 2013. p. 4.

54. Ted Anthony, *Chasing the Rising Sun: The Journey of an American Song.* New York: Simon and Schuster, 2013. p. 25.

55. Ibid., p. 27.

56. Krist, *Empire of Sin*, p. 77.

57. Ibid., p. 78.

58. Ned Sublette, *The Year before the Flood.* New York: Lawrence Hille, 2009. pp. 178–84.

59. Krist, *Empire of Sin*, pp. 138–39.

60. Michael Ondaatje, *Coming through Slaughter*. New York: Vintage, 1976. pp. 14–15.

61. Ibid., p. 15.

62. Ibid., p. 22.

63. Ibid., p. 86.

64. Ibid.

65. Ibid., p. 54.

66. Ibid., p. 127.

67. Ibid., p. 133.

68. Natasha Trethewey, *Bellocq's Ophelia*. Minneapolis: Graywolf Press, 2002. pp. 18–19.

69. Ibid., p. 24.

70. Ibid., p. 20.

71. Ibid., p. 24.

72. Ibid., p. 29.

73. Mark E. Crutcher, *Tremé: Race and Place in a New Orleans Neighborhood*. Athens, GA: University of Georgia Press, 2010.

74. Ibid., p. 15.

75. Ibid., p. 10.

76. Dewulf, *From the Kingdom*, p. 50.

77. Crutcher, *Tremé*, p. 33.

78. Kim Chatelain. The First Real New Orleans Saint? Henriette Delille's Path to Canonization. March 2, 2017. www.nola.com

79. Holly Devon, "Right of Way: Navigating the Past, Present, and Future of the Claiborne Corridor." *Antigravity Magazine*, March 2020.

80. Jordan Hirsch, "Sacred Ground: What Converting Municipal Auditorium into City Hall Could Mean for Congo Square and Tremé." *Antigravity Magazine*, June 2021, 31.

81. Judy Adams, *The Johnny Adams Story*. New Orleans: Self-published, 2009. pp. 46–47.

82. Tony Scherman, *Backbeat: The Earl Palmer Story*. Cambridge, MA: DaCapo Press, 2000.

83. Max Weinberg, *The Big Beat: Conversations with Rock's Greatest Drummers*. New York: Hudson Music, 2004.

84. Michael Tisserand, *Krazy: George Herriman, a Life in Black and White*. New York: Harper Publishing, 2016. p. 426.

85. Arthur Pfister, *My Name Is New Orleans: 40 Years of Poetry and Other Jazz*. Donaldsonville: Margaret Media, 2009. p. 133.

86. Steve Cannon, *Groove, Bang, and Jive Around*. New York: Grove Press, 1969. p. 219.

87. Colin Moynihan, "Steve Cannon, Whose Townhouse Was an East Village Salon, Dies at 84." *The New York Times*, July 16, 2019.

88. Kirsten Greusz, "Converging Americas: New Orleans in Spanish Language and Latina/o/x Literary Culture" in *New Orleans: A Literary History*. Ed. by T. R. Johnson. New York; Cambridge University Press, 2019. p. 142.

89. Kalamu Ya Salaam, ed., *New Orleans Griot: A Tom Dent Reader*. New Orleans: University of New Orleans Press, 2018. p. 361.

90. Erna Brodber, *Louisiana*. New York: New Beacon Press, 1994. p. 86.

91. Ibid., p. 88.

92. Ibid., p. 98.

93. Ibid., p. 125.

94. John Wharton Lowe, ed., *Summoning Our Saints: The Poetry and Prose of Brenda Marie Osbey*. Lanham: Lexington Books, 2019. p. 1.

95. Ibid., p. 21.

96. Brenda Marie Osbey, *In These Houses*. Middletown: Wesleyan University Press, 1988. pp. 46–47.

97. Ibid., p. 55.

98. Ibid., p. 4.

99. Ibid., p. 25.

100. Tracy Watts, "Haunted Memories" in *Summoning Our Saints: The Poetry and Prose of Brenda Marie Osbey*. Ed. by Charles Wharton Lowe. Lanham: Lexington Books, 2019. p. 90.

101. Albert Woodfox, *Solitary*. New York: Grove Press, 2019. p. 220.

102. Ibid., pp. 26, 99.

103. Ibid., p. 149.

104. Ibid.

105. Ibid., p. 209.

St. Charles Avenue – Blood and Money

1. Lilllian Hellman, *An Unfinished Woman*. Canada: Little, Brown, and Co., 1969. pp. 10–12.

2. Ibid., p. 17.

3. Ibid., p. 4.

4. Ibid., p. 5.

5. "News of the Stage." *The New York Times*, February 3, 1940.

6. Lillian Hellman and Peter Feibleman, *Eating Together: Recipes and Recollections*. Boston: Little, Brown, and Co., 1984. p. 32.

7. Ned Sublette. Canal Street: A Hemispheric Boundary. *64 Parishes*. https://64parishes.org/canal-street-a-hemispheric-boundary

8. Thomas Brothers, *Louis Armstrong's New Orleans*. New York: Norton, 2007.

9. Richard Campanella, "Faubourg Revival." *The New Orleans Times–Picayune/New Orleans Advocate*, May 2, 2021.

10. Ibid.

11. Richard Campanella, "The Warehouse District of 200 Years Ago Was Called the St. Mary Batture." *The New Orleans Times–Picayune*, July 22, 2018.

12. Richard Campanella, "The Widening of Poydras Street." *The Times–Picayune's Inside Out*, December 11, 2015, 6–7.

13. Richard Campanella, "When Lafayette City Became New Orleans." *The New Orleans Times–Picayune Inside-Out*, June 9, 2017.

14. Sarah Laskow. For 15 Years, New Orleans Was Divided into Three Separate Cities. *Atlas Obscura*. January 6, 2017. www.atlasobscura.com/articles/for-15-years-new-orleans-was-divided-into-three-separate-cities

15. Ibid.

16. Richard Campanella, "Robb's Folly: Lost Palazzo of the Garden District." *Preservation in Print*, April, 2017, 12–13.

17. Ibid.

18. Grace King, *New Orleans: The Place and the People*. New York: Macmillan Co., 1895. p. xxi.

19. Tennessee Williams, *Plays: 1957–1980*. New York: The Library of America, 2000. p. 101.

20. Ellen Gilchrest, *In the Land of Dreamy Dreams*. Fayetteville: University of Arkansas Press, 1981. p. 23.

21. Truman Capote, *Music for Chameleons.* New York: Random House, 1980. p. 184.

22. Katherine Ramsland, *Prism of the Night: A Biography of Anne Rice.* New York: Plume, 1994. pp. 6–10, 43–54.

23. Ibid., pp. 110–50.

24. Ibid., p. 156.

25. Ibid., p. xi.

26. Ibid., p. 106.

27. Ibid., p. 147.

28. Ibid., p. 314.

29. Ibid., p. ix.

30. Laura D. Kelley, *The Irish in New Orleans.* Lafayette: University of Louisiana at Lafayatte Press. p. 68.

31. Cory MacLauchlin, "A Flaneur in the French Quarter and Beyond" in *New Orleans: A Literary History.* Ed. by T. R. Johnson. New York; Cambridge University Press, 2019. p. 298.

32. Cory MacLauchlin, *Butterfly in the Typewriter: The Tragic Life of John Kennedy Toole and the Remarkable Story of Confederacy of Dunces.* Cambridge, MA: Da Capo Press, 2012. pp. 5, 211.

33. Ibid., p. xiii.

34. Ibid., p. 3.

35. Ibid., p. 53.

36. Ibid., pp. 18–20.

37. Ibid., pp. 53–56.

38. Ibid., p. 86.

39. Ibid., p. 170.

40. Ibid., p. 175.

41. Ibid., p. 189.

42. Ibid., p. 299.

43. Ibid., p. 226.

44. Elizabeth S. Belle, "The Clash of Worldviews in John Kennedy Toole's *A Confederacy of Dunces." The Southern Literary Journal,* 21.1, fall 1988, 15–22.

45. Tom Bissell, "The Uneasy Afterlife of *Confederacy of Dunces." The New Yorker,* January 5, 2021.

46. Helen Prejean, *River of Fire: On Becoming an Activist.* New York: Vintage, 2020. pp. 253–59.

47. Joyce Duringa, *Helen Prejean: Death Row's Nun.* Collegeville: Liturgical Press. pp. 1, 4.

48. Ibid., p. 38.

49. Ibid., p. 29.

50. Ibid., p. 41.

51. Richard Campanella, "When Carrolton Became New Orleans." *The New Orleans Times-Picayune Inside-Out,* September 8, 2017.

52. Richard Campanella, "How New Orleans Took Uptown from Jefferson Parish." *The New Orleans Times-Picayune Inside-Out,* July 14, 2017.

53. Richard Campanella, "Before Tulane, before Loyola, There Was Leland University." *The New Orleans Times-Picayune Inside-Out,* May 8, 2015.

54. Ibid.

55. Huntington Cairnes, "James Feibleman's Two-Story World." *The American Scholar,* 42.3, summer 1973, 477.

56. Miller Williams. *Poets.Org.* https://poets.org/poet/miller-williams

57. Gandulf Hennig (dir.), *Gram Parsons: Fallen Angel* (DVD). Rhino, 2006.

58. Ibid.

59. Jason Walker, *Gram Parsons: God's Own Singer.* Los Angeles: Helter Skelter Press, 2002. p. 201.

60. Mark Burford, *Mahalia Jackson and the Black Gospel Field.* Oxford: Oxford University Press, 2018. p. 40.

61. Mahalia Jackson Prompts Martin Luther King, Jr. to Improvise 'I Have a Dream' Speech. *This Day in History,* August 28, 1963. www.history.com/this-day-in-history/mahalia-jackson-the-queen-of-gospel-puts-her-stamp-on-the-march-on-washington

62. William Ivy Hair, "Henry H. Hearsey and the Politics of Race." Louisiana History: The Journal of the Louisiana Historical Association, autumn 1976, 17.4, 393–400.

63. William Ivy Hair, *Carnival of Fury: Robert Charles and the Race Riot of 1900.* Baton Rouge: Louisiana State University Press, 1976. p. 96.

64. Ibid., p. 115.

65. Ibid., p. 51.

66. Ibid., p. 116.

67. Ibid., p. 154.

68. Ibid., p. 155.

69. Ibid., pp. 184–85.

70. K. Stephen Prince, *The Ballad of Robert Charles: Searching for the New Orleans Riot of 1900*. Chapel Hill: University of North Carolina Press, 2021. p. 1.

71. Ibid., p. 166.

72. Peter Hernon, *A Terrible Thunder: The Story of the New Orleans Sniper*. New Orleans: Garret County Press, 2010. p. 276.

73. Ibid., p. 269.

74. Jason Berry, Jonathan Foose, and Thad Jones, *Up from the Cradle of Jazz: New Orleans Music since World War II*. Lafayette: University of Lousiana at Lafayette Presse, 1986. p. 58.

75. Ibid., p. 60.

76. Jeff Hannusch, *The Soul of New Orleans: A Legacy of Rhythm and Blues*. Athens, OH: Swallow Publications, 2001. pp. 58–59.

77. Ibid., p. 60.

78. Tom Aswell, *Louisiana Rocks: The Genesis of Rock n Roll*. Gretna: Pelican Books, 2010. p. 104.

79. Matt Miller, *Bounce: Rap Music and Local Identity in New Orleans*. Amherst: University of Massachusetts Press, 2012. p. 45.

80. Ibid., pp. 76–78.

81. Ibid., p. 82.

82. Ibid., pp. 82–83,91–92.

83. Ibid., p. 98.

84. Ned Sublette, *The Year before the Flood: A Story of New Orleans*. Chicago: Lawrence Hill, 2009. p. 195.

85. Ibid., pp. 199–200.

86. Ben Westhoff, *Dirty South: Outkast, Lil Wayne, Soulja Boy, and the Southern Rappers Who Reinvented Hip Hop*. Chicago: Chicago Review Press, 2011. p. 130.

87. Sublette, *The Year before the Flood*, pp. 218–19.

88. Westhoff, *Dirty South*, p. 126.

89. Sublette, *The Year before the Flood*, p. 214.

90. Ibid., p. 215.

91. Westhoff, *Dirty South*, p. 117.

92. Ibid., p. 134.

93. Big Freedia with Nicole Balin, *God Save the Queen*. New York: Simon and Schuster, 2015. pp. 59–65.

94. Ibid., p. 84.

95. Ibid., p. 132.

96. Ibid., p. 156.

97. Ibid., p. 236.

98. Sublette, *The Year before the Flood*, p. 186.

99. Gwendolyn Midlo Hall, *Haunted by Slavery*. Chicago: Haymarket Press. p. 210.

100. Ibid., p. 215.

101. Ibid., pp. 2–10.

102. Ibid., p. 3.

103. Ibid., p. 6.

104. Ibid., p. 44.

105. Ibid., p. 52.

106. Ibid., p. 55.

107. Ibid., p. 58.

108. Ibid., p. 74.

109. Ibid., p. 62.

110. Ibid., p. xviii.

111. Ibid., p. 99.

112. Ibid., pp. 105–10.

113. Ibid., p. 112.

114. Ibid., p. xvi.

Outskirts – Writing through Loss

1. Paul Chan, *Waiting for Godot in New Orleans: A Field Guide*. New York: Creative Time Books, 2010. p. 26.

2. Ibid., p. 308.

3. Ibid., p. 28.

4. Ibid., p. 146.

5. Ibid., p. 147.

6. Dennis Formento, *Looking for an Out Place*. Kanona, NY: FootHills Publishing, 2010. p. 31.

7. John Gregory Brown. Personal correspondence with this author.

8. Andy Horowitz, *Katrina: 1915–2015*. Cambridge, MA: Harvard University Press, 2020.

9. William S. Burroughs, *Junky*. New York: Penguin, 1953/1977. p. 68.

10. Katharine Coldiron. I Got a Sign from New Orleans Herself: An Interview with Jerika Marchan. *Southern Humanities Review*. www.southernhumanitiesreview.com/i-got-a-sign-from-new-orleans-herself.html

11. Karisma Price. On Returning: Going Home to New Orleans after Hurricane Katrina. *Rookie*. August 27, 2015. www.rookiemag.com/2015/08/on-returning

Index

Page numbers in italics indicate illustrations